The International Politics of
Surplus Capacity

The International Politics of Surplus Capacity

*Competition for market shares
in the world recession*

Edited by
SUSAN STRANGE
ROGER TOOZE

London GEORGE ALLEN & UNWIN

Boston   Sydney

First published in 1981

GEORGE ALLEN & UNWIN LTD
40 Museum Street, London WC1A 1LU

© Susan Strange and Roger Tooze, 1981

British Library Cataloguing in Publication Data

The International politics of surplus capacity
  1. Surplus commodities
  I. Strange, Susan   II. Tooze, Roger
  338   HD31
  ISBN 0-04-382034-4

Set in 11 on 11 point Plantin by Performance Typesetting Ltd, Milton Keynes
and printed in Great Britain
by Biddles Ltd, Guildford and King's Lynn

Contents

page

Preface

This book is the end result of a conference held in May 1979 to consider the management of surplus industrial capacity in the international system of the 1970s. The work leading up to the conference and the conference itself was undertaken under the auspices of the International Political Economy Group (IPEG). IPEG is a 'working group' of the British International Studies Association and has been supported since its inception in 1972 by the Social Science Research Council.

Funds for the actual conference were provided jointly by the Nuffield Foundation and Shell International Petroleum Company Limited to whom we are deeply grateful for putting their trust into an enterprise that at times looked extremely risky. We can only hope that we have justified their faith in us.

Many people have been involved in the genesis and production of the book. Some attended our conference but for various reasons were unable to contribute to the final version. Special thanks to Jeff Harrod for his particular insights, to Philip Hayes for the benefit of his extensive research and to Miriam Camps for her constructive optimism. The success of the conference was aided greatly by the geniality of our surroundings at Cumberland Lodge and thanks are due to Ruth Norton and the staff at St Catherine's.

The book was prepared and typed only through the patience and understanding of Pauline Kelly, who has been involved from the earliest stages of planning.

Finally, we would like to thank all our students and colleagues who have listened and talked: if this makes them think, then we have succeeded.

SUSAN STRANGE
ROGER TOOZE

Part One: Introduction

1

States and Markets in Depression: Managing Surplus Industrial Capacity in the 1970s

SUSAN STRANGE and ROGER TOOZE

An academic enterprise that began very modestly by simply seeking to bring together people of conflicting opinions, different disciplines and assorted professions and nationalities to discuss an international issue of common concern ended with rather more than a friendly, but sometimes heated, exchange of views. We were the entrepreneurs of the venture and it seems to us to have produced an implicit but resounding challenge to much conventional thinking about the study of international problems.

In these introductory pages we shall try and explain why we think so, and why the chapters, taken as a whole, challenge some generally accepted ideas about 'international relations' as a discrete branch of the social sciences. Although this sounds as if it might be a conclusion of interest only to academics who teach the subject, we are inclined to think that it may also be relevant to people working in government, business and organised labour, holding out the prospect of a much more fruitful approach to research into international problems – one much more likely to meet their practical needs than some current theorising. Some non-academic readers, of course, will want to skip ahead and see what our assorted contributors have to say about the nature of the problem of surplus capacity and how it has been handled – or mishandled. But some of them we hope will bear with our introductory attempt to show where we think what follows is leading. Even if the world of universities and seminars seems distant, they, too, often need to think of better ways to assess problems and make choices.

Conventionally the prime concern of people interested in the relations of states in the international political system was with issues of war and peace, and with the behaviour and policies of states as they bore upon that issue. We feel that this is a narrow and restrictive conception. Our presumption is that international politics today is, to borrow from Lasswell, about who gets what, and how they get it, 'who' including not only states but all sorts of groups of people – producers and consumers, pensioners and children, workers and investors, rich and poor, farmers and financiers, as well as all the subjectively defined groups which feel themselves joined by common race, religion, or political purpose. If 'who' is broadly defined, so is 'what'. 'What' must start with security, and security meaning not just the absence of war between territorial states but the absence of all physical violence, from civil war and revolution to terrorism and criminal assault. It should also include security as expressed in the general concept of order – the confidence that there will be some minimal measure of social, political and economic stability, the presumption that change will not be so great or fast as to be totally unmanageable. For in real life, since man is distinguished among animals by his awareness of time and the future, all the material aspects of 'what' are not simply enjoyed or desired in the present. People also want the expectation of them in the future – whether they think of food and drink, clothes, houses, books, amusements, or travel – and for that, security is a necessary condition. So it is for the means to these material ends – the opportunity to work, the resources of land, capital goods and knowledge to work with. For not the least part of 'what' in as technologically advanced a society as ours is access to knowledge of all kinds – technology, education, medicine, market information and political information.

In short, international politics is not just about war and peace any more than domestic politics is about the issues of law and order within the state. Consequently, the student of international relations must redefine and enlarge the problematic of his or her subject. The alternative is to contemplate and be reconciled to its inexorable decline into comparative insignificance among the social sciences.

The original justification for international relations as a separate discipline – if there was one at all – rested on the presumption of the separability of domestic politics and foreign politics. Almost all political outcomes, it conceded, lay within the domain and control of the territorial state – outcomes regarding material life, the generation and distribution of wealth, the acquisition and use of knowledge, the definition of liberty and duty, the manner in which private goods and goals and public goods and goals were created and pursued, all these lay within the domain of each state. Only one major political outcome, but some would say the fundamental outcome – the achievement of security from external attack – required the state to engage in foreign intercourse and depended on how successfully it did so. So, to understand the resulting unique behaviour patterns of interstate politics, the alliance building and bargaining characteristics of what Hedley Bull calls the 'anarchic society', a special mode of analysis had to be developed and special knowledge of the historical background built up (Bull, 1977). And while one set of theories could be developed to explain the internally determined outcomes within states, or within particular types of states, quite another set of theories had to be developed to explain and clarify the outcomes of their external behaviour and the manner of their coexistence, given the assumption of anarchy, itself derived from the claims of states.

Of course, the presumption that each state had complete control of everything within its frontiers and that national and international politics were therefore so totally different was itself always something of a fiction – or at least a convenient exaggeration. It reinforced the ideology of the nation-state by making a principle – a virtue, almost – of national interest. By putting so much emphasis on state sovereignty, rather than autonomy, it grossly over-stated the ability of most nation-states to do exactly as they pleased, both domestically and internationally. And this one basic fiction inevitably gave birth to a whole lot of subsidiary fictions concerning all sorts of things like a man's nationality or the 'territorial sea' or the nationality of ships at sea.

Once it is conceded that it is a fiction, however, it becomes much harder to argue that the study of international relations is separate from the study of politics in general and can be pursued independently of it. Wolfram Hanreider, among others, implies much the same from a study of policy. Referring to his perception that domestic and foreign policy are now becoming fused he maintains that this fusion 'reflects a process in which the traditional boundaries separating the nation-state from the environing international system are becoming increasingly obscured and permeable' (Hanreider, 1978, p. 1280). Given this, it seems difficult for international relations to claim its traditional distinct academic niche.

Moreover, recent work on foreign economic policies of states has implicitly suggested that the approaches of comparative politics may be more suited to explaining the contemporary world (Katzenstein, 1976). Katzenstein admits the usefulness of broad, systematic interpretations of the world economy – Marxist, liberal and mercantilist – in focusing attention on the limitations imposed on the world economy state policies. But he adds: 'These interpretations are not so helpful *in explaining the different strategies which advanced industrial states actually pursue*' (Katzenstein, 1977, p. 14, our italics). For Katzenstein this explanation is facilitated through a focus on domestic structures rather than on the constraints of international systems. It is, however, more likely that *neither* a systemic *nor* a comparative politics perspective *on its own* will be totally satisfactory for our purposes.

Much of the initial, and we think largely successful, questioning of the assumed separability of domestic and foreign policy, of national and international politics, has derived from international political economy, specifically the writings on transnational relations (Keohane and Nye, 1972; Kaiser, 1971), although there has also been a much 'lower profile' challenge from the world system approach led by the Sprouts and now reinforced by ecologists, demographers and the world modellers led by Deutsch (see Sprout and Sprout, 1971; Pirages, 1979; Cipolla, 1978; Deutsch, 1977). After all, separability makes little sense if the domains of both are comprehensively linked by interdependence and transnational relations.

There is no need here to recall the extensive literature on transnational relations and interdependence. In numerous ways, and emanating from a wide variety of starting points, it has revealed and stressed the permeability of state authority in an increasingly integrated world economy (see, especially, Cooper, 1968; Bergsten, 1977; Camps, 1975; Gilpin, 1976; Vernon, 1971; Morse, 1975; Keohane and Nye, 1977). One particularly salient consequence of the impact of transnational forces on the autonomy of the state, as first perceived and explained by Keohane and Nye (1977), was the importance in such situations of the sets of rules, laws, or customs agreed by states which allowed them to enjoy the economic benefits of international trade, production, transport communication and investment while still proclaiming their autonomy and sovereign power within their territorial frontiers. These sets of rules they called regimes. And since the regimes accepted by states (and often requiring the creation and functioning of international organisations) then limited the choice of policies open to states in both domestic and foreign policy-making, an important question became 'What causes regimes to change?'. The regime changes taking place in the real world, in the Bretton Woods system of rules for monetary exchange rates, in the Law of the Sea, in international trade, all gave topical point to the question.

Their book *Power and Interdependence* suggested one possible analytical framework for answering the question, using four sources of change (the overall power structure, the economic context or process, the relative power of states in any 'issue area' and the international organisation concerned) that might explain a regime change. The use of the method was demonstrated by applying it to US-Canadian and US-Australian relations over a fifty-year period in the issue areas of money and oceans. Although it breaks interesting and important new ground we feel that this approach begs many important questions (see pp. 8–9).

In this context the significance of interdependence for the study of international relations has been neatly and concisely explained by Chris Mason. 'A condition of interdependence tends to compel states to discuss, and make agreements about, how each is to regulate a wide range of economic activities within its own territory as well as how each is to regulate international trade in order to ensure that the results of the transactions which flow between them are as consistent as possible with what each is trying to achieve within its own territory' (Mason, 1979, p. 3). Mason also points out that concern with the form and content of regimes is not only consistent with the realist view of international politics but also an extension of it. 'For regimes are not only a means by which states can control outcomes *abroad* by influencing the behaviour of other states but also a means by which states can increase their power *at home* by means of agreements with other states about how economic activities are to be regulated, and by whom' (Mason, 1979, p. 4).

In its original formulation 'regime' referred to the agreements made between states, such as the Bretton Woods Agreement or the General Agreement on Tariffs and Trade or even implicit agreements never formally expressed in a treaty or an institution. But the definition of regime as a set of rules, norms, or institutional expectations governing a social system did not, and of course, could not, exclude rules made other than by inter-governmental agreement. (One could instance the Teheran Agreement of 1971 between the oil companies and the OPEC states, agreements between producers or unilateral rules effective abroad but accepted by others, such as US Anti-trust Laws.) Inevitably, as it has been applied to more and more aspects of international political economy, the concept has been substantially stretched.

This is particularly evident in one recent study of the global political economy of food, edited by Hopkins and Puchala (1978) who identify the United States as a decisive source of the global food regime, with the multinational agri-business corporations as important sources of influence on the regimes. But, as they rightly point out, the main usefulness of the regime concept is as much in the kinds of questions it raises as in the order it lends to analysis (Hopkins and Puchala, 1978, p. 598). In other words, it is important less because it gives the right answers than because it helps to redefine the problematic of international relations. For example, they see the most significant questions as: what kind of global food system do regime norms create, where do they originate, and how does it affect participants? Significantly, they also strongly express their contributors' vehement concern that analysis should proceed to prescription and be informed by certain basic moral or political principles.

Implicit in both the Hopkins and Puchala and the Mason analyses, and indeed in much other recent work, is a fundamental shift in perceptions of authority. The 'classical' presumption is that domestic politics are characterised by one single authority – the state – or at least by its overwhelmingly predominant influence, in the final resort, in determining who gets what; while international politics are characterised by a total absence of any authority at all. Both presumptions are now under question, with the work of Robert Dahl and Charles Lindblom of particular importance in the analysis of the domestic political economy (Dahl and Lindblom, 1953; Lindblom, 1977). What we are now saying is that, on the contrary, international

politics are characterised by a multiplicity of authorities, from diverse
sources, which can be seen as sources of influence on global regimes.
Moreover – and this is a point not brought out by Keohane and Nye –
the sources of influence may as often be negative as positive. They may
show an emphasis towards inaction, non-regulation, towards creating a
'non-regime' (which is not, therefore, the realists' 'anarchy') rather than
towards creating any coherent set of values. We have seen that this is, in
fact, a normal bias in the liberal, free-market international political
economy, and that non-regimes are consequently extremely important.
As John Pinder pointed out ten or more years ago, in relation to the
building of a European union, it is much easier for governments to
agree on measures of negative integration – knocking down differential
barriers so as to create a common market – than it is for them to
proceed to measures of positive integration and the co-ordination of
government policies to restrain, manage, or compensate for the
operations of a market system (Pinder, 1968). 'What causes regimes to
change?' is still an important question, but we need a prior question,
'What causes regimes, and why do some areas produce non-regimes?'.

It follows, then, that in any single state and for any class outcomes
for social groups will not be determined *either* by domestic politics *or* by
international politics but by a mix of the two. Owing to the
asymmetrical sensitivity and vulnerability of different national
economies (as pointed out by Keohane and Nye, and others) the
dependence of states on an international regime, or non-regime, will be
highly unequal. And, since regimes are, in Mason's words, 'intermediate
factors between the power structure of the market and the political and
economic bargaining that takes place within it' (Mason, 1979, p. 8), it
also follows that the less intermediation, or 'governance', or
'magistracy' there is (see Kindleberger, 1978), the more vulnerable
groups within states will be to the power structure of the market and to
all the other economic forces which the *dependencia* writers and the
structuralists insist upon.

It therefore becomes almost impossible to generalise about the nature
of the mix of domestic and international politics affecting all sorts of
different states and social groups within them. Faced with such a flood of
unpredictable variables, such cross-currents and contrary tides, no
wonder some prefer to seek security in the old certainties about
international politics. No wonder the search for a general system theory
becomes more and more difficult. Indeed, it has been suggested that
because systems 'may be composed of different actors at different times'
(Lampert *et al.*, 1978, p. 152) it becomes necessary to disaggregate
'system' into different systems for theory to make any sense at all. The
rationale for this disaggregation is that the notions of an all-inclusive
system or a regional 'sub-system' (i.e. 'a system which is *entirely*
swallowed up within ... another system') do not actually help us to

understand what is happening in the world. The concept of system is successfully resurrected through the idea of 'multiple issue based systems', which allows us to identify many different systems the membership and behaviour of which varies according to the issue in hand. This is indeed progress; but we wonder if it goes far enough.

Nor is the problem really solved by looking at outcomes in different 'issue-areas', as Keohane and Nye and many others have done. This may work for certain limited questions where states have little or no choice but to come to some mutual accommodation and therefore agree that they must create some sort of regime – as, for instance, with fisheries and oil rigs in the North Sea. But this approach ultimately fails because it accepts 'issues' at face value. To borrow from a political science debate of nearly twenty years ago: 'By presupposing that . . . there are significant issues in the political arena, [it] takes for granted the very question which is in doubt. [It] accepts as issues what are reputed to be issues' (Bachrach and Baratz, 1962). In other words, issue-areas tend to be status quo biased because the relevant political structure determines what are and what are not issues – 'some issues are organised into politics while others are organised out' – invariably to the benefit of the strong (Schattsneider, 1960, p. 71, quoted in Bachrach and Baratz, 1962). An analysis that ignores this inevitably fails to identify much of the real political struggle of getting issues recognised, or on to the agenda – whether it is the right of blacks to travel in the front of buses, dissidents to leave the Soviet Union, or the need for a just international economic order.

The elaboration of issue-area analysis in the United States seems to us to reflect a consensual perception of the nature of politics – in both the substantive and procedural sense – in which consensus not only reflects the appropriate issues to be decided, but who is to decide them. The problem with consensus is that the most important task becomes the explanation of the internal workings of the consensus itself, through the analysis of regimes and issues, without reference to the set of conditions, or structure, upon which that consensus depends.

This is really the basic position of the structuralist and all those, Marxist or non-Marxist, who argue that outcomes are as much determined by the economic structure, the capitalist mode of production that dominates the world system, as by a political structure in which the fiction of state sovereignty is preserved by a reciprocity of interest among governments. As Peter Gourevitch has said in comparing Wallerstein's work with contemporary *dependencia* theories, '[in both] . . . international market forces rely upon and accentuate inequality. Weak states, unable to control the terms on which their countries relate to the international economy, are confined to a subservient role which perpetuates their weakness' (Gourevitch, 1978, p. 426).

So far so good. But merely adding the economic dimension to the political hardly solves the problem any more than does resort to issue-areas. It may, and does, serve as a polemical purpose to castigate the economic structure for creating and prolonging (if not perpetuating) poverty. But it throws no light on the practical problems of LDC governments negotiating with the United States or with United Fruit; nor for that matter on what either of the latter should seek to do in their own long-term interest. In other words, it does not take us very much further in answering the question of *how* structures actually affect policy choices. And this is for the good reason that a political economy, global or national, is made up of multiple structures as well as subject to multiple authorities.

What does this mean? Negatively, we are questioning the notion of a 'single monolithic international "power structure"' and its national equivalent. As David Baldwin has suggested, in a discussion of international power that draws lessons from domestic politics: 'It is time to recognise that the notion of a single overall international power structure unrelated to any particular issue-area is based on a concept of power that is virtually meaningless' (Baldwin, 1979, p. 193). Positively, the best way of showing what we mean by 'multiple structures' is to suggest that these structures are related to the basic political functions which authority – using whatever power of coercion or persuasion it has, whatever resources of force, money, moral or intellectual leadership it commands – may conceivably exercise in relation to the system of production, exchange and distribution of goods and services. Some authorities will use certain means to certain ends; others quite different means to rather different ends. But there are certain broad functions common to most organised societies which can be distinguished, even though the outcomes in each may be very different. First, there is the provision of security and order – what can be called the security structure. Then there is the organisation of productive effort – which may be either by planned direction of resources, or by regulation of access to and order in the market, or by a mixture of both. This can be called the production structure. The more freedom of choice there is in the production structure – the more production is subject to market forces – the greater the importance of the monetary structure, the management of which has been the second most important function of political authority from the earliest days of capitalism, and indeed of all empires. The choice of public goods and the method chosen to provide them – whether it be roads or education, satellites or defence – suggests another set of structures determining outcomes within a political economy. And then, finally, there is that most inherent function of authority, the provision of justice and a system of political arbitration as an alternative to power bargaining. There is no need – nor space here – to elaborate the idea any further. But it really amounts to the same questions as those asked by Hopkins and Puchala about international regimes in their particularly elastic use of the term. Where do the rules come from? What bargaining processes lie behind them and what costs, risks and benefits are conferred on what groups as a result of their mediation between the structures of the market and those affected by it?

Perhaps for the moment we can best explain the complementary character of the concept of multiple authorities and that of multiple structures by likening the world system to a great big iced cake. The icing on top is multi-coloured and corresponds to, and could even look like, a political map showing the hundred odd states and their territorial limits. Beneath the icing the cake also has multi-coloured layers that correspond to the multiple structures – security, money and credit, trade, communications and transport, knowledge, production, welfare. The richness, colour and flavour of each layer will depend on the inputs of multiple ingredients corresponding to the choices made by the multiple authorities governing the provision of security, the management of money, the regulation of trade, the organisation of production and so forth, not forgetting the provision of welfare and justice.

For the study of international political economy to progress beyond the barrenness of the purely descriptive or the fruitlessness of the dogmatically polemical, we believe that serious analysis has to be given to each of these layers. But to pursue the analogy just a little further, it seems to us also that the layers are of uneven thickness and richness throughout the cake. In some places and for some states the provision of security is very thick indeed, in others quite thin. In other parts, the global monetary and financial structure very substantially affects many outcomes, in others much less so. And this is true whether the cake is cut downwards following the frontiers of states indicated by the icing, or whether it is cut in wedges that correspond to *sectors* – like fish, grain, copper, automobiles, textiles, or tourism.

In each of the wedges, the significance of the basic structures will be slightly different, and the input of authority will come from a different mix of sources. And much of that difference will result from the differential perception of states as to how their interests are affected and how important it is to have a regime of a certain sort or to leave it pretty much to the market structures.

For in this we would emphatically not wish to jettison the insights of the realists. Even in a multiple authority system the nation-state still commands the most authority and the ultimate authority based on the combination of force and loyalty. Salience to the state and the conclusions drawn by state decision-makers from it is therefore almost the first question which sectoral analysis must answer. Until we know whether states consider their national interests to be vitally involved in the fortunes of a particular sector we cannot possibly hope to analyse the pressures and constraints they are likely to put on the forces of the market, either directly in national regimes or through international bargaining.

Other related questions, such as perceptions of salience, and questions on the nature of the product, who operates in the sector, the modes of the market and its character as a mechanism of exchange, all need to be considered. Implicit in all this is that sectoral analysis (by which we mean any study of the political economy of a specific industry in its world context, or of specific markets for goods and services) will illuminate the key bargains, whether these are inter-governmental, company–government, inter-company or intra-company, or between the company and its labour force or its financial backers. Of course, these bargains often lie outside the field of international relations. But it is important to stress that the international political bargaining will still often be very important, and even when it is not, the very absence of an issue from the international agenda requires some understanding of the appropriate 'power structure' of the international political system.

Moreover, because not all states are equally involved in, dependent on, or concerned about all sectors of the world economy, and because the impact of structures on particular sectors is so uneven, we also conclude that some awareness of both sectors *and* structures is absolutely vital to analysis of the international political system – as is, of course, some understanding of the historical process within which sectors and structures have evolved and continue to evolve. In this we share the perspective of those development economists who comprehend world development as historical process in a *theoretical* sense: understanding of the IPE cannot be arrived at outside a historical framework. As Bernstein points out in the context of understanding world development, 'The use of such a perspective goes beyond the notion of "historical background" to the *theoretical comprehension of development and underdevelopment as historical process,* that is to say, as opposed to static conditions or processes embodying a non-historical conception of time and movement (as in system theory for example)' (Bernstein, 1973, p. 15). We do not yet know enough of behaviour within and among sectors, structures and the international political system to begin to assume the existence of specific 'systems' of behaviour, or to want to use ahistorical, non-institutional 'laws' and theories, such as those used in many versions of the theory of international trade. This means that in the following chapters the study of the problem of surplus capacity needs history, not as mere 'historical background', which Bernstein rightly dismisses, but as an integral part of our explanation and appreciation of the processes by which surplus capacity has arisen and the processes by which it can, or cannot, be managed.

Surplus Capacity and the International Political System

Surplus capacity is by no means a new phenomenon, but by the mid-1970s a long list of sectors were experiencing problems, as demonstrated by unemployment, adjustments by firms within the sector, economic studies of capacity, or the political reality of demands for company and government action, the latter usually in the form of domestic support coupled with effective protectionist policies. The list includes ships, steel, textiles, chemicals (particularly ethylene production), shoes, colour television sets, automobiles, ballbearings and refrigerators. And this list is expected to grow (Nowzad, 1978, p. 37). Whatever the sector, the appearance of surplus capacity has produced conflicts of economic interests between states. This, in itself, is not new – the protectionism and competitive depreciations of the 1930s were in many ways concerned with national management (and the international non-management) of surplus capacity. Yet the extent, persistence, depth, or just plain stubbornness of the problems encountered in the 1970s (see Figure 1.1) suggest that, at a minimum, the national, international and transnational environment within which surplus capacity has developed and is now managed is vastly more complex and is, perhaps, qualitatively different from earlier periods.

In an earlier article, which forms the basis of this discussion, Susan Strange has defined surplus capacity as 'a situation in which demand is insufficient to absorb production at prices high enough both to maintain employment and to maintain profitability for all the enterprises engaged' (Strange, 1979, p. 304 fn.). We see no reason to differ from this except to point out a few considerations when using this concept. The actual measurement of surplus capacity is problematic because there is no 'unique measure' of true capacity. Many variables enter into 'true capacity', not the least being the nature of the technology and the historical pattern of investment. As *The Economist* (21 July 1979) has pointed out:

> The figures suggest that all major economies bar the United States and Canada are still short of average, let alone peak, capacity utilisation for the pre-OPEC decade to 1973; but after a quinquennium of low investment, nobody really knows what the true level of usable capacity is.

But in many cases the 'true level of usable capacity' is not central to the problem. What matters is that within the relevant market many sectors exhibit a 'persistent long run excess of productive potential over effective demand' (Pickering and Jones, 1979, p. 3), and that the perception of this elicits responses from a wide variety of groups in society (including unions, firms and governments) which because of the nature of the world economy involves bargaining at the level of the international political system, as well as at many other levels.

Utilisation of Industrial Capacity

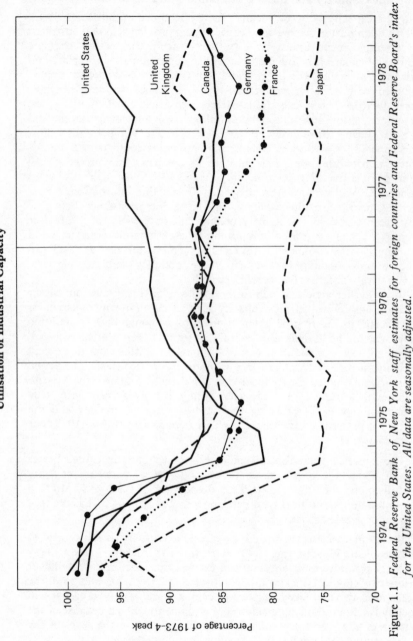

Figure 1.1 *Federal Reserve Bank of New York staff estimates for foreign countries and Federal Reserve Board's index for the United States. All data are seasonally adjusted.*

Significantly, in their paper entitled 'The problem of excess capacity in British industry', Pickering and Jones identify five major sources of surplus capacity, all of which are open to political influence and effect, either in the form of government policy, the effects of international regimes, or the result of specific political bargains. Some economists go further. Many 'liberal' assessments lay the blame for the creation of surplus capacity, and the failure of national economies to adjust to new challenges, squarely on the increasing levels of government intervention in the economy (see Chapter 18, by Jan Tumlir, and Blackhurst, 1977). Other economists, however, show no surprise that governments continue to intervene or that the system produces surplus capacity. For them this is the nature of the system of 'monopoly capitalism'. And we cannot dismiss this Marxian analysis just because its conclusions are pessimistic about the continued existence of the system or its methodology is not accepted by 'conventional' economists. For Baran and Sweezy, under monopoly capitalism 'the *normal* condition is less than capacity production. The system simply does not generate enough "effective demand" (to use the Keynesian term) to ensure full utilisation of either labour or productive facilities' (Baran and Sweezy, 1968, p. 146, our emphasis). If the internationalisation of the world economy makes possible an extension of their analysis from America to the whole of the system, clearly what they have to say is important and presages even greater conflicts of economic interests between states in the future, as more states and more people become integrated into the world economy.

Our conceptualisation of surplus capacity is, of course, difficult to apply to the service sectors – no product is produced, so no surplus is possible in theory. Yet, as Jonathan Aronson shows in his sectoral study in this book (Chapter 10), surplus capacity, however defined, is a reality in banking and insurance. Both these sectors have experienced a period of mergers and acquisitions in the 1970s, nationally and internationally, and it is possible that here we shall quite soon see the problems of service 'surplus capacity'. In general, as more of the industrialised countries' GDP is produced by the service industries it is likely that international conflicts of interest and/or international attempts at control will spread out from manufacturing and increasingly involve these sectors. The present rumblings over international air transport rates and fare structures and demands to 'control' the Eurocurrency markets are perhaps indicative of this.

So, precise measures of surplus capacity are not ultimately all that important. What matters for us is a general perception of the problem and the transformation of this perception into economic and political action – often indistinguishable. Much adjustment to surplus capacity takes place within the industrial structure itself, which means it is not 'politicised' in the sense of needing or attracting government action. But this does not mean that it is not *political* in the sense we have used: investment and operating decisions taken by firms within the market structure clearly do influence 'who gets what and how they get it'. Much of the current 'politicisation of economics' debate misses the point that liberal economic structures have always been political, and that, as E.H. Carr has pointed out, 'The science of economics presupposes a given political order' (Carr, 1939, p. 149), and that on the international level traditional economic analysis is insufficient and misleading. As Constantine Vaitsos (1976, p. 113) cogently explains,

> The structure of relations between countries and foreign controlled transnational enterprises is interpreted in traditional economic analysis as, fundamentally, involving a harmony of interests ... Alternative conclusions are reached if economic analysis is enriched to allow for imperfect world markets, distortions induced by certain government policies, costly and inequitably distributed productive knowledge, concentration of resources and the effects of transnational enterprises on unequal exchanges between and within countries as well as classes.

Whether adjustment to surplus capacity takes place within industry or is aided by a government, at the level of the international political system we are faced with all the ingredients of a 'classic' management problem because surplus capacity presents for us:

(1)   an economic phenomenon, the symptoms of which have a clear, important and immediate political relevance;
(2)   a phenomenon that varies by country and by sector, and the possible and acceptable solutions to which also vary by country and by sector;
(3)   a problem that is neither purely domestic nor international in origin or cure, but that can be partly ameliorated by making someone else bear the burden of change; this is commonly a different national group, because the major power to shift the burden is exercised by states;
(4)   a problem that existing international regimes (and the institutions set up to 'police' them) do not really help to solve;
(5)   a problem that is perceived differently by the major participants in the management process: US perceptions sometimes differ from European and government perceptions may differ from companies; and the overall perception of the problem is not helped by the fact that economists of different persuasions inevitably differ in their analysis and policy advice.

The process of managing surplus capacity, however, although

important and interesting in itself, also allows us to comment on the theory of international politics and international political economy. If we have experienced a qualitative change in the international political economy as we believe (although this itself is problematic; see Strange, 1979, pp. 307–8), how well does the wisdom of the 1960s stand up to the problems of the 1970s, and can this comparison help us to improve our understanding of the 1980s? Susan Strange has already attempted to evaluate certain theoretical implications of surplus capacity (Strange, 1979), and we will not repeat that discussion here. In our conclusions we shall discuss some broad problems of managing surplus capacity in the light of the evidence presented in the book, but we can now also briefly mention other concerns which focus primarily on the claims of and possibilities for theory itself.

The first is that although we are explicitly concerned with theory for purposes of explanation we remain sceptical as to the present possibilities of an all-embracing, all-explanatory theory of IPE. As yet we simply do not know enough about the significant variables and the links between them. What is reasonably clear, though, is that we will not find much relevant theory in the analysis of the overall international political system as such. We need to undergo a process of analytical disaggregation before we can reconstruct our theoretical statements – it was, after all, such a process of disaggregation (analysis by economic sector rather than on a macro level) that led the MIT team to some surprising conclusions on the nature of long-wave change (see Chapter 2 by Manfred Bienefeld). Moreover, current research on the international power structure tends to support the necessity of disaggregation (see particularly Goldmann, 1979).

Finally, we would argue that many of the failings of present theory stem from attempts to make theoretical statements that are ahistorical and non-institutional. Many of the statements of neo-classical trade theory, for example, are 'assumed to apply to all kinds of human societies'. One of the major contributions of 'post-Keynesian' economic analysis has been its denial of the all-embracing nature of such claims and its demonstration of the relevance of 'historical time'. Consequently the universe to which neo-classical trade theory applies is much smaller than previously assumed (see particularly Burbidge, 1979), as even a cursory consideration of mercantilism would indicate (Viner, 1946; Heckscher, 1936–7). The implication is that, at the very least, we need to be much more cautious in what we claim to be the scope of our theoretical statements, and to be aware of the limits and dangers of stretching theory too far. If history and institutions matter, ahistorical generalisations are merely an extension of historically specific cases to the level of a law (Waltz, 1979, pp. 1–13). More directly we need to develop theoretical statements which incorporate 'historical time'. Our existing statements and categories may no longer be adequate – if they are found wanting they should be discarded without the sentiment usually reserved for the old and the comfortable.

The outline of the book
We would like to be able to say that we had developed for our contributors a coherent and logical framework from the preceding analysis. That, however, as is the nature of these things, did not happen. What we did provide was a working brief with an important presumption, and the structure of the book took shape from the material we then received. The presumption is important: for us any analysis of surplus capacity needs to involve a broad range of different perceptions, not only academic but national as well – hence the relatively large number of contributors of varying intellectual persuasion, from different organisations and from different parts of the world. Despite this number of distinct contributions, and, perhaps, almost because of them, the structure of the book makes sense, not only in relation to the overall perspective we have outlined, but as an 'issue study' in itself.

In 'introductions' to books of this sort it is customary to say how each contributor links in with the overall theme and briefly summarise his/her contribution. This we will not do as we feel much of the point of the exercise lies in showing the process by which each of our contributors arrives at his/her various perspectives and conclusions. What does need some explanation is the relation of the sections to each other and the overall framework itself. The contributions are grouped under five headings: analysis, sector studies, practice, policy options and prescription. Each heading should be self-explanatory and each provides a clue – an intellectual 'way in' – to the problem at hand, and each needs the others. No real understanding of the problem of surplus capacity seems possible without at least taking account of the various themes we have identified. Other factors are also relevant but what we have listed here is the minimum we should cover – we have to start somewhere.

We felt it important to begin with as broad an analysis of the phenomenon as possible, including, of course, whether we should consider surplus capacity to be a problem or not. Only in this way could we hope to place 'surplus capacity' into some kind of perspective – historically and analytically. Each contributor has provided a different perspective and reached different conclusions, but it is this very difference that is important. One of the real problems in working towards policy within issues such as this is the complex nature of what is happening. If the analyses which form our starting points are so different, what chance is there for successful national policy harmonisation?

The sector studies provide the 'nitty gritty' of the problem, in line with our overall emphasis on the importance of the sector approach. These studies are broadly comparable in that we have asked contributors to look at three main questions.

- To what extent does surplus capacity exist?
- What are the sources of this surplus capacity?
- What has been done about it – either by groups within the sector, or by government action at both national and international levels?

Without pre-empting any conclusions, the answers to these questions, emphasising the differences among sectors, seem both highly suggestive (in terms of how we think about issues in the international political economy) and highly significant (for our understanding of the problem of surplus capacity).

After we have disaggregated our analysis through sectors we need to see how the international system has coped within the more traditional framework – the state, international organisations and the corporation itself. The analyses here present a view from these three standpoints, emphasising different problems, different processes and, most important, different goals. So the complexity of the management problem arises not only from the differences among the sectors (with some sectors being highly salient to some states and almost irrelevant to others, while other sectors are almost 'self-correcting', involving little or no overt direct governmental action) but from the nature and characteristics of the units within which it is experienced.

Similarly, the discussion of policy options indicates that further complexity arises from the differences in national goals and value hierarchies. The distinctions between the American and the Japanese analyses serve only too well to highlight the sometimes insurmountable problems of different national perceptions and values. At the very least, we need, with some urgency, not just a checklist of national hierarchies of goals, but some indication of the gaps in perception itself.

Our final substantive heading – prescription – both mirrors and develops the themes we have identified so far: complexity, diversity and, perhaps, a nagging doubt that any 'solution' is possible. In line with our concern with values and goals our final question must be: what can and what should we do now? This section illuminates our options but does not offer a magic way out. We can only leave our readers to ponder on what that might be in the knowledge that we have merely provided a tentative and incomplete framework.

References: Chapter 1.

Bachrach, P., and Baratz, M. S. (1962), 'Two faces of power', *American Political Science Review*, vol. 56, pp. 947–52.

Baldwin, D. A. (1979), 'Power analysis and world politics: new trends versus old tendencies', *World Politics,* vol. XXXI, no. 2, January.

Baran, P. A., and Sweezy, P. M. (1968), *Monopoly Capital* (Harmondsworth: Penguin).

Bergsten, F. (1977), *Managing International Economic Interdependence* (Lexington, Mass.: Lexington Books).

Bernstein, H. (ed.) (1973), *Underdevelopment and Development: The Third World Today* (Harmondsworth: Penguin).

Blackhurst, R., Marian, N., and Tumlir, J. (1977), *Trade Liberalisation, Protectionism and Interdependence* (Geneva: GATT).

Bull, H. (1977), *The Anarchical Society* (London: Macmillan).

Burbidge, J. B. (1979), 'The international dimension', in A. S. Eichner (ed.), *A Guide to Post-Keynesian Economics* (New York: Sharpe).

Camps, M. (1975), *'First World' Relationships: The Role of the OECD* (Paris: Atlantic Institute for International Affairs).

Carr, E. H. (1939), *The Twenty Year Crisis* (Cambridge: Cambridge University Press).

Cipolla, C. (1978), *The Economic History of World Population,* 7th edn (Harmondsworth: Penguin).

Cooper, R. N. (1968), *The Economics of Interdependence* (New York: McGraw-Hill).

Dahl, R. A., and Lindblom, C. E. (1953), *Politics, Economics and Welfare* (New York: Harper).

Deutsch, K. (ed.) (1977), 'Ecosocial systems and ecopolitics' (Geneva: UNESCO).

Gilpin, R. (1976), *US Power and the Multinational Corporation* (London: Macmillan).

Goldmann, K., and Sjösted, Y. (eds) (1979), *Power, Capabilities, Interdependence* (London: Sage).

Gourevitch, P. (1978), 'The international system and regime formation', *Comparative Politics,* vol. 10, no. 3, April, pp. 419–38.

Hanrieder, W. F. (1978), 'Dissolving international politics: reflections on the nation-state', *American Political Science Review,* vol. 72, December.

Heckscher, E. F. (1936–7), 'Mercantilism', *Economic History Review,* vol. VII, no. 1.

Hopkins, R. F., and Puchala, D. J. (eds) (1978), 'The global political economy of food', *International Organisation,* vol. 32, no. 3, Summer.

Kaiser, K. (1971), 'Transnational politics: toward a theory of multinational politics', *International Organisation,* vol. XXV, no. 4, Autumn, pp. 790–817.

Katzenstein, P. J. (1976), 'International relations and domestic structures: foreign economic policies of advanced industrial states', *International Organisation,* vol. 30, no. 1, Winter, pp. 1–46.

Katzenstein, P. J. (ed.) (1977), 'Between power and plenty: foreign economic policies of advanced industrial states', *International Organisation,* vol. 31, no. 4, Autumn.

Keohane, R. O., and Nye, J. S., Jr (eds) (1972), *Transnational Relations and World Politics* (Cambridge, Mass.: Harvard University Press).

Keohane, R. O., and Nye, J. S. (1977), *Power and Interdependence* (Boston, Mass.: Little, Brown).

Kindleberger, C. P. (1978), 'Government and international trade', *Princeton Essays in International Finance,* no. 129, July.

Lampert, D. E., Falkowski, L. S., and Mansbach, R. W. (1978), 'Is there an International System?', *International Studies Quarterly,* March, pp. 143–66.

Lindblom, C. E. (1977), *Politics and Markets. The World's Political-Economic Systems* (New York: Basic Books).

Mason, C. M. (ed.) (1979), *The Effective Management of Resources: The IP of the North Sea* (London: Frances Pinter).

Morse, E. L. (1975), *Modernisation and the Transformation of International Relations* (London: Collier Macmillan).

Nowzad, B. (1978), *The Rise in Protectionism* (Washington, DC: IMF), Pamphlet Series no. 24.

Pickering, J. F., and Jones, T. T. (1979), 'The problem of excess capacity in British industry', paper presented to European Association for Research in Industrial Economics, Nuremberg, September.

Pinder, J. (1968), 'Positive integration and negative integration: some problems of economic union in the EEC', *World Today,* vol. 24, pp. 88–110.

Pirages, D. (1979), *The New Context for International Relations. Global Ecopolitics* (N. Scituate, Mass.: Duxbury Press).

Schattsneider, E. E. (1960), *The Semisovereign People* (New York: Holt, Rinehart & Winston).

Sprout, H., and Sprout, M. (1971), *Towards a Politics of the Planet Earth* (New York: Van Nostrand).

Strange, S. (1979), 'The management of surplus capacity: or how does theory stand up to protectionism 1970s style?', *International Organisation,* vol. 33, no. 3, Summer.

Vaitsos, C. (1976), 'Power, knowledge and development policy: relations between transnational enterprises and developing countries', in G. K. Helliner (ed.), *A World Divided: The Less Developed Countries in the International Economy* (Cambridge: Cambridge University Press).

Vernon, R. (1971), *Sovereignty at Bay* (Harmondsworth: Penguin).

Viner, J. (1946), 'Power versus plenty as objectives of foreign policy in the seventeenth and eighteenth centuries', *World Politics,* vol. 1, no. 1, pp. 1–29.

Waltz, K. (1979), *Theory of International Politics* (London: Addison-Wesley).

Part Two: Perspectives on the Problem

2

Interpreting Excess Capacity

M.A.BIENEFELD

> Depressions have been times of excess capacity in nearly every economic sector. Depressions occur immediately after capital capacity has been fully rebuilt. When a peak in the long wave is reached, industrial countries are capable of producing more than they have ever produced before ... It should be a golden age, the time towards which society has been striving.
>
> Instead, the end of rebuilding has always led to a depression, a time of economic disaster, with hunger, unemployment, and social breakdown. (Forrester, 1978)

It is easy to view the existence of excess capacity as an inevitable consequence of the fact that full capacity refers to some hypothetical ideal which one should expect to find in practice only in exceptional circumstances. Furthermore, the fluctuations in this measure are generally understood simply as manifestations of the business cycle, so that an increase in the amplitude of such variations merely represents a change of degree, and not one of kind. The same explanations and the same policy measures are therefore invoked in response, and the analytic importance of decreasing levels of capacity utilisation becomes relatively limited.

A discussion of the potential significance of the phenomenon cannot therefore be based primarily on a detailed empirical investigation. Instead it must focus on the context within which such changing levels of excess capacity have been observed. In this chapter the experience of the 1970s will be broadly discussed, in order to consider the significance to be attached to this issue during the period.

The relative lack of concern with the empirical detail of this question not only reflects the above observation that a rising level of unused capacity is not necessarily of any particular analytical importance. It also reflects the acute difficulty of measuring the phenomenon, since the task is bedevilled by the need to quantify the essentially hypothetical notion of 'full' capacity. As a result all measures in this area are particularly ambiguous and subject to interpretation, and comparisons are perilous indeed. Under these circumstances the empirical statements which retain the greatest significance are those which identify trends over time, based on some standardised definition.

This discussion will consequently simply proceed from the observation that, by any measure, the 1970s have produced relative levels of excess capacity which were unprecedented since the war and which have at times simultaneously affected all of the most important economies, and many of the most important manufacturing sectors, including steel, chemicals, textiles, shipbuilding and others. The question is whether this has any significance, beyond indicating that over much of the 1970s the major industrial economies had shifted to a lower trend rate of growth.

It is not surprising that businessmen and economists should have a tendency to view this problem somewhat differently. Since the former tend to view developments in relation to their direct consequences for investment and profit in particular sectors of the economy, they are quicker to appreciate the difficulties inherent in such a development. For them the emergence of a substantial degree of excess capacity is a particular problem because installed production capacity has a long life in relation to inventories or order books and is generally highly inflexible. Its existence is therefore a major and protracted impediment to investment, especially when low variable costs within total costs encourage continued production below actual cost, so long as variable costs are more than covered. In this case there are good economic reasons (quite apart from social and political ones) for the inefficient to linger on, undermining the profitability of all others, and possibly pre-empting even the technical changes which might otherwise have been viably introduced.

For the economist, on the other hand, distance from the direct competitive struggle allows him to take a more 'objective' or, alternatively, a more irresponsible view. To the extent that he is concerned with the economy as a whole such sectoral problems merely indicate the need for adjustment, and hence seem to reinforce the importance of allowing the market to operate freely. The more dogmatic exponents of this position thence glibly assert that 'there is no problem' – or at least no problem that could not be readily solved by weeding out a few lame ducks. The problem of any potential social and political consequences can 'in theory' be dealt with by compensation, while the problem of alternative economically viable activities into which resources are to be shifted cannot in general arise either because of some variant of Say's Law (that supply creates its own demand) or because of the Keynesian notion that if it should fail to do so the demand can readily be created.

This, at least, was the view that dominated the 1960s, when economists were generally afflicted by a hubris which appears rather pathetic in retrospect. It was captured nicely when Tinbergen (1962, p. 68) wrote:

> Of course, problems remain, but they cannot be compared to those that existed during the great depression. Then the role of government was imperfectly understood, and mistakes were made. Too much importance was attached to the restoration of 'confidence' as a factor making for investment demand . . . Public expenditures were reduced in the erroneous belief that the solvency of the state depended upon a balanced budget. However, the decline in public spending undermined confidence in the future because of its direct impact.

The 1970s have seen this orthodoxy peremptorily swept aside. The failure of Keynesian solutions in the face of high levels of unused capacity was the most dramatic signal that something was amiss, and that the reigning mechanistic perceptions of the economic process were quite simply inadequate. (For an eloquent and devastating critique of the mechanistic nature of postwar economics see Georgescu-Roegen, 1971.) The search for alternative perceptions which could encompass the diverse phenomena that emerged over this period provides the context within which the potential significance of existing excess capacity has to be established.

The phenomena which have appeared to challenge existing perceptions include: the combination of inflation and unemployment which has accompanied, and indeed survived, Keynesian interventions; a pervasive and generalised fall in profit rates in the OECD countries; a sharp increase in unemployment within the industrial nations, together with an increasing pessimism (although with differing reasons) as to the possibility of reversing that trend; the emergence of volumes of investible resources accumulating in financial institutions whose capacity to identify viable borrowers, even at very low real interest rates, appears to confront increasing difficulty; the emergence of economies whose running of persistent large trade surpluses is associated with a remarkably good economic performance; and, of course, the reduced trend rate of growth mentioned earlier.

Furthermore, these developments have been associated with increasing economic nationalism, involving, apart from the above-mentioned 'mercantilism', protectionism, competitive devaluations, export subsidies and the beginnings of an 'interest rate war'. They have also led to the formal demise of the Bretton Woods gold-based dollar, and hence to an opening of the flood-gates to the debasement of the coinage. The waves of speculation which have swept gold, currency and commodity markets ever since have spilled over into all manner of things, from property, to stamps, to outdated 'worthless' stock certificates ('scripophily'!). In short, most of the problems which the negotiators of the Bretton Woods arrangements were concerned to forestall, so as to prevent a recurrence of the 1930s depression, seem to have returned with a vengeance (see particularly Gardner, 1956).

Attempts at explaining these events range from those that merely see the consequences of some exogenous disturbance, like the Vietnam War or the oil crisis, to those that perceive a fundamental and endogenous imbalance within the system, which will involve a painful restructuring process if it is to be rectified. The significance of the level of excess capacity and the difficulty of its 'management' follow from the view one takes of this question.

In this debate, the most significant division is between those who continue to see Keynesian demand management as the way forward, and those who think that a restructuring, involving some destruction of existing capital, higher unemployment and substantial recession, is an inevitable result of the current situation. Because this last group includes such odd bedfellows as neo-classical monetarists, exponents of the long wave, and Marxists, and because most neo-classicals eschew talk of crisis and prefer to speak of adjustment, while those who believe in some form of Keynesian solution often speak of restructuring and of crisis in the strongest terms, this division may not always appear obvious. It is nevertheless crucial, since it separates those who perceive the possibility of a non-conflictive, mutually beneficial resolution to current problems from those who are convinced that such a universally desirable and beneficial solution is unfortunately an idealistic dream whose short-term palliatives may merely pave the way for a more severe crisis to follow.

Alternatively, it is only the neo-classical position which sees the resolution of the conflicts inherent in this situation as resolvable essentially through the market mechanism, while all the other positions are united in their acceptance of the need for political initiatives to facilitate such restructuring and thus to moderate its adverse consequences. In this sense, these latter positions imply a qualitative change in the nature of the problem, which ceases to be understood as merely a larger trade cycle. The implication is that beyond some point economic mechanisms are no longer adequate to reverse such a cyclical trend, because beyond this point the minimal rules formerly governing trade, finance and production are smashed by intense economic and political pressures. Ironically, it may be that in this situation, as the need and the rhetoric for international management and collaboration increases, so the possibility of achieving it recedes, with the danger that, globally, national conflicts sharpen perhaps to the point of war, while within nations political polarisation sharpens inter- and intra-class conflicts, and threatens both the welfare state and the liberal democratic framework itself.

Of these positions, it is the Keynesian one that deserves to be considered first, since if it were feasible it would certainly represent the most desirable solution to the problem. Currently this position is still espoused, either by those who see it as feasible nationally, if and when external deficits are not a problem, or internationally, if and when appropriate international agencies are created. In spite of the potential attractiveness of this position the argument carries less and less conviction. With respect to the 'national' impediment it is decisive to note that those economies with no foreign exchange constraint are also suffering from unemployment and from excess capacity. Furthermore, the tendency of these economies to use persistent trade surpluses to economic advantage suggests a different set of problems.

Those who put their faith in global Keynesianism must explain why the Eurocurrency and related markets are not adequate sources of international liquidity; why the risks which are now threatening to reduce those flows would not apply to any Keynesian funds disbursed; how the costs of Keynesian disbursements would be borne in the short run in view of the intense pressure on profits already; and why such disbursements should differ from the disbursements which national economies can no longer make without inflationary consequences. Furthermore, in a setting where trade relations have already become politicised and the subject of national conflicts and where even the strongest economies have substantial levels of excess capacities, the unevenness of the consequent distribution of benefits would have to be considered a major problem.

Even if all of these questions were answered a further problem would remain, namely, that of primary inputs. The growth required to absorb all existing excess capacities and productive possibilities, especially in view of the current wave of technical changes, would be so enormous as to cause severe dislocation, even if one were to deny the ultimate scarcity of resources. And, finally, in a situation where a substantial imbalance exists between real income, the stock of capital, the mass of profit or surplus value and levels of effective demand it is not clear that such a Keynesian infusion would restore this balance, though this question will be further discussed below. In short there are many reasons to believe that such an initiative would indeed largely serve to fuel inflation.

The other views of the current crisis do reach just this conclusion. The monetarist position indeed sees the Keynesian solutions as the very source of the problem, and the inadequacy of profit as a mirror image of an excessive social and direct expenditure on labour and its reproduction, as a result of the excessive creation of capital which becomes possible once money has become pure paper money.

However, while this analysis is probably correct as far as it goes, it does not encompass the whole of the problem, and it becomes pure ideology when it proposes policies to resolve the problem. Its inadequacy will be discussed in considering the phenomenon of the long wave. Its ideological content is not difficult to see since it involves a declaration of war on labour in the broadest sense. From its perspective the brunt of the adjustment is to be borne by labour, and the chief culprit is the public sector. Furthermore, salvation is thought to lie in some idealised version of the market, which is seen as capable of rectifying the situation if only this flood of money is turned off. This faith is a little difficult to take seriously when markets have been so thoroughly destabilised and politicised, when excess capacity has reached such high levels, and when their own deflationary policies restrict demand and confront heavily indebted economic actors with astronomical interest rates. In short the problem is not one of economics, but one of political economy, and it will not do to propose economic solutions without recognising the political consequences as endogenous issues.

To be sure if such advice were followed through rigorously it would lead to the restructuring it seeks, but at a cost which no sane person would readily accept. Historically the struggle to see who would bear the brunt of such a process has often led to war and there is little reason to believe that could not recur. Certainly if this is the path to be taken, and if monetarism comes to be applied at a global level, there will be a depression in which the weak will go to the wall and in which many economies looking reasonably prosperous now will be crushed by the debts which have until recently been supportable only because of inflation and their expanding exports.

The inadequacy of the monetarist analysis derives from the level of aggregation at which it operates. This leads it to propose causes which are not sufficient explanations, and solutions which are horrendously crude and extremely wasteful. A more convincing analysis emerges from a consideration of the concept of the long wave, which has a chequered intellectual past but which has been squarely placed on the agenda by the events of the 1970s and by recent highly empirical work done at MIT's Sloane School of Management.[1] What is emerging clearly from this debate is a concept of the long wave that involves the appearance of a widening imbalance between the capital stock (where capital refers to any physical or financial assets seeking to generate a return on investment), the level of output, the mass of profit and the level of effective demand. Unlike the monetarists, the proponents of this view see that imbalance as being generated endogenously by the market mechanism itself.

Put simply such an imbalance can be rectified mechanically by either increasing profit or increasing demand. If our earlier discussion has been sceptical about the possibility of increasing demand, what is the problem with the monetarist proposal to solve it by increasing profit through a reduction of wage costs? The answer is that this solution defeats itself by further restricting demand. The traditional reply to this point has been that profit also generates demand, but this reply is inadequate because it treats demand as some undifferentiated aggregate. In fact the demand generated by capital is for goods or services that in turn will yield a return. This demand encourages the progressive build-up of the capital stock, but the process of building machines to build machines must eventually be validated by a demand for the final goods, and it is this latter demand which is constrained by the imbalances.

Of course, these limits are neither fixed nor precise. With liberal credit facilities, long-term gestation periods and 'Keynesian' authorities this process can continue for a long time. Furthermore, by the time the risks of further infusions have become more clear, the costs of withholding them have grown. Once that pressure has torn money loose from its commodity base, the possibilities of increasing the stock of financial 'capital' multiply and the consequent instability further undermines the conditions for efficient, productive investment. It is at this point that crude monetarism once more comes into the limelight, not to solve the problem, but merely to deplore it and to prescribe the ensuing convulsions as the cure.

The recent work done at MIT has documented this process in a detailed and compelling manner. The team constructed a macroeconomic model by aggregating a series of detailed sectoral models, each of which took account of that sector's particular responses to changes in other sectors. This represents a major advance over the usual models built directly from macroeconomic trend statistics, and it allows structural shifts to be monitored. The results came as a surprise (Forrester, 1978, p. 5):

> In fact, I [J.W. Forrester] was unaware of the scant literature on the long wave while we were initially formulating the Model. But when we assembled a consumer durables sector along with a sector that produces capital equipment, we found that the Model exhibited strong fluctuating growth and collapse in the capital sector with about 50 years between peaks of capital output.
>
> After we analysed the reasons for the 50 year mode of behaviour in the National Model, we concluded that the underlying assumptions still seemed reasonable. It was only then that the literature on the Kondratieff cycle became a part of the investigation.
>
> We now believe the National Model provides a theory for how the economic long wave is generated. The process involves an overbuilding of the capital sectors in which they grow beyond the capital output rate needed for long-term equilibrium. In the process, capital plant throughout the economy is over-built beyond the level justified by the marginal productivity of capital. Finally, the over-expansion is ended by the hiatus of a great depression during which excess capital plant is physically worn out and financially depreciated

on the account books until the stage has been cleared for a new era of rebuilding.

Further work by this group has subsequently produced a wealth of empirical evidence from the United States which strengthens these conclusions. With this evidence, the proposition that the 1970s marked the climax of a long wave becomes extremely persuasive. It is theoretically comprehensible, historically plausible and now technically demonstrable. More important, it is best able to explain, or at least to make sense of, the contradictory developments of the 1970s.

Two aspects of this debate deserve further brief mention. The first concerns the empirical relationship that undeniably exists between the expanding phase of the cycle and the application of new technology. It has frequently been argued that it is the introduction of these technologies, or in some versions, of new associated products, which explains the secular expansion (see Freeman, 1977). The formulation of the argument presented here turns this on its head by saying that it is the expansion which leads to the application of the technology. This liberates the argument from the unsupportable burden of having to show that apart from current and expected income constraints there is some major difficulty about inducing people to consume new products. That is not plausible, though it might be desirable. The second point concerns the strict periodicity of the National Model's cycles. This should be seen as a consequence of what is after all a simulation built on one set of assumptions. In the real world there are enough variables capable of affecting the process that it would take an excessively mechanistic view of the process to anticipate strict periodicity in practice. One is after all not dealing with a natural law, but with a tendency built into a decentralised, fragmented social system.[2] There may be no logical necessity for crisis, but at the same time there may be something approaching a historical necessity.

When these processes are studied at a global level, and compared with similar processes at an earlier time, there are reasons for believing that currently, at the global level, they are likely to be more severe and more intractable. This contrasts with the common view that in some general way things have changed so that earlier processes will not be repeated. The reason why they should be more intractable at a global level lies simply in the fact that at that level national policies can be formulated and implemented to shift the burden of the emerging problems on to others so that the consequences of such developments can be held at bay by the strongest economies.

The reasons for suggesting that these arguments might weigh more heavily today than in the distant past of the 1930s are these:

(1) Vast increases in project scale and gestation periods reduce flexibility and encourage large disequilibria and slower responses.

(2)   Scale increases facilitate mobilisation of institutional and political defences, and encourage direct and indirect subsidisation and other policies which blur price signals.

(3)   The internationally widening gap in labour costs creates a potential threat to social and political conditions in the industrial countries as competitive pressures induce their investors to accept the higher risks of investment in the cheap labour economies. The medium-term result is almost certainly intensified national conflict.

(4)   Oligopolistic structures facilitate 'perverse' economic reponses. Prices may be raised in response to falling turnover – although international competition may threaten such solutions – with the consequent protectionist pressures. Alternatively, producers may use speculative pressures to their sectoral advantage by using control over inputs or technologies to shift relative prices in their favour.

(5)   More integrated financial structures may further expand credit facilities by spreading risk more effectively. As a result price signals may be further distorted or obscured. Keynesian thinking and the optimism bred by the historically unprecedented boom of the 1950s and 1960s may add to this effect.

Such an interpretation leads to the conclusion that the resolution of the crisis will occur primarily through a considerable destruction of capital. This in turn suggests intensified conflict, and the need for major political initiatives to divert this process away from a creation of those conditions in which the seeds of war could germinate. Pleas to leave things for the market to solve ignore the endogenous nature of the problem. Pleas to cure things by a monetarist straitjacket cannot be separated from the political developments that would accompany such an economic purge.

This leaves political initiatives, which recognise the need for some destruction of capital, and which set about accomplishing that task explicitly and in a socially less costly manner. In theory this should be conceivable even from the point of view of capital, since the destruction of capital is already very much in progress in any case. However, in practice this option is likely to be resisted most fiercely by the most powerful concentrations of capital for it is they who have the least to lose by the other route. It is after all a sobering thought that most of the largest concentrations of German and Japanese capital survived the total war of the 1940s in remarkably good condition.

Without doubt there is a political basis for such a struggle since the mass of our populations have a great deal to lose. But the likely prospect is that crude nationalistic slogans will once more carry the day, and send forth the multitudes to defend civilisation as they know it.

Internationally too there should be a basis for such political solutions, since without it the weakest will go to the wall first, and that includes a few slipping industrial countries and a large chunk of the developing world. However, here, too, the particular perspectives of their ruling classes and groups, and the siren song of the high-debt, high-growth economic miracles, undermine a realistic assessment of the situation.

Meanwhile everyone will struggle for things that are impossible in the context of the current contradictions. A growing army of well-meaning futurologists will paint wonderful pictures of the creative leisure societies they see as technically available, only to be disillusioned by harassed politicians and businessmen operating under intense competitive pressures and unable to respond, however sympathetic they might be. Developing countries will demand more concessions from rich countries already imposing draconian deflation on their own populations. Workers facing 20 per cent inflation will demand 20 per cent wage increases, and no redundancies, from firms suffering losses and unable to pay the mounting interest charges on their accumulating debts. The problem lies in the fact that capital is unable to countenance such concessions under existing conditions. It is a matter of the economic survival of each unit of capital involved, not a matter of morality or of intent.

If in this situation positive political initiatives do not succeed in reconciling the interests of capital with the needs of people, then the monetarist policies now everywhere espoused are likely to reap the whirlwind. In many cases they will eventually be swept from power by charlatans who will unite the people behind those simplistic, nationalist slogans which have served so often to lead the troops to the front. Only this time may be the last.

In short, on this interpretation the management of excess capacity will be a monumental task indeed.

Notes: Chapter 2

1   This work has appeared in a series of monographs prepared by the System Dynamics Group of the Alfred P. Sloane School of Management at the Massachusetts Institute of Technology (Cambridge, Mass). The earlier debate on the long wave began essentially with Kondratieff's paper in the *Review of Economic Statistics* (vol. XVII, 1935). The ensuing debate soon petered out, having been mesmerised by the question of the periodicity of the cycle. A recent revival has occurred with the changed conditions of the 1970s, but the MIT work represents a most important recent contribution to that debate, which links up with the work being done by European Marxists like Mandel and Altvater, and with work emanating from the study of technical change being done in Sussex around Chris Freeman.

2   This formulation of the argument comes very close to the Marxian discussion of the tendency for the rate of profit to fall:

We have thus seen in a general way that the same influences which produce a tendency in the general rate of profit to fall, also call forth counter-effects, which hamper, retard, and partly paralyse this fall. The latter do not do away with the law, but impair its effects, otherwise it would not be the fall of the general rate of profit, but rather its relative slowness, that would be incomprehensible. (K. Marx, *Capital*, vol. III (London: Lawrence & Wishart, 1972), p. 239)

References: Chapter 2

Forrester, J. W. (1978), 'Innovation and the long wave', paper presented at an MIT Symposium on Technology, Innovation and Corporate Strategy, London.

Freeman, C. (1977), 'The Kondratieff long waves, technical change and unemployment', in *Proceedings: OECD Meetings of Experts on Structural Determinants of Employment and Unemployment* (Paris: OECD).

Gardner, R. N., (1956), *Sterling-Dollar Diplomacy* (London: Oxford University Press).

Georgescu-Roegen, N. (1971), *The Entropy Law and the Economic Process* (Cambridge, Mass.: Harvard University Press).

Tinbergen, J. (1962), *Shaping the World Economy* (New York: New York University Press).

3

Contending Perspectives on the Problem of the Management of Surplus Capacity

MARTIN GILMAN

The present chapter addresses itself, at a general level, to the different perceptions of the nature and principal determinants of the excess industrial capacity observed in most of the OECD countries since at least the mid-1970s. The focus will be on the factors and issues common to most of these countries rather than to the specific problems faced by individual countries (or regions). Likewise, the emphasis will be placed on the microeconomic underpinnings of widely observed macro-economic phenomena rather than on the experience of individual industries or sectors such as steel, textiles and shipbuilding. It is maintained that a focus exclusively on the problems of particular industrial sectors or regions, while invaluable to a proper appreciation of the impact of the recent economic difficulties, would not provide an adequate framework for the formulation of politics to manage the adjustment to surplus industrial capacity in a multilateral context. The contributions of other participants in this volume deal with the experience of individual countries and industries.

The overview of the issues presented here contrasts with those pundits who view recent developments as a crisis in Western civilisation or the ineluctable result of the transition to the post-industrial society. As in the case of other adherents of the 'decline and fall' school in the past, these observers of contemporary events may soon find their dramatic predictions confounded. Much will depend upon a correct economic analysis of problems and the political hindsight to learn from past mistakes.

It is contended that the problems faced by most of the industrialised countries are not, in essence, new as economic phenomena, but that the policy prescriptions may require some fundamental rethinking of social and industrial policies whose good intentions (and longer-term consequences) have become a part of the present problems by creating impediments to normal structural and cyclical adaptation.

This view can be summarised in the following manner. Structural changes are an inherent feature of any dynamic economy. The market mechanism supplies signals to adjust to these changes and excess capacity in any market would only be a temporary phenomenon. Cyclical changes interact with structural parameters to facilitate or deter adjustment in a dynamic economy. The responsibility for the present problems of adjusting smoothly to structural changes would seem to lie, in large measure, with governments who may have unwittingly sown the seeds for the present developments. The maintenance of relatively fixed exchange rates up until at least 1977, despite the opportunities for pursuing more independent monetary policies, may have played an important part in the transmission of American inflation to other countries. The consequent application of anti-inflationary policies exacerbated unemployment which, being politically unacceptable, forced governments to intervene increasingly in economic activity to present their policies from having full effects. This led to the rescue of lame-duck industries and greater recourse to subsidies in some countries, lowering the incentive to work through higher taxes and higher unemployment compensation. Due to job security provisions, the incentive to employ workers has been lessened and there have been increasing resorts to protectionism, sometimes disguised, as an alternative form of subsidy to maintain activity. Such measures may, in many cases, simply postpone rather than moderate some of the more difficult aspects of adjustment. In so doing, governments may be involved in the making of their own present and future problems.

Dimensions of the Problem

Comparisons between the pre-1974 economic indicators and those since then are illustrative of the dimensions of the recent problems of surplus capacity. From 1963 to 1973, for instance, the growth of real GNP in the OECD area covered 5 per cent per year, whereas the growth rate from 1975 to 1978 was just over half of that, or 2·75 per cent. Unemployment, which averaged about 2·8 per cent of the labour force of the OECD area in 1962–73, almost doubled with a rate of 5·4 per cent in 1975–8. Productivity in most OECD countries has fallen sharply as indicated by the figures presented in Table 3.1.

While the growth in real aggregates was much lower than in the pre-1974 period, inflation accelerated markedly in the OECD area. From 1960 to 1969 the annual rate of increase of consumer prices was 2·8 per cent. The rate more than doubled in the following four years (1970–3) to about 6 per cent, and in 1974–8 it averaged 10·4 per cent.

Although a great deal of caution is needed in interpreting aggregated data such as these (the situations in individual sectors or countries at different times may diverge significantly from these averages), a general picture of the situation since 1974 emerges. The 1960s can be portrayed as a period of relatively sustained growth of GNP, productivity, invest-

Table 3.1   *Productivity in selected OECD countries*

	Average Annual Rate 1963–73	1974–8
United States	1·9	0·1
Japan	8·7	3·3
Germany	4·6	3·1
France	4·6	2·7
United Kingdom	3·0	0·5
Canada	2·4	0·5
Italy	5·4	1·5

Source: OECD, *Economic Outlook,* July 1979.
   UK excludes contribution from North Sea oil.

ment, employment and trade with moderate rates of increases in consumer prices. By contrast, especially since 1974, there has been slow growth in GNP in most countries and a drop in productivity, with labour hoarding and lower investment, including R & D. Unemployment has been high although supply bottlenecks are predicted in some sectors. International non-oil trade has grown more slowly with a greater resort to selective, protectionist measures. Huge balance-of-payments disequilibria have occurred despite generalised 'floating' of exchange rates since 1973. High rates of inflation have been an enduring problem. These weaknesses in most OECD economies have been manifested, in part, in excess capacity in product and factor markets, especially acute in certain sectors and regions.

A Cyclical or Structural Approach?

In the discussion of complex phenomena it is useful to go back to basic theoretical constructs. A few elementary notions concerning supply and demand can be of assistance. In the modern, mixed economy, firms operate in often imperfect markets for products and factors where long-run profit maximisation can be assumed. Prices and quantities are determined by supply and demand factors in each market. Governments intervene to a greater or lesser extent on the supply and demand sides, directly or indirectly, and often set prices or quantities in product and factor markets. Using the nation-state as the unit of analysis, the modern economy is composed of a large but finite number of markets. In the open economy many of these markets transcend national borders (e.g. steel, shipbuilding, textiles) whereas others are usually localised (e.g. construction, retailing). Technological progress in telecommunications and transportation is opening up more and more local markets to the influences of external prices and quantities, as the integration of financial markets has provided a striking illustration.

Adjustment is a permanent feature of any dynamic economy in response to changes in supply and demand conditions in specific product and factor markets, whether local, regional, national, or international. It is a necessary response to changes in tastes and the pattern of demand (e.g. away from goods towards services), to changing technology, to changing relative costs and prices (e.g. higher energy prices, relative price changes reflecting differential productivity growth), to changes in comparative advantage between countries and to changes in the composition of the labour force.

Where these changes in supply or demand are expected to be temporary (e.g. when the demand for labour or automobiles declines as a result of stringent credit conditions, excess inventories or an over-valued exchange rate), the economic and social problems may be characterised as being conjunctural in nature and amenable to treatment by demand-management policies. In market economies which are characterised by cyclical swings in the levels of aggregate demand, and longer-term structural changes in the pattern of demand and production, it may be difficult to distinguish whether the causes in shifts of demand and supply curves are, in fact, a result of cyclical or structural factors (or both).

From this perspective, surplus capacity even in present circumstances is not a new or elusive phenomenon in the majority of cases. It should be recalled that the notion of excess supply implies imperfections in the market for that product or factor such that the equilibrium price is maintained above that which would obtain if demand and supply were to find a market equilibrium. Oligopolistic competition in product markets and union power, job security and minimum wages in labour markets tend to prevent adjustment and lead to allocative inefficiency. 'Excess supply' is an old economic problem, but the political cost of the rather 'ruthless' market solution may now be judged to be unacceptable.

Towards a Structural Approach

Before examining a plausible explanation of the contribution of cyclical factors, particularly of anti-inflationary policies pursued at the national level to contain largely externally induced inflation through relatively fixed exchange rates, it is necessary to acknowledge the role of certain structural factors in the creation of surplus capacity. After all, even where reflationary demand-management policies have been implemented, excess capacity in some factor and product markets has continued. In the late 1960s and throughout the 1970s several structural parameters (i.e. the established or hypothesised relationships between two or more economic variables) have probably changed. In a dynamic economy this would be expected and is not a phenomenon particular to this period.

Changes in both the micro- and macro-structure (capital/output ratio, labour force participation rate, etc.) are taking place all the time as a result of changes in consumer tastes, new discoveries and inventions, changes in the willingness of labour-market participants to provide services at prevailing wages, installation of new productive facilities, new government programmes and in many other ways. However, structural change does not necessarily mean that there is a structural problem. One of the most important features of a market economy is its flexibility and resilience in handling structural change.

On the other hand, there is no assurance that adjustment to any and all structural changes will occur smoothly, within an acceptable time period and at an acceptable cost (both economic and social). The structural 'problems' associated with the economic difficulties since the mid-1970s may be a result of the dislocations, high costs and long lags of the adjustments. The perceived structural problems do not arise only from changes in the domestic economic structure. They may equally, perhaps even more frequently, be a result of a failure of the domestic economic structure to adjust rapidly enough to changing needs imposed from abroad. Changing terms of trade or comparative advantage and the quintupling of oil prices would be examples.

Without analysing their impact on specific sectors or countries, it is useful to set out some of the principally mentioned actual or potential structural issues that may have contributed to the surplus capacity in factor (especially labour) and product markets since 1975. These 'structural' changes, for present purposes, can be grouped into four categories:

(1) shifting geographical patterns in production, especially in manufacturing industry;
(2) uncertainties concerning the prices and availability of certain raw materials and agricultural produce, and, in particular, the quintupling of oil prices in 1973/4;
(3) the increasing role of government intervention and growth of the public sectors;
(4) changes in the attitudes, training, composition and representation of the labour force.

In this brief overview, some of the key changes in the parameters supporting the economic structure are indicated.

In many industries, but especially manufacturing, there has been a *shift in the geographical pattern of production* both within and between countries. Within countries, manufacturing industries have moved from inner cities to suburbs and outlying regions, and national distribution has ended the local production of many standardised products. Perhaps in part due to the allocative patterns suggested by exchange rates, but mainly due to changing comparative advantage and terms of trade, international trade has created global markets for many relatively homogeneous products, such as textiles, steel, bulk carriers and consumer durables. This shift has been accelerated, no doubt, by the rapid growth of international direct investment in the 1960s and by the increasing transfer of technology on a non-equity basis outside the OECD area. The rapid growth of the so-called NICs (newly industrialising countries), the large number of compensation agreements and turn-key projects in state-controlled economies (which are now adding to excess capacity in some sectors by their payments in kind and exports), and the changing trends in direct investment (more in the United States, less in some parts of Europe, etc.) are evidence of these shifts. It should be noted that the displacement created by these changes has not been significant at the macroeconomic level for most OECD countries, but the sectoral impact has sometimes been considerable and very rapid compared to allocative shifts in the past.

The increasing amounts of international liquidity and the worldwide inflation associated with the excess of dollars may have been partly responsible for an *agricultural and commodity boom* in 1972–3. Poor harvests and simultaneous boom conditions were also responsible. Uncertainties concerning future demand and the sometimes long gestation periods to bring on new supplies may have made these traditionally volatile industries even more so in what are now increasingly global markets with little segmentation as transportation costs have dwindled on a per unit basis. The declining purchasing power of their revenues may have also encouraged the OPEC countries to *raise oil prices five-fold* in 1973–4, although this was probably not the main consideration at that time. As a consequence, the price of oil produced elsewhere and other forms of energy also increased (although not always to the same extent, usually because of government price controls). The large rapid shift in the relative price of energy, as well as OECD and OPEC balance-of-payments imbalances, increases in LDC debts and the deflationary aspects of rendering some energy-intensive activities obsolescent, were all structural changes which have been reinforced in 1979 by the oil price increases associated with the events in Iran. The real adjustment to these developments, masked in part by the anti-inflationary policies pursued by many OECD countries, has only been partial. The future availability and prices of energy are largely political and difficult to forecast.

There may be a hard to quantify but a none the less noticeable *growth of government involvement* in the economy that interferes with market signals and affects incentives. Social concerns such as health, discrimination, pollution and the desire to protect employment have tended to be accompanied by an increasing resort to political processes and government regulations (e.g. wage and price controls) rather than market signals to resolve questions of resource allocation, wage and price determination, and the achievement of social objectives. At the same time, the growth of the public sector has increased the burden on tax-payers whose willingness to accept working at high marginal tax rates has become problematic. There is some recent evidence in the United States, the UK and France, for example, that this trend is now being reversed.

Changes in the labour market have been particularly rapid in recent years. The composition of the labour force has been altered not only by the arrival (and subsequent partial departure) of migrant workers in Western Europe, but also and especially by the entry of larger percentages of married women, teenagers and even the re-entry of retired persons. In terms of training, the social attitudes of the late 1960s and early 1970s may have created greater concerns with ecological issues and the humanisation of work, but fewer marketable skills. High taxes and inflation may have also affected attitudes towards work, while higher per capita incomes and unemployment compensation may have influenced the preferences for leisure as opposed to paid employment.

A Cyclical Analysis

The structural factors mentioned above have no doubt played a considerable role in recent economic developments, especially in certain industries and regions. On the other hand, it could be argued that the excess capacity recently witnessed in factor markets (lower demand for labour and excess productive capacity) and in product markets is a result of the restrictive policies, taken in most countries starting in 1974, to combat inflation, which was seen as a national problem caused by national factors, notwithstanding the apportioning of blame to OPEC for the quintupling of oil prices at the end of 1973. Given the difficulty of lowering inflationary expectations and the determination of many governments to use traditional demand-management policies in combatting the twin evils of unemployment and inflation, there was a greater recourse to selective policies. However, contrary to expectations, there was little improvement in the growth of real aggregates (except in the United States). On the inflationary front, the rate of increase in consumer prices was only partially brought under control – from a record 15·1 per cent at an annual rate in the first half of 1974 in the OECD area, down to a rate of 8·8 per cent in the twelve months to April 1979, whereas the OECD average over the period 1961–70 was 3·4 per cent.

What has been surprising is the tenacity of policy-makers in many countries in adhering to an inflation–unemployment trade-off framework and their reluctance to avail themselves of the independence created by the floating of exchange rates in February 1973. It is recognised that in a system of fixed exchange rates, or where floating is managed to keep relative rates more or less fixed, a sustained inflation in a reserve currency country must spread itself throughout the system. The only escape available for the others is through either the floating of exchange rates, or frequent and co-ordinated currency revaluation against the inflating country. The same mechanism worked in reverse in the 1930s to transmit the severe deflation of the reserve-currency countries worldwide. For a system of fixed, or nearly fixed, exchange rates is, in itself, neutral, and simply serves to channel inflationary or deflationary disturbances through the world economy in a certain pattern (although it is debated whether the transmission operates through the price-specie-flow mechanism or more directly through a price-transfer mechanism).

The essential point is the acceleration of the rate of inflation in the United States. Beginning with the 1966 fiscal year, rapidly growing budget deficits financed by excessive domestic credit expansion in the United States created increasing supplies of international reserves relative to the demand for reserves. Consumer prices in the United States rose from rates below 2 per cent per year before 1966 to 2·9 per cent that year, 4·2 per cent in 1968 and 5·9 per cent in 1970. Domestic credit creation in the United States continued at a rapid pace, particularly in 1970, and to the extent that other countries were reluctant significantly to alter their exchange rates, they were faced essentially with a world-determined inflation rate.

Not only were the strains largely responsible for the breakdown of the Bretton Woods system, but the excess creation of dollars transmitted inflation to other countries whose subsequent policies were fighting inflation as a national problem, the resulting deflation creating excess capacity and social tensions, leading to the use of selective policies that may have made adjustment more costly, longer and more intractable. At least initially, exchange rate changes *vis-à-vis* the dollar were minimised, probably from fear of loss of competitive position in most countries and compounded in Europe by fear of offending neighbouring countries. Many of the European countries were accustomed to viewing exchange rate changes as being directed against their immediate neighbours, even though expressed in terms of the dollar exchange rate, rather than as a co-operative European effort directed against the United States.

While other factors were no doubt affecting national inflation rates in the short run (e.g. the state of aggregate demand, wage and price controls, expectations, etc.), the differential rates of inflation among OECD countries could be explained by the extent to which exchange rates against the dollar were altered. Hence the significant relationship between exchange rate policies and inflation in Germany and

Switzerland as contrasted with Italy and the UK from 1973 until recently.

However, in reacting to this externally induced inflation, policy-makers in most countries were strongly influenced by the standard theory of anti-inflationary policy – often expressed as the empirically derived so-called Phillips curve – which assumed a closed national economy and a sociologically determined level of nominal wages. As a result, inflation was viewed as a national problem, to be dealt with by national fiscal and monetary policies which could be supported by national incomes–prices policies. On the other hand, with relatively fixed exchange rates, it is argued that the national rate of inflation may have little or no connection with the state of the national labour markets. In the admittedly extreme case, with relatively fixed exchange rates, there may not even be a short-run inflation-unemployment trade-off, but merely a choice of how much excess capacity to suffer along with an exogenously given rate of inflation. In such conditions, the pursuit of anti-inflationary policies will lead to surplus capacity in product and factor markets, having the greatest impact on those par-ticularly weak areas such as school-leavers, migrant workers, outlying regions and industries producing uncompetitive, income-inelastic goods: in other words, these policies will create 'stagflation', confounding Key-nesian economists and policy-makers.

This international monetarist analysis, developed by Harry Johnson, David Laidler and Alexander Swoboda, among others, linking exchange rate policies and demand management as offering a cyclical explanation of the recent economic difficulties, would appear to be supported by the experience of those countries which, albeit reluctantly, did not accept the equilibrium rate of inflation implied by a fixed exchange rate to the dollar. In retrospect, Jacques Rueff may be vindicated.

Combination of Cyclical and Structural Perspectives

From a purely sectoral or national point of view, it is likely that the problem of excess capacity appears to be largely structural and without common elements in past experience. The similar features across sectors and countries suggest that, while generalisations of this kind are difficult, cyclical factors are also involved and that the structural aspects are not in themselves entirely new, but it is the speed and the displacement of the adjustments that are responsible for the 'problem'. As in the past, most of the changes in economic parameters mentioned above would probably be self-correcting over time.

So the real question, and perhaps the novel one, is: *why is the cost of adjustment to structural change now viewed as being unacceptably high?*

The present chapter has not attempted to answer this question. Its purpose is more limited in identifying some of the cyclical and structural factors that may explain the problem of 'excess capacity'. The international factors, exchange rate rigidities and changing comparative advantage are felt to play a major role.

In leaning too heavily on structural explanations, it should be remembered that, at the depth of recession, many problems that appear to be structural are not that at all, but simply a reflection, first, of the uneven impact on different sectors and regions of a reduction in aggregate demand, and, secondly, of the fact that adjustment to structural change becomes slow and difficult during recessionary periods. Recovery from the recent recession would undoubtedly demonstrate, as in the past, that economic expansion is itself a cure for at least some of what now appear to be 'structural' problems. Even where not cured, structural adjustments are more manageable in the context of economic expansion as in shifting capital and labour from declining to expanding sectors or regions.

Note: Chapter 3

The views expressed in this chapter are strictly those of the author and are solely his responsibility.

4

Recessions and the World Economic Order

VICTORIA CURZON PRICE

Is international economic co-operation a fair-weather phenomenon? Are sovereign nations only prepared to entertain open and co-operative economic relationships with each other from a comfortable position of security? Do they not, at the first sign of trouble, run for shelter? In a broad sense, the barometer of international economic co-operation does seem to follow the economic cycle. Certainly periods of comparatively low growth and high unemployment (1880s, 1930s, 1970s) have all been accompanied by a partial or complete breakdown of the pre-existing international economic order, the extent of the breakdown being seemingly linked to the depth and duration of the cycle.

Inversely, the construction of a viable international economic order appears to need a protracted period of growth and full employment. This has occurred twice in the course of a century, once in 1860–80, when free trade was organised on the basis of the *système des traités* and the gold standard, and again in 1945–70 when virtual free trade, payments and investment developed on the basis of the General Agreement in Tariffs and Trade and the International Monetary Fund. The 1920s period proved too short and indecisive for an international economic order to be brought into being.

However, correlation is not causation. Where does the process start? Is it that freer trade policies help to engender growth, which in turn creates a favourable climate for more growth, which in turn creates a favourable climate for more liberal trade policies, and so on? Or is it that a favourable economic climate promotes freer trade which in turn reinforces the positive growth process? Conversely, is it that restrictive trade policies (introduced for whatever reason), by helping to reduce real incomes and resist structural change, create the type of economic climate in which protection flourishes, thus reinforcing pre-existing tendencies? Or is the initial factor in a recession/breakdown phase a deteriorating economy?

Intuitively speaking, the second hypothesis appears more plausible: namely, that the state of the world trade order (whether it is moving towards free trade or away from it) is a function *(inter alia)* of the state of the world economy, rather than the other way around. Indeed, it would be difficult to explain the ups and downs of the international economic order in terms of the first hypothesis, for the interactive nature of its vicious or virtuous circles implies steady and irreversible progression in one or the other direction – a result that manifestly fails to fit the real world.

Naturally, no hypothesis as simple as the one suggested could hope to encompass the whole range of observed empirical reality. The state of the world economic order is a function not only of the state of the world economy, but also of the political climate, in particular the degree to which political leaders are in the habit of appealing to national sentiment in order to mobilise their populations behind them. However, our purpose is not to explore all the possible foundations of a world economic order, but to concentrate on one only, in the hope that it is of sufficient importance to prove useful in explaining both past and current events.

What are some of the implications of the hypothesis? For one thing, it follows that however strong the institutional and legal edifices may be that are built up during expansionary periods they will be quite unable to withstand the earth tremors of the downswings. This is because the hypothesis implies that the outward, legal manifestations of the underlying international economic order grow from it quite naturally, and reflect it faithfully. As long as the members of the international community see it as in their interests to pursue policies that are generally compatible with those of their neighbours – and this, in practice, means open trade and monetary policies – the international legal order will reflect this attitude, and conflicts, such as they are, will be relatively easy to solve. The moment members of the family of nations see their links with other members of society as an onerous burden, impinging on their welfare, necessary links that remain will be fraught with tension and the outward and legal manifestations of the pre-existing legal order will begin to droop.

This may seem to be a commonplace observation, yet it is not unusual to come across people who believe that by multiplying international conferences, by drawing up and discussing numerous agenda of desirable objectives, even by signing international agreements of growing length, complexity and triviality, we can improve, or at least preserve, the world economic order. But is this really so? One can also interpret a notable increase in economic diplomacy and 'conferenceering' as a sure sign that the underlying international economic order is in distress, for those responsible for this delicate plant note its unhealthy appearance and multiply the outward signs of co-operation in the hope that this will somehow stop the rot.

Indeed, it is the theme of this chapter that it was not the *système des traités* which made trade free in the 1860s, but free trade, or the desire for it, which made the *système des traités*; although Britain was the moving spirit, other countries followed because they saw it as in their interests to do so. A century later, it was not the Bretton Woods system which made trade, investment and payments almost free in the 1950s and 1960s, but the recognition of the desirability of virtual freedom of movement for goods and services which made the Bretton Woods system possible. As in the earlier period, although the United States was the prime mover, other countries considered it advantageous to themselves to follow the leader.

Conversely, it will be argued that the move to protection after 1875, the complete breakdown of world economic order in the 1930s and the reversal of liberal trade policies in the 1970s can be traced in part to prolonged periods of economic stagnation brought on by major structural 'shocks'. Until these shocks have worked their way through the system, most governments will attempt to prevent or hinder the redistribution of income they imply, either by protection or by any number of domestic measures with equivalent effect, thus leading to a noticeable deterioration in the world trade order. The reason why governments adopt such policies is not to be sought in economics (which teaches that they will reduce the national income) but in politics: a government's power base, whether democratically elected or not, derives from people whose status and incomes are linked to the *pre-existing* economic structure, and who feel threatened by the new one. Government policy will change to reflect their new concerns (Downs, 1957). (It is, of course, central to this thesis that governments do not represent the 'general' interest, however defined, but only some, important, subsections of it.) Once the process starts, it will be reinforced if the structural change engenders a serious recession, because otherwise unaffected groups will begin to feel anxious about their own status and future earning power, and will demand equivalent protection from the secondary effects of structural change. Power, under these assumptions, will go to those who promise to do this, and the world trade order will take another turn for the worse.

We are at present in the middle of a breakdown phase. The signs are unmistakable:

- the multiplication of fruitless international conferences (no names, no packdrill);
- protracted negotiations which by any normal input–output measure have been extraordinarily unproductive and disappointing (MTN in particular, although worse cases could be cited);
- growth of a parallel system based on the free and unchallenged use of unilateral subsidisation policies and various other non-tariff barriers; selective bilateral agreements to limit trade; and 'excep-

tional' sectoral arrangements of a discriminatory nature (in textiles).

No amount of international commercial diplomacy can halt this trend, as long as the majority of Western governments continue to react to the problem of 'overcapacity' in a defensive and inward-looking manner. Indeed, this visible deterioration in the underlying order intensified in the last five years, during which our governments devoted much effort to improving its outward appearance. The fact that governments should be found pursuing two contradictory and incompatible objectives at the same time is not surprising. Indeed, it is the nature of modern democratic government to try to satisfy as many claims on its resources as possible, and the balancing act can be elevated to a true art by satisfying several conflicting claims at the same time, in the hope that the inherent contradictions can be contained, ignored, or postponed until after the next election.

Three Breakdowns Compared: 1873–95, 1930–39 and 1973 to the present day

The nineteenth century saw a gradual and virtually uninterrupted growth in national product and international trade until 1873 (Clapham, 1961; Kindleberger, 1964). This growth was of course favoured by the free trade movement, which began as a unilateral act of faith by Britain in 1846 and spread to the more sceptical continental powers by virtue of a series of mutually advantageous and interlocking commercial treaties which culminated in the *système des traités* in the 1860s. Just as important as free trade for this world economic order was the existence of a world currency (gold), free convertibility, free capital movements and free movement of labour (Röpke, 1942). Without wishing to analyse this period in detail, it is perhaps noteworthy that it contained no serious economic discontinuities and that growth based on technical innovation spread at a sedate, nineteenth-century pace from Britain to the continent without provoking sudden changes in the income-earning potential of pre-existing assets. Even wars did not disturb the steady upward trend in incomes (Röpke, 1942).

The lengthy depression which began in Europe in 1873 and lasted the rest of the century is usually thought to have been initially caused by the sudden flood of cheap cereal imports from the United States and Canada, due to a radical fall in transport costs (Clapham, 1961, p. 178). This had the dual effect of (1) endangering the real incomes of farmers, and large landowners and (2) raising the real incomes of the urban population (industrialists and their workforce alike). Since farmers and landowners at that time represented just over half the estimated population it is possible that, on balance and in the short run, cheap food from

America meant a slight net reduction in real incomes for continental Europe as a whole, until a structural shift towards industry had taken place (Maddison, 1980, p. 47). Most continental European countries did not wait to find out, however. Their ruling elites were still firmly based on land and they saw no reason to transfer large chunks of real income to the up-and-coming urban population which was quite enough of a threat as it was.

Barriers to the import of cheap grain were erected, maintained and intensified from 1873 onwards in all but a handful of countries. Some chose to continue with their free trade policies (Britain, the Netherlands and Denmark) and accepted the structural and real income shift towards industry (Britain) or towards high value-added farming (Netherlands, Denmark). British industry's real costs declined relative to those continental European powers, where industry had to bear the burden of agricultural protection. As a result, these countries soon found that they could only industrialise behind growing tariff barriers, and what started off as a specific protective measure to cope with a crisis in farming soon spread to industry as well: Germany's infant-industry 'Bismarck tariff' was introduced in 1879 and France's comprehensive Méline tariff in 1892 (Gerschenkron, 1943, p. 44).

Although the spread of protection in the last twenty years of the nineteenth century represented a break with the past and a noticeable change in trend and emphasis, it would be an exaggeration to say that it constituted a breakdown of the world economic order. Tariffs were not so high as to seriously impede trade or halt the process of adaptation and structural change. They were not accompanied by quotas, exchange controls, or any of the sophisticated non-tariff barriers that were to become commonplace in the course of the twentieth century (Röpke, 1942, p. 24). World trade continued to grow in real terms, and by the end of the century the worst of the process of adaptation was over.

The period 1894–1914 was once more of general growth and prosperity, despite the gathering storm (Maddison, 1977, p. 111). The world did not return to the free trade position of the 1860s and 1870s, but international investment, migration and trade all flourished under currency convertibility, freedom of initiative and security of contract provided by numerous independent but mutually compatible national legal systems, which with few exceptions had not yet been taught to distinguish between nationals and foreigners.

This system was swept away for ever in 1914 and a new and much more divisive world emerged in 1918. The inheritance of the war included restrictions on trade and international payments, inflation and an increase in the number of nations, all anxious to assert their identity. Yet world trade grew in the postwar decade and in 1929 stood 30 per cent higher (in real terms) than in 1913 (Röpke, 1942, p. 24). The pattern of world trade was still determined largely by the price mechanism, tariffs tended to be a flat-rate across-the-board tax on trade rather than a differential instrument of industrial policy. The currencies of the important countries were convertible into each other, and some of them were convertible into gold.

This workable economic order came to an end in the 1930s, a period which saw successively (1) the enactment of the prohibitive Smoot–Hawley tariff in the United States, (2) the introduction of quotas in France (an innovation in commercial policy which proved to be one of France's most durable and successful export products), (3) the introduction of tariffs and imperial preferences in Great Britain, (4) the pursuit of economic isolationism in Germany and (5) the collapse of the gold exchange system (Röpke, 1959, pp. 35–6). From then to the outbreak of war the quality of international relations deteriorated steadily, forcing trade into self-balancing bilateral channels and reducing it by some 20 per cent in quantum terms at the depth of the trough in 1934. In the meantime, unemployment and deprivation stalked the industrial world from California to Eastern Europe.

The causes of this immensely complex disaster, in which random events and discontinuities, such as the 1929 Wall Street crash or the bumper wheat crop in Australia, interacted with a fatal succession of human errors, has yet to be subjected to all the rigours of modern scientific analysis, and it is certainly not our intention to do so now. However, at some risk of oversimplification, it is still possible to trace the leap towards protection in these leading countries to an attempt to stop the fall in real incomes of particularly powerful groups: the industrial sector in the United States; the farmer in France; and the dominions in Great Britain. What was not anticipated was the snowballing of the process, once it had started. The Great Depression differed from the earlier phase in the intensity of both the economic recession and the legal breakdown. Unlike the 1870–90 phase, it was caused by an unlucky convergence of several separate events instead of only one clearly identifiable 'shock'.

After the Second World War a workable economic order gradually emerged from the wreckage, but it is perhaps significant that the real forces making for growth and prosperity – US Marshall Aid and the transfer of technology via the US multinational corporations – were not part of the Bretton Woods system. In other words, the economy had first to be mended before the legal instruments drawn up in 1944–7 could come into play, from December 1958 onwards.

What were the essential elements of this post-Second World War economic order? Fixed exchange rates, free convertibility of national currencies, non-discrimination in tariff policy and renunciation of the use of quotas and other blatant tariff substitutes. In addition, although most countries retained controls on capital and labour movements, they were loosely applied, and the expansion of factor migration was in many respects as remarkable as that of trade. It is noteworthy, however (and in support of the general theme of this chapter), that this period of considerable world integration in real terms coincided with the highest recorded rates of income growth the world has ever known (Maddison, 1977, p. 114).

Turning now to the 1970s, we see that there was a noticeable change in atmosphere. Labour force migration ceased to be an asset and became a liability to be discouraged by host and home country alike; discriminatory trade arrangements multiplied; informal and selective trade restrictions were introduced to stop the growth of manufactured exports from developing countries; subsidies to failing firms in developed countries grew in both volume and value; capital goods' exporters vied with one another in offering potential customers ever more attractive credit terms while new restrictions of the export of capital in other forms were introduced (e.g. in the United States); all countries, whether capital-rich or capital-poor, with few exceptions, competed fiercely for investments by large private corporations, while for the most part criticising their impact on the local way of life; technology, which in the past had moved freely around the world on the basis of commercial criteria, became subject to control and regulation in importing countries (which needed it most); cartelisation of the world supply of certain products was actively encouraged by responsible organs of the United Nations, and actually achieved on a regional scale by the EEC (in steel); in a word, the flow of goods, factors of production and ideas became noticeably less free and more subject to political manipulation (Johnson, 1974; Balassa, 1978; Tumlir, 1979; Krauss, 1979; Nowzad, 1978).

Two things are clear:

(1) Once begun, these policies tend to snowball, since the cost of *not* acting defensively when others *are* appears intolerable (the speed of adjusting to import competition, for instance, is accelerated, because trade gets diverted on to a diminishing number of open markets).
(2) Such policies can only reduce world income in the long run.

However, it should be emphasised that, as in the previous breakdown phase a hundred years earlier (almost to the year), the deterioration in world economic order was one of nuance. It was by no means utter and complete, like the 1930s. Trade continued to grow; international capital movements not only grew but performed the apparently impossible task of recycling oil revenues; technology continued to spread; several developing countries graduated to the status of 'newly industrialised countries'; although currencies fluctuated, the important ones remained convertible for most international transactions. By the end of the 1970s the world economic order had deteriorated but was far from total collapse. In many respects it had stood up to the negative interactions of a breakdown phase surprisingly well.

Is it possible to pin down some of the reasons for the change from the build-up phase of the 1960s to the partial breakdown of the 1970s?

Most of us, if asked to identify the single most important economic event of the 1970s, would reply: the oil price rise. Indeed, it compares, in terms of structural upheaval, with the advent of cheap grain from the United States in the 1870s. But with an important difference for the importing area: instead of bearing within itself the prospect of higher real incomes in the long run due to a fall in food costs, the oil price rise reduces the real incomes of almost every section of society with no prospect of improvement once the painful adjustment is over. In global terms, of course, the loss of income of oil-importing countries shows up as an increase in the income of the oil-producing countries, but this is cold comfort for the populations in the former group, who are, willy-nilly, obliged to work harder and consume less. This unpalatable fact has, on the whole, not been emphasised by governments, which have sought for ways of disguising it, notably by hindering the process of structural adaptation to new conditions and by expanding public spending. These policies alone are enough to account for much of the deterioration in the world economic order, namely, subsidies to failing firms, credit and investment grant races, capital export controls, immigration restrictions and currency fluctuations. But this is not the whole story.

A parallel development, this time closely analogous to the arrival in Europe of cheap grain in the 1870s, is the emergence of new low-cost manufacturing centres in the developing world which threaten the incomes of established producers in developed countries, but offer the prospect of higher real incomes for all concerned once the painful process of adaptation is complete. As in the 1870s however, many developed countries are not taking any chances, and have introduced formal or informal, general or selective, restraints on trade to halt the process, as mentioned above.

Thus, when studying the 1970s breakdown phase one is struck by both contrasts and similarities as compared with historical experience. Like the 1870s, the current breakdown is only partial (but perhaps it is still in its infancy). Like the 1930s, an examination of the mechanics of the turning point leads to the conclusion that there has been a *convergence* of at least two major structural changes, implying loss of income for large and important sections of the population; as in both earlier phases, most governments have attempted to save their political skins in adverse circumstances by resisting this inherent redistribution of income; as in the 1870s, some governments have taken the risk of allowing the redistribution and reduction of income to occur (Japan, Germany, the Netherlands, Switzerland).

Conclusion

If it is true that the non-adjusting industrial countries are likely to continue their negative policies until the structural shock of the oil price rise and competition from newly industrialising countries (NICs) has had time to work its way through the system, then the world economic order is in for a prolonged period of relative decline. The problem of the NICs is here to stay, and so is the rising price of energy. Because a handful of developed countries *are* adjusting, the non-adjusters will soon find that their labour- and energy-intensive industries cannot even compete with those of their immediate neighbours, let alone distant Japan, Korea, or Mexico. The cry for increased protection will go up. Will it be heard by the government? On past record, the answer is likely to be yes, even if everyone knows that protection is no solution. Why? For the well-known reason that protection greatly benefits the few and imperceptibly injures the many, with the result that 'there will be a cohesive, well-financed, articulate special interest group to support it, and a large, poorly informed majority that, if it is informed correctly, will be weakly opposed, but often this majority will be simply unaware of the proposal' (Stigler, 1979).

Another problem is that the 'losers' in the freer trade game feel their acute loss immediately, while the 'winners' will only reap the full gains over time. This means that in the short run (i.e. until factors of production have moved out of uncompetitive and into competitive sectors) the net effect of freer trade may be to reduce incomes. In the long run, even the initial 'losers' benefit – but in the long run, as Keynes so rightly put it, we are all dead. Thus, it takes an immense amount of political maturity and economic understanding to pursue freer trade policies in the teeth of an economic recession. Yet, in present circumstances, the consequences of not adjusting rapidly to structural change are far more serious than in the past.

Our entire industrial experience has been one of replacing an expensive source of energy with a cheaper one. That this has been a prime source of growth is obvious. That this should have assisted adaptation to change is also clear. Ever lower energy costs enhanced our speed of progress, just as a downhill slope makes cycling easier. Now energy prices are rising for the first time since the industrial revolution began – we have to pedal uphill. The same effort as before yields a slower rate of progress. In these circumstances, the economy cannot afford to carry any extra weight, especially that due to inefficient activities, or it will collapse.

Perhaps I err on the side of optimism in thinking that some of the non-adjusting countries of the 1970s are coming to grips with this unat-tractive reality and are at last taking appropriate measures, namely, France (already since 1978), the United Kingdom (since 1979) and even the United States (since 1980). This raises the intricate question of whether a shift away from protection and towards 'market realities' can occur during a recession – an entirely novel event which is incompatible with our hypothesis.

Only time will tell if the 'tough' policies introduced in France, Britain and the United States will prove successful in electoral terms. If they do, then we shall have to modify the cornerstone of Anthony Downs's economic theory of politics, namely, that electorates are the victims of imperfect information, and thus lay themselves open to unprincipled vote competition by political parties which gain power by promising more than they can deliver. It is conceivable that after repeated disappointments electorates are becoming less gullible. Perhaps they have begun to realise that, as Samuel Brittan has put it: 'Each of us suffers from the concession to the groups to which we do not belong. We would all be better off in the not-so-long term if we could achieve the only horse-trading worth doing, i.e. an agreement by every group to relinquish its special privileges on the understanding that other groups did the same' (Brittan, 1980, p. 43). If so, the hypothesis outlined in this chapter would only help to explain events up to 1980, an outcome in the interest of all concerned, except the author, who would nevertheless be prepared to waive her special interests in this rather unlikely event.

References: Chapter 4

Balassa, B. (1978), 'The "new protectionism" and the international economy', *Journal of World Trade Law*, vol. 12, no. 5, pp. 409–36.

Brittan, S. (1980), 'Hayek, new right and old left', *Encounter*, January, pp. 31–46.

Clapham, J. H. (1961), *Economic Development of France and Germany 1815–1914*, 4th edn (Cambridge: Cambridge University Press).

Downs, A. (1957), 'An economic theory of political action in a democracy', *Journal of Political Economy*, vol. LXVI, pp. 135–50.

Gerschenkron, A. (1943), *Bread and Democracy in Germany* (Berkeley, Calif.: University of California Press).

Johnson, H. G. (ed.) (1974), *The New Mercantilism* (Oxford: Blackwell).

Kindleberger, C. P. (1964), *Economic Growth in France and Britain, 1851–1950* (Cambridge, Mass.: Harvard University Press).

Krauss, M. (1979), *The New Protectionism: International Trade and the Welfare State* (New York: New York University Press).

Maddison, A. (1977), *Phases of Capitalist Development* (Lavoro: Banca Nazionale del Lavoro, June), pp. 103–20.

Maddison, A. (1980), 'Economic growth and structural change in advanced countries', in I. Leveson and J.M. Wheeler (eds), *Western Economics in Transition* (Boulder, Co: Westview Press).

Nowzad, B. (1978), *The Rise in Protectionism,* IMF Pamphlet Series, no. 24 (Washington, DC: International Monetary Fund).

Röpke, W. (1942), *International Economic Disintegration* (London: Hodge).

Röpke, W. (1959), *L'Economic mondiale aux XIXe et XXe siècles* (Geneva and Paris: Droz & Minard).

Stigler, G. (1979), 'Why have the Socialists been winning?', *Ordo,* vol. 30, pp. 61–8.

Tumlir, J. (1979), 'The new protectionism, cartels and the international economic order', in R.C. Amacher, G. Haberler and T.D. Willett (eds), *Challenges to a Liberal International Order* (Washington, DC: American Enterprise Institute).

5

Tariffs as Constitutions

ALAN MILWARD

Could mid-nineteenth-century free trade economists see the grip they still had on our historical understanding they would surely be well pleased. Their position is not unmerited; they formulated a theory so simple and powerful linking international trade and political evolution that it still provides the only intellectual context in which the history of the economics and politics of international trade can be comprehended in a unified system. Otherwise we are forced to catalogue it as a series of disjointed historical events, tending sometimes in one direction and sometimes in another, swayed by the winds of chance, jolted by wars and revolutions, propelled by merely technological innovations and always at the mercy of the fluctuations of international goodwill.

The prevailing interpretation of international trade in history owes almost everything to their perception. In the early nineteenth century, it is usually assumed, countries were highly protectionist as they always had been, seeking advantages from international trade at the expense of others. As the extent to which the process of international development depended on mutually beneficial international exchanges was comprehended under the forceful influence of the industrial revolution in Western Europe, so were European tariffs increasingly modified to a point in mid-century where goods and factors flowed across frontiers with relative ease, at least until they reached Russia. It is still quite commonplace to discover the highly romanticised and entirely inaccurate image of the traveller of the 1860s setting forth across Europe, probably by the new international express trains, with no passport and no need of any other medium of exchange than gold francs or sovereigns. By the 1880s this image of peace and progress has dimmed. The world is explained as having slipped back to protectionism and its inevitable concomitants — nationalism, imperialism and militarism. In the interwar period this protectionism did not at first diminish and after 1929 reached new levels which made war inevitable. The United States Department of State based much of its planning for peace during the Second World War on the assumption that a peaceful world could not long endure the sorts of trading policies practised by Nazi Germany. The link between low tariffs, multilateralism and international peace thus received the most powerful of all official blessings. From 1958 onwards these goals were increasingly achieved, to the enormous economic and political benefit of much of the world, but the failure to cleave firmly enough to those policies threatens again to bring all the inevitable political disasters of protectionism in its train. 'We are now', argued a long anonymous article in *Le Matin* in January 1979, 'in 1932.' The article was headed 'Demain, la guerre?'.

Set against the historical record this is no more than a crass popular simplification. That is by no means to say that it is entirely or even mostly wrong. But it does not always match the accurate historical record, where we have that record, and there are important areas where we do not have that record. It rests therefore on some errors and on much ignorance, as well as on some accurate perceptions. This is not much of a foundation for so sweeping an interpretation and it certainly encourages the search for a more sensitive theory of the relations between international trade and political evolution. The one offered here really amounts to no more than a different perception of these events which necessarily implies a different perception of what is happening now. Before any interpretation can be accepted as having any real validity, however, it would be necessary for historians to concern themselves much more with the history of nineteenth-century tariffs and their meaning than they have so far done. One reason they have avoided the issue so much is probably because tariffs are extraordinarily uninteresting things unless related to the political events which give them meaning. The economic historian knows full well that there are always other far more important influences on the flow of trade and that the most important obstacles to that flow were very seldom tariffs but almost always non-tariff barriers. Other historians seldom work up sufficient interest in the humdrum detail of tariff setting and bargaining to be able to say what such bargains effectively represent in terms of social and political interests. None the less a more accurate historical account of the long-run development of tariffs than the foregoing is possible, even though it still leaves much obscure.

The trend towards lower tariffs and towards the reduction of non-tariff barriers to trade only obtained real momentum in 1860. The unilateral lowering of tariffs by Britain before that date and the reduction of the Belgian tariffs in the 1850s was certainly the start of this process, as is always pointed out. But it would probably turn out, were someone to make the calculations involved, that the lower tariffs which began to emerge before 1860 were offset by the impact of falling prices of many manufactured goods on specific tariff rates, even though there was a brief period in the 1850s when average prices seemed to have risen again. The Anglo-French commercial treaty of 1860 was the real starting point of trade liberalisation, because it was signed between the two greatest international traders and because it embodied for the first time the most-favoured-nation clause. Similar clauses were included in the network of trade treaties signed in the immediately ensuing period between all the more developed Western European countries.

One reason for the ease with which this process was accomplished was that the developing economies of early nineteenth-century Europe, the NICs of that period, had already developed favourable trade balances with protected Britain, the largest industrial producer and exporter. Their judgement of the situation in the short term was an accurate one – the balances remained in their favour even when they reduced their own levels of protection. The judgement was perhaps drawn from the previous symbiosis between the two largest producers and traders, Britain and France, still between themselves responsible for 60 per cent of world trade in the 1870s. Between them tariff reduction was a relatively painless affair. France had been the biggest market in most years for British manufactured exports and Britain always the biggest market for French manufactured exports. It was the extent of French trade surpluses with Britain which permitted the increasing imports into France of raw materials from elsewhere in Europe and the increasing outward flow of foreign investment which often financed their production. As for Britain, its deficits on commodity account with France were insignificant compared with the size of its total export surpluses. Europe was still in the 1860s the major supplier of food and raw materials to the eager British and French markets, and the European NICs of that period such as the Zollverein or Sweden had large intra-European primary export trades.

Bairoch's figures show rates of expansion of international trade for some countries in the 1860s which were never surpassed – 6·4 per cent for Belgium, 5·7 per cent for France and 7·3 per cent for Sweden. Of course these are rates of expansion starting from relatively low levels and represent a lower absolute growth in trade than the lower percentage rates recorded in the protectionist 1890s. None the less, as far as a limited area of industrialising north-western Europe was concerned, trade liberalisation proved painless and rewarding, although it did not by any means bring peace to the region. The inherent limitations on the whole process, however, should also be considered.

The larger territorial units were scarcely touched. Russia and the United States did not take part. The Habsburg Empire did enter the network for a few years but its tariffs had so high a starting point and its absolute and per capita levels of international trade were so low that its brief moment of trade liberalisation made little difference. Secondly, a major question remained unanswered in this period: what would be the response to the emergence of a larger international trader than Britain or France? It was not a hypothetical question. The situation was drawing nearer rapidly and came into existence after 1880 when German exports suddenly appeared in much greater quantities on world markets at the same time as both the British and French economies began a decade of virtual stagnation. Thirdly, how would the liberalised European trade system cope with the arrival of cheaper food and raw materials from outside Europe on European markets?

As German exports relentlessly displaced those of Britain and France from European markets, and then after 1900 began to compete effectively with them on extra-European markets, the frailty of the agreements of the 1860s became very clear. There were popular agitations against imports from Germany and claims of unfair trading practices by Germany strikingly reminiscent of those now made against Japan. Furthermore the period of tariff liberalisation had made no worthwhile concessions other than those which Britain had already made before 1860 to opening trade with colonies and it made no worthwhile concessions to other primary exporters. In one way the close preservation of colonial markets was fortunate – without India's surpluses on trade with continental Europe and the United States the multilateral payments system that accidentally evolved and that we have come to call the 'gold standard' would have been deprived of one of its main pillars. The British colonial system was relatively liberal but every sort of non-tariff barrier from the most specific to the most nebulous guaranteed that the lion's share of India's manufactured imports would come from Britain.

Other colonial powers had more rigidly exclusive rules. Algeria was incorporated into the French tariff in 1884. The 1892 French tariff incorporated all other French colonies which were considered 'developed' enough to stand the shock, that is to say all those that made any significant contribution to the French export trade: Martinique, Guadeloupe, South-East Asia, Gabon and Réunion. The French African colonies were usually governed by highly profitable and exclusive shipping and trading companies – the Société Commerciale de l'Ouest Africain and the Compagnie Française de l'Afrique Occidentale. The valuable Cuban market remained closed to all but Spain until the Spanish-American War. As the pressure from German, and other European, exporters mounted, the share of British and French exports going to colonies and dominions increased. Between 1890 and 1900, 9 per cent of French exports went to the colonies, and between 1906 and 1912, 15 per cent. Algeria became as much the instrument of preservation of the French cotton goods export trade as India did of that of Britain. Food and raw material exports from 'colonial' markets, however, competed all over developed and developing Europe.

In spite, therefore, of the advent of protection in the later 1870s and its rapid development in the 1880s, about which so much critical ink has been used, the contrast between the mid- and late nineteenth century was more apparent than real and the tariff history of the late nineteenth century in some ways an easily forecastable result of the seemingly more hopeful developments of the 1860s. In another way, too, the contrast was much less than most writers suggest. The higher nominal tariffs between the developed Western European states continued to be modified by conventional agreements. Indeed, like the French tariff of 1892 – the Méline tariff, usually regarded as the wickedest of them all before 1914 – they were designed expressly for that purpose. The Méline tariff embodied two separate sets of rates on each article, the lower intended for all conventional partners. Nominal tariff rates, or in the French case after 1892, the higher stipulated rate, were applied only to those who were outside the charmed circle and had always been outside it. In so far as the chief sufferers were the fresh generation of next-to-be-industrialised countries the situation had changed dramatically, if not surprisingly; in so far as they were LDCs it had not changed at all. When the existence of fixed nominal tariffs as bargaining points led to tariff wars these were, with only one exception, launched against NICs or LDCs. The most vicious was that waged by France against Italy from 1888 to 1896 when the Italian government tried to join the club by abandoning low tariffs and legislating its own high nominal rates. The French government simply refused to negotiate and applied its highest rates to all Italian exports – one reason for the virtual cessation of economic growth in Italy in those years. Compare this with the consequences of the British refusal to sign any tariff convention based on the French rates of 1892. They were simply that Britain and France continued through third parties to apply most-favoured-nation treatment to each other's exports. The weaker the primary exporter, the more susceptible to victimisation by tariff warfare. The bogus veterinary restrictions applied by Austria-Hungary to Serbia's main export – cattle – was a glaring example, for 70 per cent of Serbia's exports went to the Austro-Hungarian market.

In so far as the 'Third World' entered significantly into international trade before 1914 it was preponderantly a European 'Third World'. On the eve of the First World War half of the world trade in foodstuffs and 61 per cent of that in cereals still originated in Europe. Somewhere between one-quarter and one-third of world trade in wheat originated in Russia. The eruption of North American grain surpluses and South American and Australasian meat surpluses into Europe markets, which began on a significant scale at the end of the 1870s, was not the signal for a dramatic return to protectionism which it is always represented to have been – it was only an exacerbation of the problem. In the simpler framework of the previous three decades countries like Germany, Sweden and Italy had themselves had a comparative advantage in agricultural exports. Industrialisation and development had taken place there accompanied by a growing prosperity in the agricultural sector to which exports made an important contribution. But the next wave of NICs were in no position to suppose that the admission of manufactured goods at low tariffs would sustain a similar pattern of development. They were more backward, politically weaker, faced with far more competition and themselves the victims of fiercely unfair practices. It was not merely that adherence to the multilateral payments pattern of the gold standard hurt them more than the developed countries. This it did because in the periodic deflations necessary to bring payments into equilibrium the developed countries cut back sharply on primary imports and the underdeveloped economies simply did not have access to the short-term international capital market (which might have cushioned these blows) on the same terms as the developed countries. Argentina and Russia both provide excellent examples of the traumatic consequences which moderate recessions in the developed world could produce in the developing world. But any country without the political power to prevent it was likely to have the conditions for its imports laid down by direct intervention by the developed countries, for which the immediate excuse was usually the need to guarantee the flow of interest payments on earlier capital borrowing. Turkey, Greece, Bulgaria, Egypt and China were among those who lost complete tariff autonomy for periods in this way.

If the mid-nineteenth-century period of trade liberalisation was but a brief moment when the self-interest of the developed economies temporarily suggested mutual tariff reductions at the expense of others, and if, as I am arguing here, the things that would soon bring that policy to an end were already apparent, and if the later protectionist period was merely pursuing the economic logic of the earlier liberal period, the contrast between the two periods was even less marked because of the global inadequacy of protectionism of this kind to serve its purpose. The tax-rebate certificates which German rye exporters received when traded to German grain importers served to stimulate the great surge of Russian barley exports, established the Russian barley trade and thus cheapened the price of imported feedstuffs into Denmark; and in so doing reduced in turn the cost of the breakfast of a skilled British workman making much the same things as his German counterpart.

The nineteenth century was in fact a highly protectionist century and the mid-twentieth-century period of trade liberalisation was not, in spite of much neat academic comparison, a rediscovery of the true path from which the developed world had been diverted by various domestic vested interests and pressure groups after 1875. The pattern is not one of progress after 1850, regression during the late nineteenth century, the inevitable punishment for this in the first half of our century, and the rediscovery in the 1950s of the connection between human progress and that virtuous purple twilight through which Tennyson a hundred years previously had imagined future aerial argosies dropping with bales. Indeed those bales arrived on other shares with remarkable persistence as nominal tariffs increased. Higher tariffs may have slowed down the rate of growth of imports of manufactures in the 1880s, but once manufacturers had adjusted to the increase manufactured imports rose at roughly the same ratio to industrial production that they had shown in mid-century.

As for 1931–3, with the failure of the London Conference, the cry of *sauve qui peut* and the arrival of the Nazis we must beware of allowing it to acquire the same layers of bogus interpretation that have so long clung to 1873 and the mythical Great Depression which followed the stock-markets crash of that year. The sterling area and the Reichsmark bloc certainly provided better terms for their primary goods exporters than the multilateral arrangements of 1925-30 and in each case they covered a very important proportion of world trade. That the Nazi government was an exceptionally cruel and threatening regime does not mean that its international trading arrangements deserved the moral approbrium heaped on them by Cordell Hull and the United States Department of State. Those arrangements were in any case more the result of external economic weakness than economic strength. The resolute attack of the United States administration after 1945 on the sterling area in the name of a return to trade liberalisation was likely to do far more harm than good to the growth of international trade and to the less developed economies. If the early rounds of GATT amounted to very little that was because American policy there, as at Dumbarton Oaks and Bretton Woods, was based on a liberal interpretation of the history of international trade which was entirely unjustified historically.

Protectionism seems in reality not to have been simply the consequence of certain economic pressure groups acquiring enough power within the body politic at particular moments so as to distort tariffs and trade policy in their favour but rather to have had deeper political implications and more integral connections with the long-run process of political development. It might be closer to the truth to portray it as a set of stages in the widening participation of different groups in that body politic. In this sense the transition from mid-nineteenth-century liberalisation of trade to late nineteenth-century protectionism was not a regressive, atavistic response by conservative agrarian pressure groups but a progression in democratic political participation.

The French tariff of 1892 was won because its best-known proponent, Jules Méline, who gave his name to it, stumped the country and in mass meetings brought peasants back into the political life of France with real vigour and in common pursuit of a cause for the first time since they had triumphantly bowed out of it in 1793. The cause was not purely economic, it was in the deepest sense one of political participation. The campaign was against the 'arbitrary treaties', as the conditions imposed by the most-favoured-nation clauses were called. It was against the right of the Chamber to determine, by the incorporation of such clauses in treaties, tariff policy up to two decades ahead. The campaign was mounted to take effect before the common date of expiry and presumed renewal of the major treaties and to prevent the Chamber from including most-favoured-nation clauses in these future treaties. The level of tariffs, it was argued, must be left open to repeated public redetermination within the democratic assembly. The original Franco-British treaty of 1860 had been the work of a small coterie around the autocrat Napoleon III. The agricultural sector still employed about 9,700,000 people in France in 1890 and its most valuable product was that most threatened by external competition – wheat. This is not to say that the preservation of so large an uncompetitive sector in the French economy represented a rational economic choice. But the political cause was neither ignoble nor retrogressive. The dissemination of economic development, and the opening of the prairies and of the Russian hinterland to international commerce, brought the largest group in the French population into active struggle for the defence of a position which they had long held with little sign of disturbance.

The same political point may be made about the return to higher tariffs in Germany. The demand for agricultural protection offered Bismarck the chance to base the new Reich on a more solid foundation of political support, and to achieve the constitutional compromise between essentially authoritarian government and popular support which he had sought since 1848. He was able for the first time to give certain manufacturing interests good economic reasons for continuing to support his regime, rather than having to rely on the sporadic enthusiasm generated by nationalist successes which in themselves had been very limited. Aspiring groups of businessmen and manufacturers no longer needed to espouse the cause of liberal constitutionalism in their own interest. More important, he could unite such groups in one alliance of real interest for the first time with their traditional opponents – the landowners and farmers – and cement it with the little touch of intellectual glue provided by the miscellaneous group of economists and other writers who wished to preserve something of the old German society which they saw changing too quickly under the pressures of industrialisation and foreign influence. The tariff became an alternative to the constitution, as well it might for the constitution demonstrated that the existence of assemblies elected by universal suffrage did not necessarily mean the existence of an effective forum where real economic interests could be brought to a compromise in a popularly influenced government policy. Subsequent debates over tariff policy, as at the time of Caprivi's chancellorship, were more crucial to people's real interests and generated more intense political interest than any other issues until 1917. The industrial and commercial groups who had briefly glimpsed their desire for political participation turn into reality in 1848 and then seen those hopes removed were thus brought into the active political arena on quite different terms at the end of the 1870s and in safe conjunction with an agrarian interest as large as in France. It was only the initial stages of the campaign for agricultural protection, which were financed and organised by the established rural elites. The campaign soon proved almost as popular as Méline was to make it in France.

If we ask why the movement towards trade liberalisation in the 1860s was politically as painless as it was economically, the answer again is that it represented an earlier step towards wider participation in the political nation. In Britain the repeal of the Corn Laws was the first significant permanent stake in national policy which urban and manufacturing interests were able to obtain – the stake that had been denied them by the 1832 Reform Bill. Similarly the victory of Frere Orban in Belgium in the 1850s represented the arrival to full political participation there of the same interests. There was a substantial body of manufacturing support for Napoleon's tariff *coup de main* in 1860. The tariff was conceived and presented as a step in modernisation and for its industrial opponents it was sweetened by an extensive system of grants for modernising equipment and machinery. It was one more stage in the Emperor's attempts to base his rule on what he regarded as the more modern and progress elements in the nation. Delbrück's lowering of the tariff in the foundation years of the new German Reich was likewise a political concession to gain support from the same groups.

The imperfect mechanisms of incomplete democracies made the tariff books seem as important an expression of the political balance of the nation as the constitution. They represented written compromises on real tests of political as well as economic strength. Hence the extraordinary importance of tariffs in public argument when non-tariff barriers were probably, as now, much more important in regulating and obstructing international trade. They were regarded as a written expression of what the economic and social balance of the nation should be. Like the frontier on which it was levied, the tariff was a visible expression of national unity and as that unity increasingly had to include deeper strata in the nation the tariff became the instrument of their inclusion.

The significance of such an interpretation, which corresponds more closely to the historical record than the prevailing one, lies for the present in the question whether that process of widening political participation has reached its end. The growth of all Western European economies, except possibly Britain's, between 1951 and 1974 represented a virtuous circle in which a surge of exports stimulated and maintained high rates of growth in total output. The higher the proportion of manufactured goods exported, the higher the average level of productivity in industry, the higher the level of presumed future competitiveness on international markets and the higher the rate of growth of GNP per capita. All that has come to an end. Is the renewed demand for protectionism a retrogressive move, a short-sighted defensive policy error, or is it a further stage in political participation in Western democracies, an important and necessary step in political change and adaptation? Agreement between managers and workers in British Leyland to exclude those driving foreign cars from the car parks may be the only agreement they can achieve, but what would be the influence of genuine 'industrial democracy' in the mixed economy on tariffs and trade? If liberal trade regulations no longer convince entrepreneurs, they have practically never convinced their employees. But they have rarely anywhere been able to express their views on equal terms even in labour and socialist parties whose leadership in Western Europe, presumably under the heavy influence of history, has frequently (for reasons of greater political participation) been nearer to a free trade position than their conservative opponents. As the organs of nineteenth-century political democracy become less and less adequate and responsive to the popular will it is hard to imagine that lower-level assemblies, regional parliaments, elected factory councils (or perhaps some more genuinely democratic version of the corporate state than that with which reactionaries of the interwar period toyed) would not bring to fruition another wave of protectionist agitation. This might well represent a significant step forward in democratic politics, even though it might well be bad economics. The consolation, if one is needed, is to be found, of course, in the likelihood that it may cause no more of a break in the trend of international trade from the 1950s and 1960s than existed, in reality, between the late and mid-nineteenth century. In retrospect it might, as in the nineteenth century, be an issue of much political importance but, economically, no great matter.

Part Three: Surplus Capacity by Sector

6

Iron and Steel

STEPHEN WOOLCOCK

The Importance of the Market

The problems of the steel industry are not exclusively due to the existence of surplus capacity, but they can be discussed in relation to it. Differences in the degree of surplus capacity, and the ability of steel producers to avoid or reduce it, go a long way towards explaining the differing degrees of crisis in the steel industry of the world.

The experience of the development of the industry in North America, Europe and Japan over the last twenty-five years suggests that strong and dynamic growth in demand for steel is a major factor in determining the strength of the industry and thus its ability to adjust to surplus capacity. Dynamic growth not only promotes higher productivity through the construction of new plant (see Wolter, 1977) but also eases the adjustment on the supply side.

The US industry was the first to benefit from the postwar boom in steel-intensive consumer products, such as automobiles and domestic appliances. Since the beginning of the 1960s, however, the growth of demand for steel on the vital domestic market has slowed down as demand for these products has stagnated. Steel production in the United States grew at an average annual rate of only 2·5 per cent from 1950 to 1974, with the result that steel producers adopted a cautious investment policy. In the twenty-five years up to 1978 only two new greenfield plants were built in the United States.

In comparison, Japanese production grew at an annual average of 13 per cent between 1950 and 1974, and steel demand outstripped the growth in GNP. Thanks to this dynamic growth the steel plant in Japan was newer and able to operate at higher levels of productivity than US or European plants. When the rate of growth of demand for steel finally fell below that of GNP in 1974, Japanese producers were therefore better placed to weather the recession and could operate profitably at only 70 per cent of capacity (Nomura, 1979, p. 117).

In Europe, although it is difficult to generalise, growth in demand took an intermediate position between that of the United States and

Japan (Commission of the European Communities, 1976a, p. 82). When the recession struck in 1974 the European producers were generally still operating a number of obsolete plants which had a detrimental effect on their overall productivity. Perhaps the most significant factor in determining present productivity of the various steel producers is therefore the rate of growth of demand for steel, which depends on the general growth of manufacturing industry, over the last ten years. However, the stagnating growth in steel demand in the 1970s has meant that steel producers who could not take advantage of the rapid growth of the 1960s faced especially severe problems of output adjustment in the 1970s.

Future demand for bulk steel is unlikely to solve these structural problems. Indeed the fact that demand for steel is likely to grow twice as fast in the developing world, where steel consumption per capita is about 40 kg per annum on average, compared with 500–700 kg in Western Europe (Commission of the European Communities, 1976a, p. 27), suggests that shifts in the location of steel production will add to the social and political frictions generated by adjustment under conditions of slow growth in the industrialised countries.

Trade

The 1960s and 1970s saw a progressive shift in the pattern of trade in steel. The United States became a major importer of steel from the mid-1960s with the result that various forms of import restraint were introduced after 1968. Voluntary restraint agreements were concluded with Japanese and European producers which were replaced, in 1977, by a system of trigger prices based on Japanese production costs. Despite the trigger prices US imports remained relatively high in 1978 and 1979, and there has been renewed pressure from the industry for more restrictive measures.

If the United States is the largest single import market, the Japanese producers have been the most prodigious exporters. Japan's share of world steel exports rose from 27 per cent in 1966 to 44 per cent in 1977, while that of the European Community (EC) fell from 51 per cent to 26 per cent, including intra-EC trade, and due to the difficulties in other industrialised markets the Japanese have been obliged to accept a policy of export restraint for some time. Export restraint to the EC has generally followed restraint towards the United States but the EC has concluded more formal agreements with Japan under the external measures of the Davignon plan (for the details of the Davignon plan see Commission, 1976b, c, 1977a, b). Such bilateral agreements have also been concluded between the EC and some eighteen steel-producing countries in 1978 and 1979, and will continue in 1980 for the more important industrialised steel-producing countries. With strong demand in the Third World the new steel-producing countries are unlikely to become net exporters in the 1980s but rapid growth in output in these countries will mean that import substitution will continue to deprive the industrialised countries of a large and growing export market in this region (for one estimate of self-sufficiency see CIA, 1979, p. 7).

In summary, therefore, the shifts in trade patterns and the progressive closing of traditional export markets, especially for the European steel producers, will mean that any surplus capacity problems caused by changes in demand or supply in the advanced industrialised countries (AICs) will, in the absence of access to any growing markets, have to be solved by adjustment of capacity. The option of venting excess capacity on export markets as was done in the 1960s is no longer an effective solution (Stegemann, 1977). Furthermore, the existence of excess capacity has resulted in an increased regulation of trade and above all prices, in order to tackle the short-term problems resulting from surplus capacity.

Technology and Industrial Structure

The improvements in production technology in the form of larger blast furnaces, coupled with oxygen steel converters and continuous casting, not only improved productivity for those producers who were in a position to exploit them, but also increased the pressure for concentration in the industry. The effects of increases in the economies of scale of production and the cost of capital investment, combined with the pressures caused by cyclical and structural changes in demand, led to an increase in mergers and rationalisation agreements (Cockerill, 1975).

In the UK the nationalisation of the industry provided an opportunity to rationalise production by means of a corporate strategy based on five giant coastal plants (DTI, 1973). Due to delays, largely caused by the modification of the strategy by successive governments, the UK public sector was still struggling to restructure when the recession hit in 1974. From what was the most ambitious investment programme in Europe in the mid-1970s, the flow of capital to BSC gradually slowed as losses mounted. In France there was a fairly rapid process of concentration and by the mid-1970s there were only three major steel groupings. The continued recession led to more direct public involvement in the form of partial ownership, and the restructuring of the industry around Usinor and Sacilor.

The FRG is interesting because the established economic philosophy virtually excluded the possibility of any increase in the size of the public sector. The restructuring of the industry was consequently under the control of the private sector. Through the aid of the Walzstahlkontore and later Rationalisierungsgruppen (regional sales and rationalisation groupings), assisted by a tradition of co-operation and backed by the private banks, a degree of what might be termed 'private planning' was achieved which assisted the process of adjustment. The task of phasing new capacity and thus avoiding cut-throat price competition was eased by the strength of the German manufacturing industry and the fact that the private planners were not constrained by political and social factors to the same extent as other steel industries in Europe in which public planners had more influence. When structural problems in the late 1970s necessitated further rationalisation on an international scale, the first response of the German industry was to form Denelux, an international extension of the rationalisation groups, including Dutch, Belgian and Luxembourg steel producers. This met strong opposition in France, which feared a reconstruction of a 'gigantic German cartel'. At this point, and with the encouragement of the EC Commission, Eurofer was born – an organisation that included all Community steel producers. Differences between national steel producers have, however, meant that this body could not develop into an effective cartel and, in contrast to some of the national steel associations, it has remained a rather weak lobby.

In Japan there are five major integrated steel producers who account for 95 per cent of pig iron and 77 per cent of crude steel production. Nippon Steel, with about 30 per cent of the industry, is a dominant force and effectively determines wage and price levels. As in the EC the Japanese government also provides indicative guidelines for production, and has recommended to steel companies the timing of blast furnace construction in the light of supply and demand. In this case, the large number of smaller producers has led to problems in Japan and Europe. In Japan a 'recession cartel' was formed in order to control the situation in 1977. In Europe the introduction of minimum prices started with reinforcing bars because the lack of 'discipline' of the 'Bresciani' producers was causing serious problems for the larger integrated producers in this particular market.

In the United States the industry reached a relatively high degree of concentration earlier than Europe. On the other hand, investment there generally lagged behind that in Europe and Japan. The problem of low investment persists today and has been recognised by, for example, the 'Comprehensive programme for the steel industry' (US Department of the Treasury, 1977). In Europe and Japan investment declined after the 1974 recession, although some extra capacity was added due to decisions made before 1974. In the EC raw steel capacity rose from 190m. tonnes in 1975 to about 202m. in 1979 but can be expected to remain at this level until 1982. In Japan operating capacity rose from 128m. tonnes in 1974 to around 146m. in 1978. With the addition of a further blast furnace, capacity is expected to rise to about 150m. in 1980, although estimates vary. In the non-integrated sector in Japan MITI has recommended that long product production capacity be reduced by 3·3m.

tonnes in the crisis cartel by 1980s (Nomura, 1979, p. 120). In the EC the diverse nature of decision-making on investment and the existence of various national industries within the common market has made the process of sharing the burden of adjustment more complex. Comparing the expected annual crude steel capacity in 1980 with 1975, French capacity will fall by about 2·0m. tonnes, British by about 4·5m. and Luxembourg by 0·5m. Italian capacity will be 4·0m. tonnes larger while German and Belgian will remain approximately constant − although in all cases it should be remembered that the real capacity of steel plants is exceedingly difficult to determine and is often a closely guarded commercial secret.

The Response to Structural Problems: Anti-Crisis Measures

Adjustment to changes in the pattern of demand and trade have been continuous. The above section has described briefly the longer-term response to the need for adjustment in the form of changes in industrial structure and concentration, and so on. In this section the various responses to what might be called the management of surplus capacity will be dealt with. It is useful to consider two forms of approach to the problem: the short-term measures designed to raise prices and thus mitigate the effects of surplus capacity on the financial performance of steel industries, and the longer-term restructuring measures.

While the 1970s did not see a return to international cartels as in the 1930s various forms of intervention were introduced (for the 1930s see Rieben, 1977). As we have seen, the United States changed from a policy of supporting 'voluntary' export restraint agreements concluded between the US government and foreign steel producers to a system of trigger prices. The reasons for the change were twofold: first, various steel producers had been the subject of triple damage actions under US Anti-trust Laws which dissuaded the Europeans and Japanese from any future 'voluntary restraint' agreements of this kind; secondly, the import restraint had not led to an increase in investment in US industry (*Sunday Times*, 9 October 1977). There was also concern in the US government and elsewhere that the tentative determination found against Japanese producers in the Gilmore case would lead to a series of anti-dumping actions in the US courts which would damage trade relations with Japan and Europe (*International Herald Tribune*, 4 October 1977).

In Europe the EC Commission had been pressed by the French to declare a manifest crisis as early as September 1975. But there was not enough support for such a move, which would have given power to the EC Commission, under Article 58 of the Treaty of Paris, to introduce production quotas and to take other measures to prevent imports. The fact that mandatory production quotas were not introduced derived

from Article 57 ECSC which obliged the Commission to attempt voluntary measures first. The main reason for not actually imposing production quotas, however, was German opposition to any form of market-
sharing. Until May 1977 the EC Commission applied voluntary indicative prices and production guidelines. Mandatory minimum prices were
then introduced for reinforcing bars, where the Italian Bresciani
producers had not 'co-operated' with the indicative guidelines. In
January 1978 minimum prices were also introduced for two other
products following the collapse of the market in autumn of 1977 which
has led to an intensification of cut-throat competition. No mandatory
production quotas were introduced by the EC Commission but it continued to produce quarterly forward programmes, along the lines of
MITI in Japan. On the basis of these projections bilateral undertakings
were concluded, between the steel producers and the Commission, on
how much steel should be produced. In January 1978 the EC also
introduced base import prices and began negotiating bilateral arrangements with exporting countries which regulated import volume, on the
basis of 1976 imports, and prices.

These anti-crisis measures in Europe and the United States could not
function effectively without Japanese support, which was granted by the
steel producers in late 1977. The Japanese accepted that import regulation in the United States and Europe was inevitable and that they might
as well agree to the US trigger and EC base import prices and thus raise
export revenue if not volume. These anti-crisis measures made it
possible for producers to raise prices to help cover rising costs; in the
ECSC prices rose by about 20 per cent. Imports into the three steel-
producing regions have remained stable, although at a relatively high
level in the United States.

In order to co-ordinate these anti-crisis measures in a more formal
setting, but also to seek international solutions to the problem of adjustment and restructuring, a steel committee was set up within the OECD.
The committee has set itself the objectives of ensuring that anti-crisis
measures are not unnecessarily restrictive, and that national steel
policies do not shift the burden of adjustment on to other countries
(OECD, 1978). Although the fear has been expressed that the committee might develop into an international cartel, the differences between
the OECD producers are such that this would seem very unlikely. In
addition the large number of steel producers, including the new steel
producers of the Third World, make the organisation of such a cartel
far more difficult than it was in the 1930s.

The Removal of Surplus Capacity

Faced with either increased competition from abroad, as in the case of
the US industry, or persistent surplus capacity, as in the case of the

European producers, there is therefore a need for real adjustment in the longer term. This fact was brought home to even the most optimistic in the industry by the collapse of the market in 1977. Current demand projections for the 1980s suggest that more will have to be done in the future.

In some cases adjustment occurred spontaneously before the onset of the crisis: Mannesmann in Germany had moved out of bulk steel production and diversified into engineering and higher-value-added products. In general Japanese producers are the most diversified followed by the United States and the Europeans. Some US steel producers are beginning to move out of steel altogether and into service industries. How far this process will be allowed to go remains to be seen but there are certainly those who fear that by the mid-1980s the US industry will not be able to cover domestic demand, thus rendering the United States dependent on foreign steel (CIA, 1978). The US industry has made some significant closures, first in 1977, and then more recently in December 1979; and there now appear to be more signs that the US industry is considering a longer-term policy of adjustment than was the case earlier in the 1970s. In view of the strength of Japan and the likelihood that the yen will not appreciate greatly against the dollar, there would seem to be little prospect of the US industry regaining the kind of strong competitive position *vis-à-vis* Japan which would make continued export restraint on the part of the Japanese redundant.

In Japan there has been a stabilisation of capacity expansion. Thanks to increased export prices and improvements in production techniques the Japanese industry has been able to operate profitably at some 70 per cent of maximum capacity. The Japanese producers are therefore in a position to benefit from the improbable event of a marked improvement in demand which could not be covered by other producers, while shifting to new export markets such as China.

In Europe there have been major closure programmes in France and in the UK which have been mainly due to the costs of maintaining surplus capacity or obsolete plants. In Germany there has been a slight reduction in capacity while Italy and Belgium have at least maintained existing capacity. Capacity utilisation varies; for example, West Germany was operating at a rate lower than France or the UK in 1977, 58 per cent as against 66 per cent in France and 71 per cent in the UK. This would tend to indicate that it is not so much the degree of physical surplus capacity which determines whether adjustment will take place but the ability to operate at lower levels of production without incurring excessive losses. The reasons why the Germans have been better at this are numerous. Output adjustment in Germany was eased, for example, by the ability to reduce the number of hours worked, national insurance funds being used to make up wages. In November 1975, for example, 2·3m. hours were lost in Germany compared with 85,000 in the UK where an agreement on a guaranteed working week reduced the flexibility of BSC.

The impact of redundancies in West Germany was also less. Average unemployment in steel-producing areas in the FRG was 3·2 per cent in 1977, compared with 5·8 per cent in Belgium, 4·3 per cent in France and 5 per cent in the UK. Furthermore, nearly half the redundancies in the FRG – 19,500 in 1974–7 – were in Rgierungsbezirk Düsseldorf where steel accounted for only 7 per cent of total industrial employment in 1977. In the areas where obsolete plant was situated in the UK and France, steel accounted for about 20 per cent of total industrial employment in Clwyd, Cleveland, and so on, and in Lorraine, and even more in narrowly defined areas.

In the Saar, where nearly 6,000 jobs were lost between 1974 and 1977, steel accounted for nearly 12 per cent of employment, and in this case the federal government provided DM200m. in regional aid plus a further DM900m. in investment guarantees for the reorganisation of the industry in 1978. In 1979 a further DM250m. was provided for the Saar steel industry from land and federal grants (*Metal Bulletin*, 1979, p. 37). While these public funds are not as great as those provided for the British, French, or Italian industries, and are in any case partly public investment capital and not subsidies, they do show that in the few cases when the social and employment implications of adjustment in the German steel industry have been unacceptable the state and local government have intervened. What is argued here is that while the German industry has generally adjusted better and without public assistance, the social and political problems involved in adjustment in Germany have been less than those in France and the UK. Where the socio-political environment has been less favourable, public assistance, although partly indirect via the banking community, has been provided.

Conclusions on the Structure of Authority

What can one conclude from this brief and inevitably schematic description of the various responses to the problem of surplus capacity in the steel industry? First, at the international level a greater degree of inter-governmental anti-crisis management has more or less replaced international cartels as the favoured policy of the OECD countries. This is possible within the EC due to the extensive powers of the EC Commission in the field of price and production regulation, and in Japan due to the dominant role of Nippon steel in policy formulation. While European and Japanese producers can sit down with national governments or foreign producers without anti-trust problems this is not the case in the United States, although the conclusion of the Solomon Report was accompanied by trilateral talks between producers, unions and government. The establishment of the OECD steel committee, however, does provide the opportunity to bring industrialists into the technical committees. The symposium organised by the steel committee in February 1980 recalls the ILO as a way of getting around the remaining barriers to trialogues (involving producers, governments and unions) at an international level.

There has been a higher degree of state influence over investment, production and pricing policies in the steel industry than in most others. In Japan, while direct control is no longer exercised or indeed necessary, the possibilities for indirect control still exist and have been used in all three fields during the recent recession. In the United States the government has influenced the pricing policy of the US steel industry, although with declining effectiveness since the earlier confrontations between the industry and the Kennedy Administration. In the United States, therefore, state influence over investment has been largely through its pricing policies, but with the worsening structural problems in the industry the federal government has also moved to provide capital grants, to ease environmental control regulations and capital depreciation periods, which will all influence investment. Within Europe the recent recession has seen an increase in the extent to which the state exercises direct control over the industry's adjustment plans. In France and Belgium the state has taken the industry into partial public ownership, and in Belgium a planning commission, consisting of unions, producers, government, and the EC Commission as an observer, has negotiated on restructuring. In the UK the state exercised a good deal of influence over investment before the nationalisation of the industry. Since 1967 the state has repeatedly intervened directly, and often inconsistently with change of government, in the developing strategy of BSC. In Italy something of a dual structure exists in which a large number of small private steel producers have acted independently of national or EC control, while the larger integrated steel plants are run by public enterprise.

In West Germany the industry is still controlled by the private sector but this has not meant that the state has not been influential behind the scenes when the adjustment of the industry has had a major impact of a social or political nature. In Germany, in comparison with the United States, the private steel companies have developed and implemented longer-term corporate strategies within the industry.

In terms of demand there is little the state has been able to do directly by way of public procurement, although indirectly public enterprise has possibly given preference to domestic steel and steel has also figured in foreign aid programmes. In the future the new GATT code on public procurement is likely to inhibit the development of such national preferences. The state has sometimes intervened to support the all-important captive domestic markets and thus help to ensure that the steel industry could rely on a sound domestic base.

During the 1960s and 1970s the development of production technology favoured the development of large-scale production and thus the concentration of the industry. This tended to strengthen the traditional oligopolistic structure of the industry. However, since the 1975 recession there has been a stop on investment in new, large, integrated works. With the prospect of slower growth during the 1980s, the risks involved in the construction of larger greenfield plants will deter all but the biggest, most optimistic investors, because the high fixed capital costs make such investments very vulnerable in times of recession. In the future there might be a steady growth of smaller steel plants, based on electric arc furnaces, along Italian lines. On the other hand, there will be a greater drive towards automated process control and higher rolling speeds by the larger oligopolistic producers. In sum, a degree of competition will survive despite efforts to suppress it. This would provide greater scope for new competitors. But as experience in the EC and Japan has shown, market regulation becomes more difficult when there are a large number of small producers.

The long-term developments in the pattern of demand would appear to favour the development of steel industries in the NICs. Indeed the leading new steel producers have already made rapid progress during the 1970s, increasing their share of world production from 3·5 per cent in 1974 to 6 per cent in 1979. While the NICs are unlikely to become a major factor on export markets, at least until the end of the 1980s, they will, through increased import substitution in what are the only markets with good medium-term growth potential, increase the pressure on the OECD steel producers to adjust.

References and Further Reading: Chapter 6

Central Intelligence Agency (1978), *The World Steel Market: Continued Trouble Ahead* (Washington, DC: Government Printer), May.

Central Intelligence Agency (1979), *The Burgeoning LDC Steel Industry: More Problems for Major Steel Producers* (Washington, DC: Government Printer), July.

Cockerill, A. (1975), *The Iron and Steel Industry: International Comparisons of Structure and Performance* (Cambridge: Cambridge University Press).

Commission of the European Communities:
  (1975), *Guidelines on Iron and Steel Policy*, COM (75) 701;
  (1976a), *General Objectives for Steel, 1980–85*, Official Journal C232;
  (1976b), *Guidelines on Iron and Steel Policy*, SEC (76) 2813;
  (1976c), *Community Steel Policy*, COM (76) 543;
  (1977a), *Community Steel Policy*, Official Journal C303/3;
  (1977b), Official Journal, L352;
  (1977c), Official Journal, C316.

Department of Trade and Industry (1973), *Steel: A Ten Year Development Strategy*, Cmnd 5226 (London: HMSO).

Federal Trade Commission (1977), *The US Steel Industry and its International Rivals: Trends Determining International Competitiveness* (Washington DC: Government Printer), November.

International Iron and Steel Institute (1974); *Steel Intensity and GNP Structure* (Brussels: IISI).

Metal Bulletin, 18 December 1979.

Nomura Research Institute (1979), *Prospects for Japanese Industry to 1985*, Vol. 1 (London: Financial Times Management Reports).

OECD (1978), Council Decision, 'Establishing a steel committee', Paris, 26 October.

Rieben, H. (1977), *La Bataille d'Acier* (Lausanne: Centre de Recherche Européenne).

Stegemann, K. (1977), *Price Competition and Output Adjustment in the European Steel Industry 1954–1975* (Tübingen: Mohr).

UNIDO (1978) 'The world iron and steel industry', Second Study, International Centre for Industrial Studies, UNIDO/ICIS, 8–9 November.

US Department of the Treasury (1977), report to the President: 'A comprehensive programme for the steel industry' (Solomon Report), November.

Wolter (1977), 'Perspectives for the international location of the steel industry', Kiel Institute of World Economics, Working Paper No. 60, October.

7

Textiles and Clothing

CHRIS FARRANDS

Significant Variables

While other industries can date their current problems of instability from the economic crisis of 1973–4, in textiles and clothing the instability and the attempted management of it, by both national policies and international agreement, has been more determined and of longer standing than in many other sectors. Thus, the international trade in textiles is one of the most protected and also one in which some producers have been protected for longer than in any other major industry.

The sources of instability (which, I shall argue, have not been minimised or managed, but rather exacerbated by government intervention) are both secular and cyclical. Most important have been three kinds of changes relating to production: in the raw material used in manufacture; in the techniques of manufacture; and in the location of manufacture. In 1960–1, 83 per cent of world fibre production was of natural fibres, while ten years later the figure had fallen to 68 per cent. In absolute terms the output of natural fibres increased 10 per cent while that of man-made fibres increased by 150 per cent (Commonwealth Secretariat, 1973, p. 1). This change has been associated with financial restructuring and the increasing influence on the fibres and the textile trade of a few, very large, multinational chemical companies.

Secondly, the industry has experienced some major technical revolutions in the last decade, notably the 'knitting revolution' and the change to rotary spinning, besides various advances in synthetic technology. This has given important advantages to countries coming into the market for the first time (e.g. South Korea) and those that renew their capital more often. On average, equipment in German and Japanese industry is replaced every three or four years, in French and British it has averaged about every five. Technological change has also tended to accelerate over-production wherever information about market conditions is imperfect or where assumptions about the future state of the market have been over-optimistic.

Partly as a result of the opportunities held out by the first two changes there has been a shift in the location of textile manufacturing from developed industrial to newly industrialising countries (NICs). In 1968 the developing market economies exported 9·8 per cent of total world exports of textile, yarn and thread. In 1977, this proportion was virtually doubled to 17 per cent (United Nations, vol. II, 1979 p. 123). Moreover, as can be seen from Table 7.1, world production has tended to grow more slowly in textiles and clothing than in manufacturing generally, and though some countries (notably Britain) had not shared in this growth even before 1973, the problems of surplus capacity which they had already perceived became more generally apparent after 1973. Recovery in the late 1970s has been comparatively slow. Among producers, the European Community (EEC) as a whole has a dominant role in the international market (see Table 7.3). This has helped the EEC to gain advantages in negotiations on the future of the market (see Farrands, 1979). But as Table 7.1 also shows, the Europeans found the 1973 crisis a far more traumatic blow than the United States. For Japan's textile production, the 1973 crisis precipitated a contraction, in contrast to the general tendency of her industry to ride the storm well. This was at least partly a result of a deliberate policy to put industrial effort into other sectors.

On top of these changes on the production side came the check to demand on the consumption side following the recession of the mid-1970s. The market for clothing and other textile products depends directly on household incomes. And if there is less to spend, clothing is the marginal item for many. People buy fewer clothes, or less often, when they still go on buying food and fuel. Up to 1973, as household incomes steadily rose, demand remained buoyant. But in 1973–5 demand actually fell in some countries and in general has grown far less rapidly since 1975 than it did before.

The result has been, first, that Britain, France, West Germany, Japan and the United States have all lost about a third of their workforce in textiles since the beginning of the decade. Even in the 'best' year of the decade for textiles sales, the loss of jobs continued. Secondly, some producing countries have been more successful than others, moving up-market as pressure increased from new entrants like Hungary, Czechoslovakia and Mexico as well as Taiwan, Korea and Portugal.

Japan has been the best exponent of this policy. The apparent contraction shown in Table 7.1 masks a deliberate decision by Japanese firms, with government support, to move up-market and specialise, leaving mass-production items which they made in the 1950s and early 1960s to newer entrants. In parts of Europe (especially Britain, Italy and France) lack of capital and lack of confidence have hindered a similar response. But the position is not simply one of import penetration disrupting vulnerable European industries. Hong Kong, a major

Table 7.1   *Indices of production in textiles and clothing including leather and footwear compared with all manufacturing in OECD countries*

	Textile and clothing (includes leather and footwear)				All manufacturing		
				(1970 = 100)			
	Europe	*Japan*	*USA*		*Europe*	*Japan*	*USA*
1971	103	101	103		102	103	102
1972	107	105	111		107	110	112
1973	108	111	118		116	128	122
1974	105	100	112		117	123	122
1975	99	97	105		109	109	109
1976	107	102	118		116	121	122
1977	105	98	118		119	128	129

Source: OECD (1979).

NIC in clothing, imports virtually all the raw materials it uses for reprocessing, especially fabrics for making up at the top of the market. And Britain, where import penetration has risen enormously since the mid-1960s from 15·7 per cent to 34·1 per cent in fibres, from 4·8 per cent to 22·3 per cent in yarns, from 27·8 per cent to 45·1 per cent in fabrics and from 8 per cent to 21·3 per cent in finished clothing, nevertheless remains a net exporter of textiles, although in clothing it has recently acquired a large net deficit (Joint Textiles Committee, 1976, p. 33). Britain imports clothing and exports yarn, fabrics and (along with West Germany, Switzerland and Sweden) large quantities of textile machinery, the latter mainly to the NICs.

The picture of trade and of surplus capacity is consequently complicated; easy, oversimple judgements about the NIC threat to European industry are dangerous – not least because of the opacity of accounting procedures used by multinational companies.

For it is not only the international structure of the sector, by countries, that determines outcomes. Industrial structures are equally significant in determining the distribution of the adjustment burden. Thus, while textiles (including fibres and yarns) are dominated by larger firms, the clothing trade is characterised by a much larger number of smaller producers. In Britain, for example, production of textiles is mainly carried out in firms with more than 400 employees, while the typical clothing firm has only between 10 and 100 employees (Joint Textiles Committee, 1976, p. 15). This makes it easier for the textile producers to co-operate spontaneously amongst themselves in response to surplus capacity, or for them to be brought together by government in EDC sector working parties. In the clothing industry, planning is more difficult, at best more chaotic, and the response to surplus capacity (or a miscalculation about the market) is more likely to be the liquidation of individual firms or the actual bankruptcy of entrepreneurs. And this structural pattern recurs throughout the textile and clothing industry, worldwide.

Government policy has encouraged the retention of surplus capacity, or even its expansion. This has especially been true with respect to economically weak regions. The Thompson Report on regional problems in the European Community showed how far the textile industry predominated in these regions (Commission of the European Communities, 1973). Government aid for investment in regional problems is therefore a major source of investment in the textile industry, for social as much as economic reasons. Italian government aid has funded rapid increases in capacity in synthetic textiles, for example, and has helped to make possible Italian domination of the European market for ladies' tights (pantyhose to the Americans and Australians!). Governments also play a protective role, by exercising power to grant planning permission, and/or through fiscal policy. And while they do not seem to have had great success in achieving their declared objectives, they may actually perpetuate surplus capacity through schemes to avoid labour-shedding by subsidising industry in development areas.

Diagnosis

There has been much argument over the nature of the problem and the factors and trends to be held primarily responsible for surplus capacity. It has been compounded by some widespread (and probably unavoidable) imprecision about how surplus capacity can be defined and thus recognised and even measured. This confusion accounts for disagreement over the remedial policies appropriate to the condition. Uncertainty over the distribution and extent of surplus capacity seems greater in clothing than in the synthetic fibres/textiles sector. But this may be only because larger firms, especially the multinationals predominant in synthetics, are well informed and able therefore to form a more coherent picture of the market they dominate. In woollen products or clothing this is far more difficult and surplus capacity is consequently harder to pin down. (It may be argued by a trade organisation that there is a surplus of old capital equipment in need of replacement, but that is not exactly the same thing.) Furthermore, in woollens and clothing market forces are strong and brutally effective. Small, often underfinanced firms are vulnerable to takeover or bankruptcy if they cannot cope. Because of these immediate pressures an important cause of surplus capacity, in clothing at least, has been intervention of governments protecting or subsidising jobs. However, in sectors other than synthetics, there has been more disagreement about the nature of the problem. Within the OECD bloc it has been seen as one caused by low-cost competition. Alternatively it has been attributed to the failure of high-cost producers to adapt, to rationalise, and to move on to new, more advanced and more capital-intensive technologies. This has been the view of all those in GATT, the European Community and the NICs who have opposed and criticised the growth in OECD protectionism. Perceptions are thus the key to the problem; though surplus capacity is no less real for that.

One explanation for the argument over the nature of the problem in textiles lies in the overall market system or regime. This has been crucial. In cotton there has been a controlled market since 1962, initially operated by the Long Term Agreement (LTA). This was replaced in 1973 by the Multi-Fibre Agreement (MFA) which extended the LTA regime, adding stronger rules and institutional controls and covering, besides cotton products, nearly all other categories of textile products at all stages of production (see Farrands, 1979). The 1973 MFA provided a relatively liberal framework for trade between those members of GATT who entered it. This includes the United States, Japan, Egypt, India, Pakistan, Brazil, Hong Kong, South Korea, Singapore and the European Communities (who act as a single negotiator), as well as a number of other textile trading nations. Details of market shares are summarised in Tables 7.2 and 7.3. The 1973 MFA encouraged the growth of textile trade by seeking to guarantee that, subject to certain safeguards for importers, the developing countries would be able to increase their exports by 6 per cent p.a. This was an important incentive to new investment planning in those countries; access to previously closed markets seemed open.

Table 7.2   *Total world trade in textile products 1973–9 inclusive (all in US$m.)*

	Imports					Exports				
	1973	1974	1975	1976	1977	1973	1974	1975	1976	1977
Textile yarn and thread	5·7	6·7	5·9	7·2	7·6	6·1	7·3	6·2	7·4	8·2
Cotton fabrics, woven	3·3	3·9	3·6	4·6	5·1	2·8	3·4	3·2	3·8	4·2
Woven textiles, non-cotton	6·8	7·7	7·8	8·4	9·3	7·0	8·1	8·0	8·6	9·4
Lace, ribbons, etc.	0·5	0·5	0·5	0·6	0·7	0·4	0·5	0·6	0·6	0·7
Special textiles	1·9	2·5	2·3	2·4	2·8	1·9	2·6	2·3	2·4	2·7
Floor covering, etc.	1·3	1·7	1·7	2·0	2·3	1·1	1·6	1·6	1·8	2·1
Totals	19·5	23·0	21·8	25·2	27·8	19·3	23·5	21·8	24·6	27·3

The 1973 MFA can therefore be seen as a direct contributor to increases in world capacity. However, the world market did not grow as

Table 7.3   Percentages of world markets of major textile products held by selected countries 1973–7 inclusive[a]

Imports	1973			1974			1975			1976			1977		
	i	ii	iii	i	ii	iii	i	ii	iii	i	ii	iii	i	ii	iii
EC (nine)	45.4	35.3	40.4	46.2	39.7	39.4	48.5	41.5	40.9	49.0	43.2	38.6	49.8	43.4	39.9
UK	5.1	7.7	5.6	6.8	7.7	6.1	6.1	7.7	6.2	5.9	7.3	5.5	n.a.	n.a.	n.a.
US	4.5	9.5	8.9	2.9	9.0	6.9	2.2	6.1	5.7	2.7	8.4	6.3	n.a.	n.a.	n.a.
Japan	3.9	n.s.	6.0	2.4	n.s.	5.7	3.3	n.s.	4.5	3.6	n.s.	4.7	n.a.	n.s.	n.a.
Developed (DDMEs) Market Economies	74.0	75.7	75.5	73.4	77.3	74.7	73.0	71.0	70.6	73.1	73.9	69.7	72.6	71.3	69.7
Developing Market Economies (DGMEs)	26.0	24.3	24.5	26.6	22.7	25.3	27.0	29.0	29.4	26.9	26.1	30.3	n.a.	n.a.	n.a.
Exports															
EC (nine)	58.6	33.6	53.4	56.4	36.0	51.9	57.6	37.6	53.1	55.5	32.6	50.3	53.8	34.4	52.3
UK	7.6	n.s.	6.9	7.6	n.s.	6.8	7.2	n.s.	6.1	6.9	n.s.	5.6	7.0	n.s.	6.5
US	4.5	9.4	4.1	5.6	11.3	5.1	4.8	12.0	4.9	5.1	13.3	5.0	5.1	n.a.	4.4
Japan	9.5[b]	6.9	19.7	11.0	7.1	20.9	9.4	8.2	21.6	8.4	8.4	22.7	10.0	n.a.	21.5
DDMEs	84.2	62.9	86.7	85.5	66.1	87.5	85.0	69.0	88.6	82.6	65.8	86.5	83.0	67.0	86.8
DGMEs	15.8[c]	37.1	13.3	14.5	33.9	12.5	15.0	31.0	11.4	17.4	34.2	13.5	17.0	32.9	13.2

[a]i = textiles yarn and cloth; ii = cotton fabrics, woven; iii = woven textiles, non-cotton; n.a. = not available; n.s. = not significant.
[b]In 1968 = 12.5.
[c]In 1968 = 9.8.
Source: United Nations (1979, vol. II, pp. 123–9).

expected and import penetration of developed countries markets by NICs proved distressing and disruptive. Furthermore the impact of the global 6 per cent p.a. growth target was uneven: NIC sales to the United States rose by between 3 and 4 per cent; to the EC they rose by over 40 per cent. Industry in France, Italy and Britain called strongly for a revision of the agreement and for greater protection, and even the force-fully anti-protectionist *Economist* called the MFA 'too liberal' on 15 October 1977. When it was renewed at the end of 1977 it took a very different form, especially in the bilateral agreements on import quotas into the EC from the major NICs, and controls were to operate more effectively. The 1977 MFA retains the principle of 6 per cent sales growth a year from NICs, but is in detail a restrictive agreement.

The following are the main courses adopted to manage surplus capacity or a tendency to surplus capacity in the textiles and clothing sectors.

Short-time working. Since 1975 there has been a steady increase in short-time working within the developed OECD states where a problem has been identified as manageable in the medium term, or where plant closure and unemployment have been mitigated by government or trade union pressure.

Plant closure. Resorted to very late in the day within the large firms for economic as well as social reasons, plant closure is wasteful and expensive as well as difficult and unpleasant. While multinationals working outside their home territory may appear to enjoy an advantage, this is certainly not necessarily the case: the French government successfully obstructed a programme of plant closures by Montedison, subsidiary of the Italian Montefibre.

Bankruptcy. This is far and away the most important control in the more fragmented sectors of textiles and clothing, especially clothing. Figures for Britain (I do not have complete figures for any other country) suggest that firms left the market at a rapidly accelerating rate after 1973. Between 1958 and 1973 the number of firms in textiles as a whole fell by 42·3 per cent, from 8,461 to 4,883, but rationalisation and restructuring were the primary cause of this except in earlier bad years (e.g. 1967) (Joint Textiles Committee, 1976, p. 15).

International Agreement. The 1977 MFA acts as both a restraint on the creation of new capacity and an agreement that will indirectly curtail some existing capacity. For example, within a year of its signature India asked for a revision of its quotas because of the slump caused in its industry by the tighter control of its sales to the EC.

Exports. The controlled regime of the MFA makes it difficult to resort to exporting on a large scale as a solution to excess capacity. In any case increased exporting cannot be a solution to a global surplus capacity such as that found in synthetics. But for the individual firm a search for new markets is one possible solution to a problem of under-used capital, one which is much emphasised by planning bodies and sector working parties in all OECD countries affected. NICs have aimed at deliberately promoting surplus capacity in textiles to help their exports and thus their development. This includes both developing states like Nigeria and Kenya, and semi-industrialised countries like Greece, Portugal and Turkey. The 1977 MFA now controls their exports more tightly.

Cartelisation. In the main area where surplus capacity can be identified – synthetics – one proposal within the EC has been for cartelisation. This proposal has come from the eleven major multinationals and has been worked out between them and the Industrial Affairs Directorate General of the European Commission (*The Economist*, 27 January 1979). Twice the Commission as a whole has overruled the individual Directorate General pointing out that the cartel would break the rules of the Treaty of Rome and the Communities' competition policy (Articles 85, 86, 89). It has been deeply divided. National governments have also been divided: France, Britain and Italy have supported the scheme increasingly strongly while West Germany and Denmark have joined M. Vouel, the Competition Commissioner, in opposition. The scheme involved market-sharing tied to planned cuts in productive capacity. This was to involve redundancies and plant closure. Since most firms, including Hoechst, ICI, Courtaulds and Azko, already had schemes for such cuts it was not a difficult plan to draw up. Some conflicts arose over the Italian position since while Italian companies were joining the scheme, they were at the same time about to receive substantial government grants to increase capacity at other plants. These problems appeared to have been overcome by mid-1979. *The Economist* (27 January 1979) guessed that the cartel would go ahead despite the Commission's avowal that it would breach the Treaty and that the Commission would then find it preferable to turn a blind eye to the cartel.

Cartelisation is only an effective option where units are large, where information is easily available about the market as a whole, and where the problem is acute enough to persuade competitors to co-operate. It was estimated that surplus capacity in synthetics has cost the eleven majors \$2·5b. since 1975. It has also helped to have the benign eye, and possible refereeing role, of M. Davignon and his staff.

By contrasting the synthetics and clothing sectors we can identify the main factors that suggest why surplus capacity has been handled as it has been in textiles and clothing. The size and number of firms in the market is a key factor, as is the role of multinationals with wide-ranging rather than nationally based definitions of the problem. Technical change has made surplus capacity harder to identify, but also harder to manage, and has been a continuing source of a tendency to surplus capacity unless other forces intervened to prevent it.

The special context of a relatively longstanding set of international trading arrangements under the LTA and MFA make this a unique sector amongst those studied in this book. The MFA has not made surplus capacity either inevitable or impossible in itself, but it has certainly affected the forms and scope of surplus capacity and made the exporting solution to national problems of surplus difficult to manage. It has also helped governments under domestic pressure to resort to protection which has encouraged surplus capacity. In synthetics the major factors have been the multinational companies and the large-scale capital-intensive nature of production. Multinationals have also had two other effects: they have moved into other sectors, taking over clothing and woollen firms and therefore having important repercussions for other sectors; and they play a major part in trade associations and regional or sector planning organisations. As such, through pressure groups such as the European industry committee COM-ITEXTIL, or the very successful American textile lobbies in Congress, they have much influence on government policy. The 1977 MFA talks in Europe were dominated by the trade associations and the large companies. Their role shows as its strongest and clearest in the talks on a synthetic cartel, and the tacit capitulation (if that is what it was) of the European Commission to their plans.

In clothing, by contrast, and despite some financial restructuring which has included takeovers by large firms, production is still largely small scale within the whole global industry. It is fragmented and has responded to surplus capacity either by bankruptcy or by moves to newer technology or to new markets. In both sectors government policy, which has generally stressed the need for job protection and re-investment, has been a factor, a direct cause of some surplus capacity. Given the context of unemployment in the European and American industries this protection has hardly been socially or politically unnecessary.

The management of surplus capacity in textiles and clothing has thus been largely in the hands of firms themselves. But only the multi-nationals have had the overview or the power to take general decisions about the future of a market as a whole. They have been joined by the European Commission and GATT Textiles Committee which also have an overview of the industry but which need the support of national governments to be effective. Governments have not in general been active in investment or ownership, with the important exception of regional investment and development policies in Europe. But their trading policies set the context for what is very much an international market. A problem is posed by the growth of NIC expectations and by NIC production: the MFA is due for renewal again in 1981, when NICs are expected to increase demands for a growing market share. No one among the developed producers seems willing to face that at present. Governments, firms and trade associations play a major role in the management of the MFA regime and hence in the way markets are divided and trade is controlled.

Trade unions, by contrast, although they exist at national level and are members of international bodies such as the European Trades Union Council, have far less influence in this fragmented, low-wage industry where many of the employees are women (and, at least according to what one is told, therefore less willing to unionise). In the synthetics cartel plan, the unions simply were not consulted until the plan was settled (interview evidence).

Structural change and the pattern of the managed market have, therefore, promoted surplus capacity in textiles and clothing. Strong pressure in international bodies such as GATT and the World Bank has not been very effective in controlling protection (World Bank, 1979), and the problem remains. If surplus capacity is to be limited, it calls for co-operation. But the social and political problems of rationalisation are enormous. Whatever economic justification there may be for the cutting of capacity, governments have to take note of these problems. It would seem that while economic efficiency demands adjustment, social and political pressure, and political will, are going to determine the pace of adjustment.

References and Further Reading: Chapter 7

Commission of the European Communities (1973), *Report on the Regional Problems of the Enlarged Communities* (Thompson Report), COM (73) 550 (Brussels: EC Commission).

Commonwealth Secretariat (1973), *Industrial Fibres: A Review* (London: Commonwealth Secretariat).

Farrands, C. (1979), 'Textile diplomacy: the making and implementation of European textile policy 1973–1978', *Journal of Common Market Studies*, vol. XVIII, 1 September.

Joint Textiles Committee (1976), *Textile Trends 1966–1975* (London: JTC).

OECD (1977), *Industrial Production: Historical Statistics 1960–1975* (Paris: OECD).

OECD (1979), *The Textile Industry in OECD Countries 1977* (Paris: OECD).

United Nations (1979), *Yearbook of International Trade Statistics 1977*, 2 vols (New York: UN).

Walsh, A. E., and Paxton, J. (1970), *Trade and Industrial Resources of the Common Market and the EFTA Countries* (London: Garnstone Press).

World Bank (1979), *World Development Report 1979* (Washington: World Bank).

8

Shipping and Shipbuilding

CHRIS CRAGG

Shipping is at the sharp end of international political and economic relations. In terms of history it is frequently thought of as a specifically national asset. Great Britain, after all, prided itself on the size of its merchant fleet and there is little doubt that the country was greatly aided by it during the period of imperial and commercial expansion. Furthermore it is unlikely that Britain could have survived two military confrontations with Germany this century without the significant merchant marine it then possessed. In terms of military and commercial strategic capability, a sizeable merchant fleet has always been a decided advantage and this remains true today.

At the same time, however, the commercial success of merchant shipping depends profoundly upon an open international trading system. This is not merely because protection and tariff barriers reduce the possibility of international specialisation, competition and profit maximisation through economies of scale. Clearly this affects all large-scale industry and shipping also. Rather it is because for shipping there is no phrase directly corresponding to the 'home market' in the way a medium-size engineering company might use it. Except for coastal tramp or product shipping, the vast majority of ships trade between countries rather than out of one in particular. As a result true protection for a national shipping fleet lies in bilateral agreement to split cargo, rather than in unilateral declarations about carrying UK exports in UK ships. To adopt the latter stance is to ensure that ships spend half their voyages in ballast and to cause an immediate doubling of freight charges, which, given the importance of fob/cif price differentials in export sales, has the effect of discouraging them.

Thus, as both a national asset and a part of an open trading system, shipping is particularly vulnerable to increases in international tension and responds more rapidly than other industries to the prospect of a decline in international trade. While ships themselves may take more than five years to finance, design and build and forward planning is crucial to their commercial success, routes, security of charter and prospect of profit can disappear with the announcement of a grain embargo or an oil price rise. Overcapacity in (say) steel can slowly emerge in response to a different economic climate or a change in the use of materials and be met by subsidies. A marginal monthly downturn in international trade, whether in oil, dry bulk, or finished products can turn a highly priced vessel into a floating liability that costs money to maintain and lay up, and mounting debt interest to keep. If the monthly downturn continues then the resale of this costly asset at a price that remotely resembles the accumulated capital debt that was required to build it in the first place will become increasingly difficult. A shipping company can thus lose turnover, followed rapidly by collapsing asset values, at a speed that would frighten less flamboyant industries.

Effectively, in times of worsening international trade the only 'bottom line' available to a shipowner is the likely scrap value of his vessels and the sure knowledge that his bank is highly unlikely to foreclose on him however large his accumulated debts. The former of course depends on the differential between the price of scrap and the cost of labour to break a ship apart and this is not always favourable to scrap. The latter depends on the secure knowledge that if 'Oil Shipping Ltd' cannot run a supertanker, then certainly neither can the 'Global Shipping Bank', and the bank does not want to try. In addition, if charter rates can fall rapidly, they can equally rapidly rise. Any bank that calls in the bailiff after a few sleepless months is financing the wrong industry.

Two further general points need to be made before analysing the specific nature of surplus capacity in merchant shipping; first, that it exists in a complex network of financial institutions, and secondly, that it is not a substantial employer in comparison to capital employed. Both these issues are directly relevant to surplus capacity in addition to the paradox of its strategic importance and dependence on open trade.

The importance of banking has already been mentioned, particularly in relation to the independent owner. Since shipping in the capitalist West has not been particularly profitable in recent years, it has undoubtedly become more highly geared. That is to say, its ratio of debt to equity capital funding has grown considerably. This has largely been due to developments in shipping itself. The increasing specialisation of ships, while greatly increasing the possible speed of cargo transit and the range of materials carried, has also greatly increased the amount of capital required to stay in the business at all. Such capital funding could not always come from retained profits or from new share issues, so it frequently came from banks. Shipping is thus tied in with any major crises of the secondary banking system and may be, in times of rapid shipbuilding expansion, a highly destabilising factor due to its nature as a speculative industry.

Shipping is often seen by those outside the industry as directly related to the health of shipbuilding and vice versa. Unhappily, however, the interests of the two industries are by no means compatible, particularly from the stance of shipowners in high-wage economies. Because shipping is a small employer (a 125,000-cubic-metre liquid gas carrier can cost over $150m. and directly employ less than thirty men), the real social cost of shipping overcapacity lies in shipyard and dock work and this is where Western governments try to alleviate it, through subsidies. The cost of this to the concept of shipping as a national asset is greatly to increase the tonnage available to competing nations and eventually further to increase surplus capacity, unless it is combined with systematic scrapping. At present, despite much high-level talk, there is little sign of this.

Surplus to Requirements

Since 1973 world shipping has been in a state of profound crisis. The statistics can be very misleading. Measured from end to end the decade between 1968 and 1978 apparently produced an increase in the seaborne trade of the five major bulk commodities – iron ore, coal, grain, bauxite and phosphate – of 5·3 per cent p.a. The carriage of oil over the same period grew by 8·7 per cent p.a. when measured in tonne-miles and by 6·5 per cent p.a. when measured in tonnes. Many would think this a satisfactory rate of growth for any major industry. Before 1973 many regarded it as excellent and could not wait to join in. Unhappily these astronomical growth rates are the mathematical computation of the classic problem of boom and slump, and most of the growth was confined directly to the earlier part of the decade. After 1973 the average rate of growth for all these commodities was nearer 1 per cent p.a.; before then oil carriage had been growing at nearer 10 per cent when measured in tonne-miles (Fearnley and Egers, 1978).

In late 1972 Worldscale, the tanker chartering index,was hiccupping upwards towards 200. By mid-February 1973 it stood at its peak at around 250, then started to tumble as the full implications of the Arab price rises finally sunk in, and ended the year around 80. It is now slowly creeping back upwards, especially in the small tanker route of Caribbean to US Atlantic coast, but it has not gone much above 140 for five years, and VLCC rates from the Persian Gulf have rarely been above 40. A slackening of demand might well have been controllable if the rapidly increasing demand for tanker tonnage, created by the lack of oil self-sufficiency in the United States, had not been so dramatic. As it was the Gulf/US route was exactly the kind of voyage where cost economics favoured the big battalions and the supertanker had just come into being.

As a result when the amount of crude to be carried fell from 1360m. tonnes in 1974 to 1259m. tonnes in 1975, 395 new tankers with an extra 22·5m. grt came off the slipway at the same time. Given the length of time required by shipbuilders these were shortly joined by 366 vessels in 1976, 283 in 1977 and a further 132 in 1978 (Fearnley and Egers, 1978). Thus even when oil carriage by sea stabilised and began to rise again at the much slower rate of around 1 per cent p.a., tanker owners had around 55·9m. new grt and no systematic mechanism for controlling who went to the wall except to lower rates and scrap older ships. Ironically the carriage of oil became cheaper while the cost of the cargo rose, thus nearly reversing the frequently held belief that the ship must be worth more than what it carries and opening up new opportunities for cargo fraud.

In the dry bulk trades matters were more confused. The oil price rise undoubtedly pushed dry bulk rates down. In 1975 the amount carried fell by 5 per cent over the previous year and those engaged also acquired a further 1·6m. new grt, especially designed for the trade. Unfortunately the tanker owners, caught between the massive collapse of Worldscale and the prospect of contracted new tonnage being launched on a depressed market, made rapid contact with the shipyards to change their orders. By 1977, while tonne-mileage of ore and other dry bulk cargoes was falling by 3 per cent, the supply of suitable ships had risen by 12·2 per cent in just over a year, to 74·8m. grt in the biggest annual increase on record. One estimate suggested that at the end of that year there was still some 7·6m. grt on order. As a result the US Gulf/ARA rate fell to $4 a ton of grain in mid-1977 and primarily recovered because of Soviet grain purchases, which are now in abeyance. The knock-on effect of a crisis in one part of the industry created a crisis in another (OECD, 1977, pp. 68–70).

The other parts of the industry, namely, the general cargo and liner trades, while not suffering the kind of gigantic rate collapses familiar to bulk traffic, also have their problems. While clearly affected by the oil crisis and the subsequent downturn in economic activity, the liner trades have an overcapacity problem more directly related to historical structure and national control. Shipowners in the West, towards the latter half of the nineteenth century, had discovered that the competition in general cargo trades could rapidly become ruinous unless they combined in preferably national cartels. Dubbed 'Liner Conferences', these worked by carefully calculated agreements to maintain rates at profitable levels and hammer any new entrant by combined rate-cutting as a quicker means of making him agree to accept only a proportion of the trade or go out of business. This worked very well for a good many decades, especially for the British who thereby built up a formidable control over strategic shipping in places like the Far East. Unfortunately in the past two decades other countries, most notably Russia and Brazil, have wanted a slice not merely of their own traffic, but of the cross- or three-way traffic as well. What has followed has been a rate-cutting war not so much connected with over-supply as over whose supply.

The impact of Soviet intervention was felt hardest on the North Atlantic routes, where in 1971 they had a mere 0·3 per cent of the total. By 1977 they had 4·4 per cent and were quoting rates between 10 and 15 per cent lower than the conferences, in spite of long negotiations about joining. In the trans-Pacific liner trades they also greatly increased their penetration, building up a triangular service between the United States, Japan and Australia and again undercutting the conferences by 10–20 per cent. They succeeded in taking some 7 per cent of the Japan–USA route, but their efforts were not confined to the major oceans. Their Besta line started a service on the Eastern Africa trade in 1976 which took 16 per cent of the southbound traffic from Europe and is estimated to have cost that particular conference $40 million in lost revenue the following year. In addition the land-bridge provided by the trans-Siberian railway is now estimated to be taking 20–25 per cent of the Europe/Far East route and Western owners complain that Soviet fleets take almost 80 per cent of all bilateral trade with the USSR (OECD, 1977, pp. 49–58).

This Soviet intervention, combined with the pressures created through the UNCTAD Liner Code by developing countries and their slowly increasing fleets, has effectively stuck Western liner shipping in the doldrums shortly after its rapid expansion into new types of capital-intensive technology. Containerships, Ro/Ro and LASH barge-carrying vessels have transformed the traditional dockside throughout the world (thereby rapidly decreasing the numbers employed in modern ports) and also increased the capital costs of the industry. However, out of twelve major freight commodity routes examined by UNCTAD in 1977, in only two had the cost of shipment remained stable as a percentage of the cost of the commodity. In all the rest it had fallen considerably, in spite of rapid rises in the bunker fuel cost. Thus while the problem of over-tonnage in the general cargo trades has not been as dramatic as elsewhere it has undoubtedly resulted in considerably cheaper costs to the consumer. It is doubtful however if the disguise of rate-cutting and selling older vessels to developing countries can continue, especially if Western governments begin to see shipping as an important strategic asset in the way the Soviet Union clearly does already.

Table 8.1   *Surplus capacity in the world's merchant fleet, 1977*

	Tonnage over-supply	% of fleet
Tankers	83·6	25·5
Combined carriers	12·7	26·7
Bulk carriers	26·4	23·4
Residual fleet	18·9	12·3
Total fleet	141·6	22·1
	(m. dwt)	

What then is the extent of surplus capacity in the world's merchant marine? The only effective way of making such a calculation is to relate the ratios of tonne-miles per dwt in a year of balance like 1973/4 and extrapolate. According to UNCTAD the result for 1977 is as presented in Table 8.1. Fortunately the situation has improved considerably since these figures were calculated, when the scrapping price was a mere $40 per lightweight ton in Europe. By November 1978 this had reached $135 in the Far East and 1978 was a record year for scrappings with 19·1m. dwt scrapped. In addition the real indicator of the imbalance between supply and demand – the figures for laid up tonnage – have been consistently falling, having reached a peak of 57m. dwt in June 1978 and now being only 11·6m. dwt. Tankers now account for 76 per cent of this total (UNCTAD, 1979).

None the less, while the situation is undoubtedly better, the fact that one estimate suggests that in 1977 21 per cent of the total world merchant marine was 'surplus' and that at the height of the crisis approximately 60m. dwt of ships were standing idle gives considerable pause for thought about the global management of surplus capacity. The fact that the international supply and demand of seaborne transport is only now beginning to come into balance (and this may well be disturbed by increasing international tension), at the cost of the employment-intensive shipbuilding industry, is perhaps even more alarming.

Shipbuilding

While shipowners saw the approaching crisis of overcapacity in a sudden and dramatic period in 1974, shipbuilders had a considerably longer span of full order books before being affected by the problems. When these did make themselves felt, however, declining orders had considerably greater social impact and thus forced governmental intervention. In 1975 global orders stood at 133·4m. grt. The order book now contains less than one-quarter of this figure and 90 per cent of the total will be ready for delivery in 1980. Only 8m. grt were ordered in 1978 and although this figure was higher for 1979, the magnitude of the problem can be gauged from the fact that this is a mere 11 per cent of the boom total, and that capacity had been increased to cope with that boom (Seatrade, 1980). New yards in South Korea, Japan, Brazil and Spain had used the tanker boom to attack the dominance of traditional shipbuilding countries like Britain, but the argument that countries like the latter should not suffer in the slump because they had not expanded in the boom could not but be regarded as special pleading because the former were vastly more efficient as a result of their newer technology. In addition the type of order has undergone a marked change with tankers dropping from 70 per cent of the total in 1974 to a mere 30 per cent in 1977.

The results of this are little short of catastrophic, and have produced in Western Europe a formidable array of subsidy devices to tempt owners of all nations to order as soon as possible even to the detriment of their own shipping interests. These work generally through the credit system. Norway, for example, offers 80 per cent delivery credit over twelve years, with no repayments for the first three, in addition to a 10 per cent subsidy on all new buildings. Around NKr 100m. is currently being expended on an attempt to subsidise the interest paid by LDC countries. Likewise in Denmark – a country with a substantial export-oriented industry – the government offers 80 per cent credit over ten years at 8 per cent interest. In the UK, an intervention fund by the government backs up British shipbuilders and up to 40 per cent of the cost of a ship for an LDC can come from development aid. Italy too is struggling to keep up orders with complex interest support systems and in addition by ordering ships for the state shipping company Finmare that some commentators feel Finmare does not really need, and thereby greatly increasing state dominance over shipping.

The move into competitive subsidies has forced the OECD to lay down guidelines about them, which effectively limit their level to the type of country for whom the ships are constructed. Ranging from 8 per cent over five years to 7·75 per cent over ten years, the guidelines suffer from the secrecy involved in the system they try to control, as well as the disadvantages, mentioned above, about foreclosing on a shipowner. Furthermore the whole problem is greatly exacerbated within the OECD itself by the very effective way the Japanese have cut capacity, while the Western Europeans have systematically blamed each other.

Japan has in fact shown the world the way to expand into an industry and then rapidly diversify away from it. In 1975 it built some 54 per cent of the global total and had a peak capacity of 9·8m. cgrt. Since then a government plan requiring permits for all new buildings has come into being with the aim of reducing capacity in an orderly way to 65 per cent of the 1975 figure by 1985. As a result between early 1978 and March 1979 the industry relocated some 20,000 of its workforce. Its capacity to produce the larger tankers has been cut by some 40 per cent. As a result Japanese shipbuilding seems likely to remain pre-eminent since it is concentrating far more on sophisticated shipping, without subsidy, and does not fear developing world competition (Seatrade, 1979).

Western European yards, in contrast, do not as yet have a coherent scheme for mutual capacity reduction. The nearest thing to it is the EEC sponsored 'scrap and build scheme' which has not yet got further than acrimonious debate. While it is generally acknowledged that European shipbuilding needs to lose 45 per cent of its capacity, a great deal of the indigenous flag fleets are comparatively new since the boom and the older tonnage can frequently be sold off profitably to countries like China. In addition the EEC forum tends to produce a strong nationalistic response where jobs are concerned and few members wish to lose capacity if others are going to keep it. Thus while the subsidy schemes are estimated to be costing around $16b. and 'scrap and build' would cost around $200m., the former does at least have the attraction of keeping the matter in the hands of local politicians. The Japanese as a result feel cynical about any OECD plans to share out capacity on a 50:50 basis with Europe while such disparate nationalistic aims prevail (Seatrade, 1980).

Outside this quarrel, however, certain other countries (notably Brazil, South Korea and Taiwan) are using a whole armoury of economic devices including protection to continue to increase their market share. The South Koreans are the acknowledged 'bogeymen' of shipbuilding, since having beaten down most opposition in the last scramble for orders at the end of the tanker boom, they then went bravely ahead with two more large shipbuilding yards in 1977. Total capacity is now 4m. cgrt, but is still growing at 0·25 cgrt p.a. with active government promotion that gives 92 per cent of the purchase price in preferential loans at 11 per cent interest over eight years. With a battery of import licence controls, indigenous shipowners have to make a very strong case before buying from abroad. In addition the government subsidises the import of raw materials for shipbuilding. Given the original price differential between Western yards and those in Korea, the high subsidies make a mockery of their Western counter-parts by simply maintaining the difference. Taiwan is in a similar position, having built up capacity with a governmental shipbuilding programme and now attracting orders from Western oil companies like Exxon by sheer price. The government projects domestic orders to be at 400,000 grt in 1980–1 and this will obviously be built at home (Seatrade, 1979).

Perhaps the most coherent governmental response to shipbuilding has come in Brazil which, rather against the trend, doubled its production of ships between 1975 and 1976 (ISE, 1977 p. 218). Here the govern-ment lays down firm rules regarding the type of ships to be built in each yard and offers a possible fifteen-year credit period at under 10 per cent interest (Seatrade, 1978a, pp. 71–3). Domestic orders – given Brazil's determination to build up a formidable merchant marine for strategic reasons – thus go straight into Brazilian yards and the order book was at 60 per cent capacity at the end of 1978 (Seatrade, 1978b, pp. 47–9).

This success looks incongruous beside the talk in Western yards about rapidly reducing capacity, but the answer effectively lies in the hands of national governments. Sadly the native merchant fleets of the traditional shipbuilding countries have either been declining in size or alternatively were the leaders in the building boom of the early 1970s. The developing nations have little if anything to lose by expanding their fleets. Unlike their rivals in the West, whose shipowners are free to hunt down the best price, Far Eastern and South American shipowners are heavily bound up with the local shipbuilders and governments pursue a conscious policy of marine expansion. The traditional shipbuilders, like Sweden or Britain, can only keep their capacity by developing new technology or by offering subsidies to foreign buyers – thus undermining their own fleets.

The problem with new technology, however, is that it is extremely expensive to develop and unless it comes at precisely the right time threatens to bankrupt any shipbuilder who indulges in it. The new call for Liquid Natural Gas carriers, to which a number of Swedish and American yards responded, turned out to be premature since nearly all the liquifaction plant on-shore suffered frightening delays. Shipowners who bought these monstrously expensive ships, from the world's most sophisticated yards, have watched them float idle for half a decade waiting for world demand for liquid gas to overcome environmental and technical pressures against it. One company, Ocean Transport and Trading, started depreciating its LNG carrier Nestor at a rate of £2·5m. p.a. in 1980, having owned it for three years during which it had made no money at all. The fact that it now seems likely that new seaborne gas routes will open up is poor consolation for the huge amount of interest already paid for the idle tonnage.

The problem of world shipbuilding capacity is thus a complex mixture of market boom and slump and national policy. The subsidy route to survival may have eventual benefits to the consumer of seaborne commodities but it is hardly calculated to reduce capacity. The idea of scrap and build has plenty of attractions, not least in reducing the number of older 'rust buckets', yet it seems politically very difficult to co-ordinate in such a national yet international industry. Certainly the idea that it can be controlled by some international body, in a manner calculated to maintain the strategic shipping status quo, would require too much calculation even if the global community could decide what the actual position appeared to be. Shipping and in consequence shipbuilding has never been amenable to bureaucratic supervision.

Furthermore the immediacies of the market have once again upset longer-term calculation since the recent rise in bulk rates in the smaller tanker, O/O and OBO markets have brought a sudden spate of fresh orders. With 33·6m. dwt due for delivery by 1984 (almost double the figure projected at the beginning of 1979) shipbuilders have some justification for seeing a light at the end of the tunnel. Combine this with hopes about diversification into the off-shore oil and gas markets, the huge potential re-engining programme currently being followed by some of the major shipowners to escape the rising costs of bunkering and the effects of IMCO regulations on safety, and the opposition towards centrally imposed cutbacks to capacity is greatly increased. Indeed, if one assumes that average speeds remain at 12–14 knots, floating storage remains at around 6m. dwt, IMCO regulations come into effect in 1981 and the vast majority of VLCC tonnage over fifteen years old is scrapped, then even the 200,000 dwt and larger range of tanker capacity should be in balance with demand in 1985 (Fearnley and Egers, 1980). The problem, particularly from the Western countries, is to hold on to capacity in the interim and to ensure that the projected figure for growth does not lead to a repetition of the 1974–8 disaster.

Conclusions

Not perhaps surprisingly, in the light of the decline in freight rates during the period of surplus capacity, the shipping industry, especially in the bulk trades, has largely responded to the crisis by becoming less 'technically efficient'. One estimate suggests that slow steaming accounted for around 45m. dwt of surplus VLCC capacity in 1979. In addition port delays, averaging around twelve days for an operation that need take only two, are thought to take another 21m. dwt out of the possible VLCC supply (*Petroleum Economist*, 1980). Given the continuing rise in bunker costs it seems highly likely that the next few years will see quite dramatic changes in the speed of transit, even in the more sophisticated container liner trades, and that this will be institutionalised by re-engining. This should quite rapidly reduce potential capacity. In addition, even if oil transport should decline (and this is by no means certain), given that a decline in crude sales frequently increases the use of product carriers as oil companies swop refined products to meet short-term demand, the predicted rise in seaborne trade in coal and gas should compensate.

These are certainly more than palliatives, but unfortunately the real solution to the cyclical problem of surplus capacity in shipping and shipbuilding and the continued growth of the industries lies in increased world trade – a prospect that seems unlikely. Without such an increase it seems likely that both industries will continue to suffer from the consequences of the abrupt downturn following 1973 and the orgy of expansion that preceded it. For shipping the primary need – now that demand and supply are slowly returning to balance – is to avoid another sudden political disturbance of that kind and greatly to increase the sophistication of planning techniques to avoid the lemming-like behaviour which produced the boom. Since it seems unlikely that those developing countries with a governmental determination to succeed in building a national fleet will simply stop because the OECD says they are not playing the free market game, the West will presumably have to write this expansion into its planning and concentrate on the trades it does best. Utter contempt for developing country aspirations, as expressed in the UNCTAD Liner Code, can only lead to mutually damaging bureaucratic delays which will further slow the growth of trade by sea.

At the same time the policy favoured by the UNCTAD Secretariat of the market for sea transport regulating in favour of developing countries involves huge costs, for it probably involves duplicating world tonnages at a time of overcapacity. While shipbuilders in OECD countries currently have the twin handicaps of hard currencies, which enable their shipowners to buy cheaply in places like Taiwan, and multinational companies which are frequently outside the direct economic control of national governments, both their shipping and shipbuilding expertise could seriously damage their counterparts in LDCs if Western governments decided to protect these industries further for employment or military reasons. The same moral applies to the expansion of Soviet shipping where the demand for hard currency has brought ludicrously low freight charges by Western standards and retaliation could seriously threaten the levels of East–West trade.

Overall grandiose plans to control world shipping and shipbuilding from Geneva, by a calculated splitting of national interests between UN states, seem likely to be stalemated given the nature of the industry. It is, for example, by no means clear that the Soviet Union is any more generous towards the Group of 77 regarding cargo-sharing than the West in spite of voting support on occasions. At the same time the issues presented by unilateral US action on pollution do not favour the development of LDC shipping simply because 'ecologically sound' vessels are frequently highly expensive in comparison with second-hand purchases. The whole thrust of safety and pollution legislation through IMCO tends to put barriers in front of developing new national fleets if there is a shortage of trained personnel and money. In addition, of course, the LDCs themselves are in conflict over the issue of flags of convenience, with countries like Panama and Liberia clearly reluctant to forego the lucrative trade in tonnage taxes and registration fees. If the nations of the world cannot maintain a system where ships actually belong to the countries whose flags they fly it seems singularly unlikely that they will be able to allocate tonnages and mitigate the effects of international competition by collective agreement.

The main potential focus for controlling and regulating surplus capacity by governments undoubtedly remains that created by IMCO's technical agreements on issues of safety and pollution. Not only does international agreement of that type increase the available shipyard work, but its enforcement could be much more effective as a means to eliminate rogue shipowners. A really successful mechanism of unilateral port–state control would force much of the older surplus tonnage off certain routes and raise freight rates accordingly. If after an initial period of retaliation other states joined in, the process of regularly renewing ships would become obligatory thus decreasing the uncertainty surrounding shipbuilding projections, reducing insurance claims, making the seas cleaner and generally increasing the professional competence of ship-management by making the cost of entry much higher.

This might initially be damaging to LDC interests (although it has to be said that some countries like the Philippines have very stringent pollution regulations in spite of their own lack-lustre record as shipowners), but it would undoubtedly be much better for them if Western responses to competition were couched in terms of safety than those of pure protection. Regulating sea trade is perhaps better done on the dockside than at the conference table. Bilateral discussions should clearly work towards this end rather than the competition of protected national interests which too frequently solves only the national political consequences of surplus capacity while reducing the total volume of capacity required.

References: Chapter 8

Fearnley and Egers, Chartering Co. Ltd (1978), 'Bulk market review'.
Fearnley and Egers, Chartering Co. Ltd (1980), 'World bulk fleet'.
Institute of Shipping Economics (1977), *Shipping Statistics Yearbook* (Bremen: ISE).
OECD (1977), *Maritime Transport*.
Petroleum Economist (1980), April.
Seatrade (1978a), *Guidelines to the Shipping Industry*, March.
Seatrade (1978b), *Scales Swing Europe's Way*, October.
Seatrade (1979), *Far East Report*, December.
Seatrade (1980), *EEC Shipping Guide*.

9

Petrochemicals

JUDITH GURNEY

The petrochemical sector is very important for the contemporary economies of the United States, Western Europe and Japan, accounting for nearly 10 per cent, on a value-added basis, of all industrial output in Western Europe in 1976 and for 12·5 per cent of Western Europe's annual oil and gas consumption. Production of petrochemicals began, on a very small scale, in the United States between the wars as an off-shoot of the natural gas industry. Stimulated by wartime shortages of such raw materials as rubber, the petrochemical sector gained momentum rapidly, and experienced a sensational boom worldwide in the 1960s. Table 9.1 which shows the role of petrochemicals in organic chemical production, tells only one side of the story – the other is an equally dramatic growth in demand for the four major categories of products manufactured from organic chemicals: plastics, synthetic fibres, synthetic rubber and detergents.

Table 9.1 *Petrochemicals as a proportion of organic chemicals (percentages)*

	USA	UK	West Germany	France	Western Europe	Japan
1921	0·01	0	0	0	0	0
1930	6	0	0	0	0	0
1941	21	0	0	0	0	0
1950	50	10	2	0	4	0
1960	88	61	50	54	58	4
1965	94	68	61	66	68	74
1971	96	90	91	90	91	93

Source: British Petroleum (1977), p. 379.

The 1960s and early 1970s saw double-digit growth rates in the petrochemical industry. Between 1960 and 1973, when total industrial production in the OECD rose at around 5·5 per cent p.a., the petrochemical sector grew at a rate varying between 10 and 17 per cent according to the products involved (butadiene 10 per cent, benzene 13 per cent, propylene 16·5 per cent, ethylene 17 per cent). World production of organic chemicals based on oil and gas, which was 3m. tonnes in 1950, reached 70m. tonnes in the mid-1970s. Production figures for 1971 included 20m. tonnes for Western Europe, 30m. tonnes for the United States and 11m. tonnes for Japan (British Petroleum, 1977, p. 871).

It is generally considered that the petrochemical sector now has a surplus capacity which is affecting the large traditional petrochemical producers in the OECD area. Concern over this present situation is aggravated by the fact that current overcapacity is expected to become much worse in the near future (if demand for petrochemicals does not increase strongly) when the many new petrochemical plants now being constructed, or in various stages of planning, come on-stream from the early 1980s onwards in the Middle East, Comecon, Europe and in a number of developing countries throughout the world.

There are several unique characteristics of the petrochemical industry which have helped to bring about the present overcapacity and which make its management infinitely more difficult. In the first place, the industry is very closely linked to the oil/energy sector and to oil/energy companies. Its raw materials, known in the trade as feedstocks, are crude oil and natural gas liquids and for this reason it is deeply affected by the highly volatile economic and political forces controlling the supply and price of oil and gas. Secondly, the industry is very sensitive to the prosperity of the ordinary man-in-the-street. The consumer market for its 'second generation' products such as plastics has considerable elasticity of demand. And finally, the structure of the industry was bewitched by its sensational boom in the 1960s and planners have tended, until very recently, to base their investment decisions on extensions of the growth rates of this period. And while OECD investment policy-makers now plan from a less optimistic GNP growth rate base, their counterparts in the Middle East, Comecon and the developing world are less willing to accept a view of the petrochemical sector as becoming less profitable in real or proportional terms. Moreover, many Western economists still insist that profits are easily come by even when times are hard. So far, many of the major products have had considerable success in passing on their higher costs; some – notably plastics materials manufacturers – have seen the upward spiral of oil prices as a god-given opportunity to raise their depressed profit margins (*Financial Times*, 22 June 1979). Such flexibility is not characteristic of an industry suffering with overcapacity, as, in theory, 'excess capacity can be expected to bring about price cutting as companies try to increase their output in a declining market to make better use of their fixed assets and achieve lower costs' (Jones, 1979, p. 39).

Structure of the Industry

The petrochemical industry in Europe and Japan developed from the supply of surplus naphtha in oil refining; and naphtha, although it is now scarce and high-priced, is still its principal feedstock. From naphtha are derived, or produced, two major groups of organic-based chemicals which form the building blocks of the chemical and plastics industry:

(1) *Lower olefins*, of which the most important are ethylene, used in the production of polyethylene, PVC and polystyrene plastics, anti-freeze, polyester fibres, ethyl alcohol and synthetic rubbers; propylene, used in the manufacture of polypropylene, solvents, acrylic fibres, polyurethane resins, nylons and plasticisers; and butadiene, used to make synthetic rubbers and nylon;

(2) *Aromatics*, of which the most important are benzene, toluene and xylenes, used in the manufacture of a number of important products such as polystyrene plastics and paints.

The petrochemical industry in the United States, by contrast, uses mostly natural gas liquids – ethane and propane – as feedstocks although naphtha is occasionally employed. As a result, the American petrochemical industry has a different mix of products – ethane and propane give a higher yield of ethylene than naphtha but insignificant amounts of propylene and butadiene – and a different cost/price structure. This means that the worldwide petrochemical industry responds to feedstock price changes. The enormous rise in the price of naphtha in the Rotterdam spot market in the first half of 1979, from $190 per tonne in January to $339 per tonne in June, resulted in lower prices and higher profits for American petrochemical companies, and a fear of low-priced American petrochemical products flooding European and third, markets, clearly expressed by a director of the German-based BASF, Dr Gernot Winter, in a speech in London in May 1979, when he said that 'US chemical companies were now making three or four times more profit on sales than their European counterparts' (*Financial Times*, 3 May 1979). The substitution of feedstocks in existing plants – natural gas liquids for naphtha, for instance – is not generally considered economically feasible.

The industry is capital-intensive and characteristically it is only multinational giants who can invest in the large-scale plants able to produce, at the lowest unit cost, an output which then requires large international markets. As BP (1977, p. 389) explains:

the industry often sizes its plants to supply larger markets than can be provided by single countries – except the USA . . . the high cost of the large plants that have now become the normal production units demand financial resources not always available to the small chemical companies. To an increasing extent, therefore, the production of petroleum chemicals will be in the hands of large, financially strong, groups.

Who are the present petrochemical producers? On the one hand, they are the chemical divisions of the great oil companies themselves – Exxon, Royal Dutch/Shell, BP, ARCO, Gulf, Mobil, Texaco, Conoco, SoCal, Phillips Petroleum. On the other, they are giant chemical companies with varying degrees of involvement in oil and gas fields which supply their feedstocks, and in the manufacture of second-generation products from organic chemicals. The world's three largest chemical companies, based on 1977 world group sales, were Hoechst AG, Bayer AG and BASF AG, all carved from the ruins of I.G. Farbenindustrie AG in the early 1950s. Other chemical giants include ICI, Du Pont, Dow Chemical, Monsanto, Montedison, Mitsubishi, Union Carbide, Rhone-Poulenc, Ciba-Geigy. The list of ethylene producers in one industry directory shows how much petrochemicals are the province of big business (*Worldwide Petrochemical Directory*, 1979, pp. 50–3).

The fact that the industry has been dominated by multinationals has made it more difficult for the warning signs of structural surplus capacity to be seen and heeded as multinationals have the financial resources to withstand market pressures in one particular sector of their activities if it is in line with their long-run corporate strategy. Well before the oil price rises of 1973–4 there were signs that petrochemical growth was slowing, due to the fact that substitution of traditional materials by synthetics had reached a plateau in some industries, and plant sizes had increased to the point at which the benefits of scale were less apparent. But these signs of structural overcapacity were not given sufficient publicity by the multinationals dominating the industry to warn off newcomers from entering the field.

Perceptions of the Problem

The concern about surplus capacity to be found in Europe is not echoed by American petrochemical manufacturers. These differing perceptions are expressed frequently in the media. 'Exxon Chemicals' Ray Nesbitt: Petrochems face strong future' reported one American journal at the end of January 1979, 'Bright future seen for the petrochemical industry in the US' it reassured in February (*Oil and Gas Journal*, 1979a, pp. 232–3, 1979b, p. 83). But 'Europe petrochemicals face new woes' it warned in January, and in March, 'European chemical industry in turmoil about prices' (*Oil and Gas Journal*, 1979a, pp. 80–2; *Financial*

Times, 8 March 1979). A British view in June 1979 was no more hopeful: 'Gloom in Western Europe' it reported (*Petroleum Economist,* 1979, p. 233).

A relatively conservative mid-1979 forecast in the United States was for a growth rate of 5 per cent for petrochemicals, not considered out-of-line in terms of the 9 per cent growth rate achieved in 1976–8. With a 5 per cent growth rate, the demand for ethylene would require the industry to work at 85 per cent capacity in the United States through 1981, an acceptable situation given that 90 per cent is considered to be the sustainable operating rate for any extended period.

Europe, on the other hand, perceives a serious threat of over-capacity. According to the European Council of Chemical Manufacturers' Federations (Cefic), ethylene capacity in Western Europe will reach 17·4m. tonnes by 1980 from plants already in use and under construction, whereas demand, even at a growth rate of 3·4 per cent, cannot be expected to reach 17m. tonnes before 1987 (*Oil and Gas Journal,* 1978, p. 71). New capacity is due to come on-stream in 1979 in France, Germany, the Netherlands and Spain, and Cefic's figures show that European producers plan to add close to 2·5m. tonnes of new ethylene capacity by 1981, despite the delay and cancellation of many projects. If both capacity increases and demand forecasts prove accurate, European operating rates in 1981 will be only slightly over 70 per cent.

Export markets are vital to the European industry which can only function efficiently with a large market. For this reason, Europeans are generally more prone than Americans to cutting prices in the face of competition in order to gain, or keep, markets in areas which they judge vital. They are presently very anxious about American petrochemical products making inroads in their markets since the explosion in naphtha prices had made American feedstocks some 40 per cent cheaper than European feedstocks. (It is not only the reduced feedstock price which makes American petrochemicals less costly; under present price controls in the United States, American chemical concerns pay some 30 per cent less than European companies for their operating needs of crude oil and gas.) The fact that the United States is considered a better prospect for chemicals is shown in the numerous recent US acquisitions and invest-ments by West European companies, such as ICI participation in the Corpus Christi ethylene cracker project, BASF planned expenditures of $700m. and Shell, Bayer and Hoechsst sizeable US expansions. Furthermore it is shown in the sales by US companies of their West European chemical interests. Union Carbide and Monsanto both sold large parts of their European plastics interests in 1978 and Monsanto announced the closure of its European nylon plants, which were reported as incurring $70m. in operating losses from 1975 to 1978, in mid-1979 (*International Herald Tribune,* 19 June 1979). Table 9.2

gives an idea of the comparative prices of petrochemical feedstocks and
organic chemicals in May 1979.

Table 9.2   *Petrochemical prices (US = 100)*

	West Germany	Japan
Naphtha	115	115
Ethylene	145	155
Propylene	120	160
Benzene	125	135
Cyclohexane	105	135

Source: Financial Times, 3 May 1979.

Europeans are also anxious about petrochemical projects planned
outside the OECD, particularly by OPEC. There are petrochemical
complexes in the design stage in Qatar, Algeria, Ecuador, Kuwait,
Libya, Iraq, Iran, Venezuela and Saudi Arabia (and Mexico), although
only those in Iran, Kuwait and Venezuela were on-stream in early 1979.
OPEC countries argue that it is logical for petrochemical plants to be
located near to feedstock sources, particularly where there is sufficient
capital resources. The OECD stock reply is to emphasise the importance
of contact with consumer markets for petrochemical second-generation
products and to point out that while petrochemical plants require
mostly energy feedstocks, capital and little labour, the manufacture of
second-generation derivative products, such as plastics, requires a completely different mix of labour and capital and a cheap semi-skilled
labour supply, not to be found in most OPEC countries. This is certainly true for Saudi Arabia, which is currently constructing four petrochemical plants (each to produce some 500,000 tonnes of ethylene) in its
gas-gathering scheme under which natural gas, now flared, will be con-
served, the more easily transportable liquids (propane, butane and
natural gasoline) exported and the remaining gases, such as ethane and
methane, becoming petrochemical feedstocks. SABIC, the Saudi
Arabian Basic Industries Company set up in 1976, is proceeding slowly
with this plan, in which Shell, Mobil, Exxon, Dow, Mitsubishi and
other OECD petrochemical companies are involved, partly, it is said, in
order to secure future supplies of Saudi Arabian crude for themselves.
The European petrochemical industry is nervous that its crude supply
arrangements with OPEC petrochemical producers may be tied in the
future to petrochemical import deals. OPEC and Third World future
petrochemical producers are nervous that OECD markets will be closed
to them by tariffs which increase with the level of processing, by quantitative restrictions and by other trade barriers.

Comecon presents another threat to the European petrochemical industry, and some believe that 'by 1985 Eastern Europe chemical industry production will be equal to Western Europe's if all the buy-back deals (by which payment for machine, plant, and technology is made in produce) are consummated' (*Oil and Gas Journal,* 1979a, p. 80). And finally, there are plants in construction and on the drawing board in many developing countries. Michael Hyde, publisher of *Chemical Insight,* claims to have identified more than a hundred ethylene projects in fifty-five developing nations. Assuming that less than half of these plants materialise by 1990, the developing nations would have, by that date, a 26 per cent share of world ethylene capacity (*Financial Times,* 22 January 1979).

Attempts to Control Productive Capacity

The petrochemical industry is vulnerable, on the one hand, to the political and economic factors affecting its energy feedstocks and, on the other, to effective demand in the world market for its second-generation consumer goods' products. Since a minimum of five years' lead time is required for the construction of new plants, it is easy for supply to get out of phase with demand. There seem few effective outside controls on decision-making in the industry, despite efforts made at several levels.

Inter-industry endeavours
Within Europe, Cefic prepares studies and forecasts for the petro-chemical industry as a whole and the OECD also serves as a convenient venue for company interaction, at least for the purpose of information-gathering and dissemination. There are indications that European petrochemical firms collaborate on investment questions and, to a certain degree, in price-setting. Such collaboration is probably less in the United States, due to American anti-trust regulations (the West German Federal Cartel Office sometimes expresses its misgivings about industry price-setting agreements in Europe), but there are inter-company meetings and conferences in the United States, often with the participation of the US Department of Energy, where problems are aired and, presumably, deals concluded.

National government involvement
Although the petrochemical industry is, in many ways, an outstanding example of independent 'big business', there is more government involvement and control than is generally supposed, even in the OECD. The Comecon petrochemical industry is, of course, government-controlled, and Third World governments have considerable, often con-trolling, shares in petrochemical companies. Through the Petrochemical Corporation of Singapore, the Singapore government has, for example, a 50 per cent stake in the planned Singapore petrochemical plant

designed to fulfil demand in Asian, Australian and perhaps Chinese markets (*Financial Times*, 30 January 1979). Most OPEC projects are government-sponsored.

OECD governments also act indirectly in response to the pressure of companies and, without conspicuous success, have tried to dissuade Third World countries from petrochemical ventures. These same governments have been less willing, at least to date, to accede to company demands for anti-dumping tariffs to prevent the arrival of cheaper petrochemical products in home markets. This reluctance may be due to fear of retaliation by crude oil producers.

Inter-governmental co-operation
The most active inter-governmental agency in the field of energy and thus petrochemical feedstocks is the IEA (International Energy Agency), an autonomous body established in November 1974 within the framework of the OECD in which twenty OECD members participate and the Commission of the European Communities takes part by special arrangement to '(a) meet oil supply emergencies, (b) reduce dependence on imported oil, (c) promote co-operative relations with oil-producing countries and other oil-consuming countries, including those of the developing world through a purposeful dialogue' (OECD, 1977, p. 1). The IEA is certainly efficient in gathering information on supplies and market conditions and its effectiveness in directing government action is being tested following its directive of March 1979 for a cutback of 5 per cent in energy demand by its members.

Despite the existence of OPEC and OAPEC, the producers of petro-chemical feedstocks and future petrochemicals felt the need for a counterpart to the IEA. One response was the Arab Energy Conference, which met for the first time in Abu Dhabi on 4–8 March 1979 under the joint sponsorship of OAPEC and AFESO (Arab Fund for Economic and Social Development) 'to try to match some of the functions of the IEA/OECD through which industrial countries work to restructure the energy systems of their member states', and decided to set up a pan-Arab Energy Committee and national energy committees to work with OAPEC and AFESO. A second energy conference is due to meet in Qatar in 1982.

The official attempt to provide a venue for discussions by producers and consumers in energy and energy-related fields, CIEC (Conference on International Economic Co-operation, generally known as the North/South Dialogue), was not a success. Four commissions were set up in February 1976 to discuss energy, raw materials, development and finance and great hopes were raised when the oil-producing and oil-consuming governments sat round a table for the first time to discuss the implications of the oil price rises of recent years. But as the North/South Dialogue developed the oil producers insisted, apparently, on linking their pricing policies to consumers' concessions in aid and trade. The producers were weakened by the price dispute within OPEC in December 1976 and the North/South Dialogue petered away without reaching any conclusions. The differences in perception of the world economy by North and South, and the varied abilities of governments to control multinationals, makes this type of inter-governmental action to control overcapacity in the petrochemical field highly unlikely to succeed.

Another inter-governmental attempt at control was made by UNIDO (United Nations Industrial Development Organisation) with a First Consultative Meeting on the Petrochemical Industry held in Mexico City in mid-March 1979 at which over 150 participants representing government, labour, industry and consumer groups from both developed and developing countries discussed marketing and transfer technology questions affecting the industry (UNIDO, 1979, p. 1).

Conclusions

Government attempts at control have been largely ineffective to date in dealing with the problems caused by overcapacity in the petrochemical industry or, in fact, with the growth of overcapacity itself. Since the industry's surplus capacity largely results from the promise of future profits comparable to those gained by the industry in the 1960s and early 1970s, it may be that only the harsh conditions of rising costs, decreasing markets and hence diminished profits, if not actual losses, will be necessary to curtail surplus capacity. International and national political organisations may prove ineffective in controlling demand and supply in an industry which is so highly capital-intensive and which has had a history of so much financial success.

References: Chapter 9

British Petroleum (1977), *Our Industry: Petroleum* (London: BP).
Jones, T.J. (1979), 'Oil refining, an EEC and UK problem of excess capacity', *National Westminster Bank Quarterly*, May.
OECD (1977), *IEA Energy, Research, Development and Demonstration: Programme for the IEA* (Paris: OECD).
Oil and Gas Journal (1978), 25 December.
Oil and Gas Journal (1979a), 29 January.
Oil and Gas Journal (1979b), 19 February.
UNIDO (1979), *Newsletter*, April.
Worldwide Petrochemical Directory (1979), (Tulsa, Oklahoma: WPD).

10

Banking and Insurance

JONATHAN DAVID ARONSON

Most recent studies of the political economy of transnational enterprises focus on the interactions of manufacturing and extractive corporations with national governments. Service industries are ignored for the most part, or grouped unceremoniously (and incorrectly) with other concerns. To understand the role of service industries within the world economy requires a different framework.[1] Service enterprises are catalysts which support the linkages between nations and transnational firms, holding together the international economic system. Without banks and insurance enterprises, for instance, the trade, monetary and investment systems would cease to function. It is therefore important that the role of service industries within the system as well as their interactions with governments be examined.

The role of service industries is growing as the percentage of industrial nations' gross domestic product produced by service transaction rises. By 1978 over 60 per cent of the US GDP was composed of service transactions. In most other developed countries services account for 40–50 per cent of the GDP (OECD, 1979). In addition, manufacturing and extractive industries are relying more on service transactions and less on existing product lines for their profits. The collapse of the Bretton Woods system has turned the treasurer's office into a profit centre for many corporations. This evolution makes it more difficult to treat these corporations within existing analytical frameworks.

It is easier to examine surplus capacity in manufacturing and extractive industries than in service industries (see particularly Strange, 1979, p. 304, fn.). Indeed, economists cannot measure, or even define, surplus capacity in the service sector. No product is produced, so no surplus is theoretically possible. Nevertheless, bankers and insurance executives insist that their industries are currently facing a serious and potentially destabilising crisis of surplus capacity (interview evidence over a six-year period).

The necessity for cogent thinking and action by industry and governments is intensified by a new conglomerate movement. Manufacturing and extractive industries are earning more and more of their profits from fee and service business. In the aftermath of the onslaught of flexible exchange rates, corporations added financial experts to their staffs to protect against foreign exchange losses. These money men taught corporations to seek profits outside their traditional product lines. The burgeoning commercial paper market and the advent of captive insurance companies are just two of the ways these executives found to make money in service areas. Banks and insurance companies also began to trespass on each other's traditional territories. As a result, large companies are no longer easily classifiable as extractive, manufacturing, or service industries. This also makes it far more difficult for governments to regulate business effectively.

This chapter describes and analyses the changing nature of surplus capacity in banking and insurance services. It assumes and argues that 'over-competition' in service sectors is the functional analogue of surplus capacity in the manufacturing and resource sectors (comment by R. O. Keohane). It then explores the implications of these surpluses for the operation of the world financial system, and it suggests that if the banking and insurance systems can be made to function more effectively, international economic regime change without crisis or collapse may be possible.

Surplus Capacity in Services

Traditional, demand-oriented analysis leads inescapably to the conclusion that there should be no such thing as surplus banking and insurance capacity. Today, many industries are crying out for new investment to maintain their previous productivity. Simultaneously, banks and insurance enterprises are hard pressed to find suitable, safe receptacles for their loans and investments. In panic, funds are flowing into short-term paper and into gold, a sure sign of diminishing confidence in the health of the economic system. In the past decade the myth and the reality of banks and insurance companies have diverged widely.

Surplus Capacity in Banking

The mythical banker sits sternly behind his imposing desk, rejecting more often than not the loan applications of the supplicants who come before him. A bank is supposed to be a conservative institution which lends money that has been deposited with it. Profits arise from the difference between the interest paid to the bank by borrowers and the interest paid by the bank to depositors, less expenses. Prudence and regulations dictate that some percentage of deposits be held as reserves and in securities. When loan demand is slack, banks might increase their holdings of securities. They should not cut the rate at which they will lend so far that they cannot make profits. Neither should they accept lower-quality borrowers simply to boost loan demand. This view of banking retained popularity at least until 1970–1 when it 'was the consensus of financial economists . . . that the following decade would likely witness strong demands for funds relative to the available supply' (Hayes, 1971, p. 39).

In the past two decades, however, bankers have in fact been globe-trotting executives seeking new borrowers wherever they might be lurking. The return of European currency convertibility and the launching of the Common Market in 1958 attracted transnational corporations into Europe throughout the 1960s. American banks rushed in after them. Others followed.

In the late 1960s Citibank introduced the concept of liability management. Banks borrowed money from other banks or central banks in order to relend it. More liquidity was created. Go-go bankers of the 1960s and early 1970s were no longer content to borrow long and lend short. It is extremely doubtful that the growth in sound borrowers came close to the growth of potential lenders eager to expand their Euro-currency operations. In Hyman Minsky's terms, national economies and the international economic system became more fragile. Most banks became willing to lend to countries and to large corporations (private or state-owned) on better and better terms. Hedge finance, where borrowers are able to repay the interest and principal from a project's cash flow, was replaced by speculative finance, where only the interest can be repaid from projected cash flow. Sometimes banks were not even assured that a borrower could repay the interest owed from the specific project (Minsky, 1975). Nobel laureate W. Arthur Lewis commented (Lewis, 1978, p. 65):

> But why should they [the borrowers] be called on to repay? A bank lends money to earn interest. So long as the interest is safe, there is no need to repay the principal. The loan can be rolled over. A customer who insists on repaying is just a nuisance who is putting the banker to the trouble of finding another customer.

Bankers on hearing this statement nod, and comment: 'And expensive too.'

The introduction of flexible exchange rates, the rising price of oil in 1973–4, and the necessity for private recycling of petrodollars disoriented the financial system. Although the collapse of the German Bankhaus Herstatt, under massive foreign exchange losses in late June 1974, re-injected some order into the Eurocurrency and foreign exchange markets, the respite was short-lived (Aronson, 1978, pp. 117–21). Banks began searching for new borrowers among previously 'uncreditworthy' nations and enterprises. Morgan Guaranty Trust Company estimates that publicised new medium-term Eurocurrency credits rose by $19b. in 1976, by $26b. in 1977 and by $40b. in 1978. The trend was most dramatic among non-oil-exporting developing countries. At the end of 1973 these nations' external debt was $75·3b., $36·8b. (49 per cent) of which was held by private institutions. By the end of 1977 these same nations' external debt had reached $160·0b. of which $91·0b. (57 per cent) was held by private creditors (Crowe, 1979, p. 29). The non-OPEC developing countries' Eurocurrency borrowings increased from $13·49b. in 1977 to $26·90b. in 1978 and $35·46b. in 1979. Their share of total new borrowings increased from 32·5 per cent in 1977 to 38·3 per cent in 1978 and to 43·1 per cent in 1979 (Morgan Guaranty, 1980, p. 16). These needs are likely to continue to rise in the face of the 1979 oil price rises. In 1974–5 the banks rescued the non-oil developing countries. They may need to continue lending in the future to heavy borrowers.

The bankers correctly point out that when these figures are adjusted for inflation, the growth of the market lending to developing countries is not quite as serious as some alarmists fear (Leftwich, 1979). For one thing, private bank lending is concentrated in the wealthiest and fastest-growing of the newly industrialising countries. Mexico and Brazil accounted for $13·7 billion of the Eurocurrency credits announced in 1979. Argentina, Korea, the Philippines and Taiwan account for another $8·5 billion of 1979 borrowing. Thus over two-thirds of banks' Eurocurrency lending to non-oil developing countries went to only six nations (Morgan Guaranty, 1979, p. 16).

Still, the liquidity glut in the markets has led to major changes in bank lending behaviour. As of September 1979 Morgan Guaranty estimated that the gross Eurocurrency market had reached $1,070b. and the net market had grown to about $600b. (Morgan Guaranty, 1979, p. 15). Banks needed to lend these funds to maintain their profitability. But, as absolute interest rates increased, actual bank international profitability narrowed substantially. Since US inflation is extremely high by historic standards, the true cost of funds to the borrowers is approaching all-time lows (1–2 per cent).

However, the lending cycle, which can reverse the excess capacity situation more rapidly than could be contemplated in manufacturing concerns, is tightening. The Iranian crisis provoked banks to re-examine their foreign political risks. The freezing of Iranian funds by the US government initiated major departures from accepted bank policy by New York banks. Citibank immediately announced that it would offset its existing Iranian loans with its Iranian deposits, in effect voiding the debt through prepayment. Chase Manhattan declared a $500m. loan to be in default despite the attempt by Iran to service the loan, and over the objections of European and Japanese syndicate participants. In effect, US regional banks were left holding the bag. Although they had loaned money to Iran, they held few Iranian deposits with which to offset.

Wells Fargo, Crocker and Security Pacific sued to recover their potential losses. European and Japanese banks, furious at being drawn into US–Iranian hostilities, are distrustful of the actions of the New York banks. There is some question whether borrowers or other lenders will feel secure in US-led syndicates in the future and whether American banks may have forfeited their leadership with their rapid, self-serving moves (*Business Week*, 10 December 1979). If this proves correct, the dynamo of foreign lending may slow down and the price of future loans may rise to match the risks. Banks may be forced to meet the glut of liquidity with reduced business rather than with increased risk to the system.

Surplus Capacity in Insurance

Largely overlooked by theoretical economists, insurance is nevertheless a vast industry and an essential mechanism for the world economy. Global 1977 premiums were estimated at just under $300b., nearly half derived from US business. The two nations with the highest propensity to insure are the United States, where in 1977 premiums as a percentage of GNP reached 7·67 per cent, and Great Britain where the comparable figure was 5·67 per cent. Moreover, insurance has expanded faster than the GNP worldwide. The ratio of insurance premiums to world GNP (excluding the Eastern bloc) increased from 4·75 per cent in 1967, to 5·15 per cent in 1972 and to 5·34 per cent in 1977 (*Sigma*, 1979, pp. 6, 10).

Unlike banking, capacity issues are central to insurance literature and operations. Insurance capacity in any business line reflects the amount of exposure available in world markets at a 'reasonable price', but this capacity can collapse immediately following a major catastrophe. Insurance is a curious business. On the one hand, it helps other industries smooth their profitability over time. On the other hand, insurance enterprises have been unable to regulate their own profit stream and depend on underwriting cycles to impose discipline. Leading insurers and re-insurers believe that most insurance services are underpriced today and that sane pricing practices will return only when catastrophe strikes the weakest and most foolish insurers. As bankers sometimes hope for another Herstatt collapse to let them correct their price-slashing, some insurers wish for another Hurricane Betsy to restore order. And, insurers insist, only a major catastrophe will help; aviation losses and oil spill claims hardly budge the rates or hinder the growth in capacity today. One major European re-insurer was of the opinion that the underwriting cycle would wipe out many of the troublemakers and his and a few other strong companies would survive and prosper.

Part of the problem is that insurers rely on two types of profits.

Underwriting profits are the difference between premium income and claims. Investment profits are the returns on invested premium income. Most insurers now rely on investment income for the vast majority of their profits. Indeed, many lines of business show consistent underwriting losses throughout the industry.

Poor results have helped change the insurance field. Traditional North American and European insurance mainstays such as motor, marine and aviation are now frequently unprofitable. Underwriting profits are made in high-risk areas and insurers are often forced to rely on catastrophe insurance premiums. In addition, insurance is becoming a truly international business for the first time, 'as previously insular insurers, worried by the saturation of their national markets and the growing severity of underwriting cycles, look abroad in an attempt to spread their risks and find the profitable business that their own countries no longer provide (Kaletsky, 1978, p. S.4).

Specifically, the frequency, amplitude and predictability of underwriting cycles changed drastically in the past decade. The harmonisation of underwriting cycles across insurance lines (e.g. fire, motor, health/accident, marine) also increased. Some critics of the industry believe cycles may have broken down completely. They argue that insurers and re-insurers are writing for premium income and for balanced books, without regard for underwriting results. As long as investment returns remain solid, and the world economy grows, the insurers are content. True underwriting profits are isolated in new, little-understood areas involving high technology and/or catastrophic risk levels. Although product liability, oil platform, kidnap and ransom, and nuclear and liquified gas facility and transport insurance remain profitable, they are all risks so unpredictable that they should not perhaps be technically insurable. Hazel Henderson suspects that many new energy projects are insured, despite their 'essential uninsurability'. She questions the conventional assumption that 'the greater the catastrophe the less likely its occurrence,' and argues that 'it might well be that the greater the accident the *greater* the chance for its occurrence! The point is that we do not know and the theoretical foundations of statistical probability modelling are now inadequate' (1978, pp. 9, 11, 12). The difficulties are underscored by the rash misjudgements, frauds and disasters that have recently shaken Lloyd's of London (Lauriat, 1979, pp. 66–9; *Business Week*, 25 February 1980, pp. 94–108).

None the less, insurance capacity is rapidly expanding even if the prospects for underwriting gains remain dim. Since the mid-1970s global insurance capacity has been augmented by: (1) the doubling of names in Lloyd's of London which began admitting women and non-British nationals and increased their demonstrated wealth requirement; (2) the re-entry of American life insurance companies into the general international insurance market (significantly, when last the US life companies entered this fray, they retreated under heavy underwriting losses at the next downturn, perhaps further destabilising the markets); (3) the organisation of the New York free trade insurance zone and the New York insurance exchange which hope to compete with Lloyd's and retain more American business in America (although its rules differ from those of Lloyd's – limited versus unlimited liability, for insurance – it provides new insurance capacity and may help offset the balance-of-payments outflows from the United States related to insurance; Gahin, 1979, p. 14); (4) the growth and proliferation of captive insurance companies owned by corporations to retain and manage industrial risks (captives have let their parents increase coverages, raise deductables and concentrate on excess loss insurance instead of day-to-day problems; some captives also write insurance for other companies and are emerging as full, integrated companies; Welles, 1979a, pp. 121–7, 1979b, pp. 81–92); (5) the growth of insurance and reinsurance companies from developing countries (while still a small part of the market, protective national regulations and increasing emphasis on LDC insurance potential has propelled insurers from developing countries on to the centre stage; Ripolli, 1974, pp. 75–105; Shelp, 1976, pp. 701–35).

In sum, banks increased their international lending faster than the growth of sound borrowers in the system and insurance capacity rose faster than insurable risks. As capacity in banking and insurance increased, the average quality of their business declined. At least until the onset of the Iranian crisis, banks narrowed their spreads and increased the tenor of their loans to keep on lending. In some cases even overheads were not covered (Bruce, 1979). A borrower's market prevailed. Insurers slashed premiums, knowing that their price-cutting would result in underwriting losses. Insurance brokers found existing surplus capacity let them hold rates stable for loss prone customers and win reductions for better risks. Insurers, even large ones, feared that brokers could deprive them of large chunks of business if they refused to participate in certain lines of business. Insurers complain that excessive market capacity has hurt their bargaining power *vis-à-vis* the brokers and their clients (interviews, London, Zurich, Munich, March – June 1979).

Inevitably, surplus capacity and unrealistic pricing will vanish, but increasing international monetary interdependence could make this correction disruptive and extremely expensive. LDC reschedulings are already a common feature of international finance. If banks failed to roll over loans to Brazil and other wealthier non-oil-exporting developing countries, the banking system could be shaken (Aronson, 1979). Iran held major deposits with the banks; the Philippines, Korea, Taiwan and Brazil do not. Similarly, earthquakes in California or Japan, a major storm, a giant North Sea wave, or even the destruction of the Arzew, Algeria, liquified natural gas facility could topple major actors in the world insurance market. More important, the crunching corrections in banking and insurance could threaten the stability of the world's monetary and economic system.

Surplus Service Capacity and International Monetary Stability

The most devastating implication of the preceding discussion is that neither the banking nor the insurance system can change the direction of their international momentum unless plagued by crisis or collapse. Just as in governments, service bureaucracies frequently augment, but rarely revoke, existing procedures (Gerth and Mills, 1946). In the past, only cycles of boom and bust reordered the markets and forced losers out. Today, however, some actors are so large that governments will not permit their failure. The handful of largest banks and insurance companies in each nation are particularly sacrosanct. Their demise, it is feared, would shake national economies; indeed, the ramifications would be international in scope. Simultaneously, banking and insurance are now so global in character that no government can regulate them alone. The comic attempts to regulate the Eurocurrency market are evidence of these difficulties (Frydl, 1979–80, pp. 11–19). The system is running out of control, incapable of self-correction and beyond the reach of national decision-makers. Yet this potential disaster remains largely unrecognised by those most concerned. The wrong questions are being asked.

The key issue involves 'regime change'. It is necessary to begin planning and implementing the orderly transformation of one regime into another rather than merely recognising such change (Keohane and Nye, 1977). In a financially interdependent world it is simply too expensive to pass hegemonic leadership from one city or nation to another following financial and economic collapse (Kindleberger, 1973).

Possible outcomes can be grouped in five classes (Robertson, 1978, pp. 15–36). First, nothing will be done and the system will collapse. Secondly, the system will chug along with its ups and downs but without catastrophe. Thirdly, growth and productivity will rebound in the developed and developing worlds, allowing the system to absorb the threatening overhang of surplus capacity. Fourthly, governments and corporations will impose and accept new limits on the growth of insurance and banking and adjust to an environment where quality replaces quantity as a measure of success. But this option implies a dramatic shift in societal consciousness, the requirements for which are fascinating but beyond the scope of this chapter.

Fifthly, centralised government control of the economy will be found necessary to save capitalism from destruction (Heilbroner, 1979; Stein,

1979). If governments believe banks and insurance enterprises are acting irresponsibly to rid themselves of surplus capacity, they will intervene. Thus, the October 1979 'Volcker' shocks imposed an additional 8 per cent reserve requirement on American banks' lending from abroad, but could not touch non-American enterprises. As a result non-US banks now enjoy a 1·25 per cent advantage in funding dollar business. Banks and corporations are grumbling about unfair competition, but most admit that Volcker's decisiveness was necessary and continue to support his lead. The banks realised that self-regulation was impossible and were forced to accept imperfect control from above.

A final possibility is a more corporatist state. Most large banks and insurance companies argue that their actions stabilise markets, which would be sounder if smaller firms stayed out. Governments should set goals for corporations to pursue, not try to dictate corporate strategy (Schultze, 1976). Corporate supporters argue that the costs of regulation exceed the benefits (Weidenbaum, 1978). Sadly, sectoral self-regulation apparently works only when an oligopoly triumphs. Competition generates risk-takers, some of which cut prices recklessly. Although most gamblers eventually fail, system equilibrium is threatened. To gain stability, free markets and true competition are abandoned in favour of size (Lindblom, 1977). The system is further undermined when promised government bail-outs allow the largest oligopoly members to take unwarranted long-term risks. The bank lending cycle and the insurance underwriting cycle are distorted beyond recognition.

Problems are telescoped in the banking and insurance sectors since all other industries depend on them. For instance, banks carefully monitor their smaller customers, but allow their big customers to do as they please. Similarly, diverse insurance investment needs can distort economic activity. For example, large-scale construction projects funded by insurance companies are going forward in the United States despite the unstable US economy, while the construction of single-family dwellings is falling.

It appears that neither a socialist state nor a corporatist economy will solve the long-term destabilising impact of surplus service capacity. Even improved governmental strategic planning is unlikely to produce well-ordered markets. And, investors must have something to invest in. Growth for growth's sake is unlikely to continue in the coming era of limits and high-priced energy. Cross-sectoral investment temporarily may buoy the service industries, but innovation is necessary for a realistic growth scenario. This is particularly true where non-polluted earth, air and water are felt to be important (Gianni and Loubergé, 1979).

Notes: Chapter 10

The author wishes to acknowledge the assistance of Peter Cowley in the preparation of this chapter.

1 Most American research on multinational enterprises is indebted to Raymond Vernon's studies of 187 US-based extractive and manufacturing firms. Comparative work on European and Japanese multinationals also has tended to focus on manufacturing concerns, and their relations with governments rather than with the system. Even Robert Gilpin's neomercantilist study of the role of the multinationals in the world economy makes little sense when applied to service industries.

References: Chapter 10

Aronson, J. D. (1978), *Money and Power: Banks and the World Marketing System* (Beverly Hills, Calif.: Sage).

Aronson, J. D. (ed.) (1979), *Debt and the Less Developed Countries* (Boulder, Co: Westview Press).

Bruce, N. (1979), 'Tracing the lead banks: who's competing hardest?', *Euromoney*, August.

Crowe, B. G. (1979), 'International public lending and American policy', in Aronson, op. cit.

Frydl, D. J. (1979–80), 'The debate over regulating the Eurocurrency markets', *Federal Reserve Bank of New York Quarterly Review*, vol. 4, no. 4.

Gahin, F. S. (1979), 'International insurance transactions in the US balance of payments', *Best's Review*, Property/Casualty Insurance Edition, October.

Gerth, H. H., and Mills, C. W. (eds) (1946), *From Max Weber: Essays in Sociology* (New York: Oxford University Press).

Gianni, O., and Loubergé, H. (1979), Geneva Papers on Risk and Insurance nos 13, 14.

Hayes, D. A. (1971), *Bank Lending Policies: Domestic and International* (Ann Arbor, Mich.: Bureau of Business Research, Graduate School of Business Administration, University of Michigan).

Heilbroner, R. (1979), 'Inflationary capitalism', *The New Yorker*, September.

Henderson, H. (1978), 'Risk, uncertainty and economic futures', *The Geneva Papers on Risk and Insurance*, no. 9, July.

Kaletsky, A. (1978), 'Hazards ahead: a survey of world insurance', *The Economist*, 16 September.

Keohane, R. O., and Nye, J. S. (1977), *Power and Interdependence: World Politics in Transition* (Boston, Mass.: Little, Brown).

Kindleberger, C. P. (1973), *The World in Depression 1929–1939* (Berkeley, Calif.: University of California Press).

Lauriat, G. (1979), 'Awash in an ocean of dollars', *Far Eastern Economic Review*, 16 November.

Leftwich, R. (1979), 'Debt problems of developing countries', paper presented at a conference on Achieving Stability in the International Monetary System, World Affairs Council, Philadelphia, Pa, 1 November.

Lewis, W. A. (1978), *The Evolution of the International Economic Order* (Princeton, NJ: Princeton University Press).

Lindblom, C. (1977), *Politics and Markets* (New York: Basic Books).

Minsky, H. P. (1975), 'Financial resources in a fragile financial environment', mimeo. for the 17th Annual Forecasting Conference of the New York Chapter of the American Statistical Association, 18 April.

Morgan Guaranty (1979), *World Financial Markets*, December.

Morgan Guaranty (1980), *World Financial Markets*, January.

OECD (1979), *Quarterly National Accounts Bulletin*, vol. II (Paris: OECD).

Ripolli, J. (1974), 'UNCTAD and insurance', *Journal of World Trade Law*, vol. 8, January/February.

Robertson, J. (1978), *The Same Alternative: Signposts to a Self-fulfilling Future* (London: Villiers).

Schultze, C. (1976), *The Public Use of Private Interest* (Washington, DC: Brookings Institution).

Shelp, R. K. (1976), 'The proliferation of foreign insurance laws: reform or regression?', *Law and Policy in International Business*, vol. 8, no. 3.

Sigma (1979), no. 5, May (Swiss Reinsurance Company).

Stein, H. (1979), 'Economics at the New Yorker', *Wall Street Journal*, 12 November.

Strange, S. (1979), 'The management of surplus capacity: or how does theory stand up to protectionism 1970's style', *International Organisation*, Summer.

Weidenbaum, M. (1978), *The Future of Business Regulation* (New York: Amacom).

Welles, C. (1979a), 'The captives: turmoil in Bermuda', *International Investor*, April, pp. 121–7.

Welles, C. (1979b), 'How remote Bermuda is captivating bankers', *Euromoney*, May, pp. 81–92.

Part Four: The Practice of Managing Surplus Capacity

11

The Response of the European Community

LOUKAS TSOUKALIS and

ANTONIO DA SILVA FERREIRA

The Paris Treaty which led to the establishment of the European Coal and Steel Community (ECSC) gave the High Authority extensive powers which included the raising of levies on production, extending loans to firms for capital investment, financing research and development and retraining redundant workers. The supranational institution was also empowered to co-ordinate investment plans, although the authors of the Treaty did not go as far as giving the High Authority the right of veto over investment decisions. Some mild form of long-term planning was envisaged, while in a period of 'manifest crisis' the High Authority had the power, with the agreement of the Council, to establish a system of production quotas. Mergers were subject to authorisation by the High Authority and all state aids and subsidies were prohibited but member states reserved the right to pursue independent commercial policies *vis-à-vis* third countries.

Although the philosophy of the Paris Treaty was fundamentally a liberal one, the High Authority was expected to play an active role in both the coal and steel sectors. This was almost inevitable given the strategic importance of the two sectors in national economies, the supra-nationalist fervour of the Schuman era and also the fact that one of the main objects of the whole exercise was to avoid the re-emergence of cartels among steel producers; hence the policing powers given to the High Authority.

Industrial policy was hardly given any place at all in the Rome Treaty signed in 1957. Here, the emphasis was on the creation of a customs union through the elimination of tariffs, quotas and other obstacles to free trade. There were also provisions for the liberalisation of labour and capital movements and freedom of establishment. The only exceptions were agriculture, transport and commercial policy, the latter being a necessary consequence of the eventual creation of a common external tariff.

Industrial policy virtually implies government intervention at the micro level. Such intervention can either take the form of a policy designed to eliminate distortions to competition or the form of planning which implies that the state has different priorities or objectives from those which may result from the free interplay of market forces. As far as the Rome Treaty was concerned, it was only the first aspect of industrial policy that was touched upon with Articles 85–9 dealing with restrictive business practices and the abuse of dominant positions, and Articles 92–4 dealing with government aids and subsidies. The treaty implied a free market economy and said almost nothing about the role of government in industrial development. The strong liberal bias of the treaty was the result of German economic liberalism and French nationalism. What we mean by this is that although France, following a long-established tradition, favoured *dirigiste* measures and experiment with indicative planning at the national level, it was, however, not prepared to accept any form of planning at the Community level. It was only at a later stage that French governments became aware of the limitations imposed on national economic decisions by the creation of the customs union.

The treaty was in clear contradiction of the trend of increasing government intervention in the economy in all EEC countries during the 1960s. But this contradiction did not become so acute because the second decade of European integration coincided with a honeymoon period for all Western European economies, characterised by high rates of growth, balance-of-payments surpluses, low rates of inflation and near full employment.

The object of this chapter is to examine Community policies for the management of surplus capacity in steel, textiles and clothing, and ship-building as distinct from purely national responses. The Community has had a well-developed external economic policy, but almost non-existent powers in the field of industrial policy – though some qualification should be made in the case of steel. How has it performed?

We have chosen the three sectors because the problem of surplus capacity is by common consent a structural one as opposed to short-term problems related to the economic cycle, which may be the case with the chemical and the motor car industries. To the extent that one can generalise about industries with different sub-sectoral trends, it can be argued that in all these three cases European industrialists have been losing their comparative advantage against foreign producers – mainly Japan and the newly industrialising countries.

We start with an *a priori* assumption that the Community, unlike GATT and the OECD, is not a typical inter-governmental organisation. It has slowly emerged as a new political and economic unit in the international system, which defies old classifications. The management of surplus capacity in these three sectors can also serve as a case study of the way in which the Community has been responding to a constantly evolving economic environment.

Steel

For almost a century the steel industry occupied a strategic position in the economic development of Western Europe. Until the Second World War the future ECSC members produced 40–50 per cent of world steel and accounted for about 80 per cent of world trade. Western Europe's share in world steel production and trade has been constantly declining since then and the Community of Nine now ranks second to Japan in terms of exports. This reached a crisis point in 1975, when the loss of comparative advantage was combined with a severe recession which hit the world steel market as a whole.

Rationalisation in the 1950s and the 1960s took place within national boundaries. The first transnational mergers, among German and Benelux producers, only started in the late 1960s. Until then, and despite the common market in steel, member states had built up 'national champions'. As a result of the 1975 crisis, the French asked for a declaration of a 'manifest crisis' in the steel industry and called for external protection and internal stabilisation measures. They were joined by the British and the Italians, while the Germans seemed to be more worried about the subsidies given by the three governments to their respective industries.

As the crisis worsened in 1976, the German producers extended their already existing 'rationalisation groupings' (Rationalisierungsgruppen) to include Arbed in Luxembourg and the Dutch steel industry in the north. A group was formed (Denelux) to represent the interests of all those producers in Brussels. But the outcry of those who had been left out, and growing anxiety within the Commission that this might lead to a cartel of producers dominated by the Germans, led to the creation of a wider cartel (or group of producers in more neutral terms) named Eurofer, which now represents about 95 per cent of total production in the nine countries. The creation of Eurofer provided the Commission with a very useful interlocutor and also made the adoption, as well as effective implementation, of the Davignon Plan much more feasible. The growing pressure for unilateral measures in the most seriously affected countries of the Community and the increasing opposition to redundancies by steelworkers in the Saar industry finally forced the Federal Republic, followed by the Benelux countries, to go along with the plan put forward by the Commission.

The anti-crisis plan consisted of internal and external measures. The former were intended to stabilise the Community market through the adoption of minimum prices for the most 'sensitive' products, and recommended prices for ten other steel products. Minimum prices were mandatory and agreed between the Commission and representatives of Eurofer. Although there have been a number of complaints about firms breaking the Commission's guidelines, the degree of compliance by European steel companies has been greater than many people would have expected. Readiness to comply must have been strengthened after the Commission took a few recalcitrant firms to the European Court of Justice.

The anti-crisis plan also included a voluntary agreement on production quotas between the Commission and individual producers. This had to remain voluntary, because otherwise the Commission would need to declare a 'manifest crisis', according to the provisions of the Paris Treaty. This was impossible because of German opposition. The fact that voluntary production quotas did not remain purely theoretical may be at least partly explained in terms of the oligopolistic structure of the industry. It is this structure which also made the creation of a cartel possible.

External measures have included bilateral negotiations with foreign suppliers, which have usually led to 'voluntary' restrictions of exports but, if this has failed, the Community has then adopted anti-dumping measures. With the worsening situation in the world market at the end of 1979, there has been increasing pressure from US producers for further measures against European imports. Meanwhile, in the OECD's permanent Steel Committee, both the Europeans and the Japanese have expressed themselves in favour of 'organised trade' through price controls and agreed market shares in international trade.

If the Commission has been relatively successful with its anti-crisis plan, in terms of the degree of conformity achieved by individual producers and the preservation of the common market in steel, the same does not exactly apply to its medium-term objective, namely, the rationalisation of production and the restructuring of the Community industry. As with shipbuilding, the Commission has never made any attempt to suggest how the burden of adjustment should be shared among member countries. The decision was, therefore, left to the Council of Ministers or to individual member governments.

The recent crisis has strengthened the links between government and industry in all member countries. Faced with the prolonged recession and rising unemployment, member governments have found it very difficult to implement their rationalisation plans, as witnessed by the long strike of German steelworkers in 1978 and the riots in Lorraine in the early months of 1979 or the more recent national steel strike in Britain. But the French rationalisation plan finally went ahead and French producers are expected to break even in 1980. German industry is already in the black and so are the Dutch and Italian private producers. The new Conservative government in Britain is also pushing ahead with its plans for a major cutback in productive capacity and an increase in productivity. However, it should be added that whatever restructuring there has been it was more the result of big financial losses rather than real pressure exerted by the Commission.

The Commission was also forced to give its blessing to open-ended subsidies, as for example in the UK and Italy, which were often meant to keep obsolescent plants alive. Since the Treaty of Paris prohibited any form of state aids, a way round this problem was found by referring to Article 93 of the Rome Treaty, which provided for exceptions. It is not, however, true that the Commission has been entirely powerless *vis-à-vis* national governments and steel producers. The fact that the Community's contribution to total investment in the steel industry in 1977 accounted for over 20 per cent, in addition to other forms of assistance coming from various Community funds, meant that the Commission had some real influence on investment decisions.

More recently, the powers of the Commission in this field were considerably strengthened with the adoption of a new code on state aids which had become a *sine qua non* condition for German acceptance for the continuation of the Davignon Plan in 1980. The adoption of the new code on state aids signified remarkable progress, which was almost unthinkable within a wider framework such as the OECD.

The Davignon Plan has provided a Community framework for a joint solution to the problem of surplus capacity in the industry, a problem shared by all major steel producers in the Community. The plan aimed at stabilising the market through a direct control of prices and imports. This was to avert two equally disastrous alternatives, namely, a series of bankruptcies in the European steel industry with the consequent heavy loss in employment, and/or the adoption of unilateral, national measures which would have meant the end of the common market in steel. In this respect, the Davignon Plan seems to have been successful. But the solution has only been temporary. Adjustment has only moved at a very slow pace and the long-term problem of a major cutback in productive capacity still remains. At least the necessity of adjustment seems now to be widely accepted. Member governments have not been able to agree on the sharing of the cost while the Commission has very limited legal and political power to enforce decisions. It might, however, be unrealistic to expect the Commission to succeed where many national governments have failed. One important factor against the survival of the anti-crisis plan in the future will be the growing opposition of the relatively efficient producers in the Community who stand to lose from the freezing of production shares.

Textiles and Clothing

Textiles and clothing have long been considered a declining industry in the Community. Low-income elasticity of demand and growing competition from foreign producers who could take advantage of low wage costs in a labour-intensive industry, coupled with low rates of investment in Europe, made textiles and clothing a declining industry in the Community long before the advent of the recent crisis.

The industry still employs about 10 per cent of the total industrial workforce in the Community, clearly illustrating the social dimension of the problem. Moreover, a large proportion of those laid off are women and relatively unqualified workers for whom there are very few possibilities of alternative employment even in times of prosperity, not to mention prolonged periods of recession see Farrands, Chapter 7).

Until 1973, with the exception of Italy, government intervention was limited to the common external protection offered to all Community producers. But faced with a deteriorating employment situation, one government after another was forced to resort to internal measures in order to arrest the decline of its national industry. General programmes, which usually took the form of relief assistance to the clothing sector, were slowly replaced by elaborate and selective schemes, which meant that governments were now forced to play a more active role at the micro level. It was only the federal government in Germany which held out for the market-oriented approach.

While government intervention spread in the member countries, the Commission tried to arrest the protectionist trend and bring about some co-ordination of national policies, with emphasis on the long-term need for restructuring. In July 1978 the Commission presented to the Council its'General Guidelines for a Textiles and Clothing Industry Policy'. This was, however, only the most recent of a long list of Commission initiatives which have met with little success. The Commission was keen to stress three basic points: (1) changes would have to rely on private initiative, (2) external protection should provide only a temporary shield for the Community industry and (3) greater competitiveness could only come through a substantial futher reduction in the existing number of jobs. But the Commission believed that the necessary process of adjustment should be eased through Community aid for the conversion of plants, job-creating, labour retraining, relocation of workers, early retirement, unemployment allowance and other social measures. This would put an end to 'conservative' national aids and would also strengthen considerably the role played by the supranational institution in the management of surplus capacity in this sector. However, the Commission did not have the necessary information and the human resources, nor did it have the political power or the financial resources to play such an active role.

We have already mentioned the fact that the Commission was not faced, as in the steel sector, with a small number of large producers who could provide an effective negotiating partner. The measures put forward by the Commission implied effective regional and social policies and financial resources far beyond those available to the Community at present. On the other hand, member countries were not keen on such a transfer of political and economic power to Brussels. Thus action ultimately remained confined within the boundaries of the nation-state. The Commission so far has had little success in bringing about some agreement on the criteria guiding the provision of aids to industry.

Man-made fibres are a special case within the textiles sector. The two main factors which distinguish it from other sub-sectors are its oligopolistic structure and its dependence on oil as the basic raw material. Thus, after 1973 man-made fibres in Western Europe were faced with rapidly rising costs and falling demand – a problem shared with the Japanese industry (if that was any consolation for European producers). Estimates of surplus capacity in the Community were about 30–40 per cent on average. But here, given the oligopolistic structure of the market and the internationalisation of production, producers adopted a co-ordinated response. In July 1978 the eleven biggest producers of man-made fibres in the Community (sharing 80 per cent of the market) signed a cartel agreement, with the blessing of M. Davignon. The agreement was based on a freezing of production shares and a cutback in productive capacity by 15 per cent. Despite the support of M. Davignon's Directorate General, the Commission failed to legalise the cartel agreement. The lack of legal powers emanating from the Treaty of Rome and the opposition of the majority of Commissioners, led by M. Vouel in charge of competition, and Germany, combined to defeat M. Davignon and the producers' lobby. But the Commission's decision was supposed to be provisional, which, in turn, meant that the agreement remained legally in limbo, while the agreed cuts in productive capacity went into effect all the same.

Where the Community has been very active is on the external front. The first Multi-Fibre Agreement (MFA) signed in 1973 proved to be a disaster for the European industry and particularly for the old-established producers like Britain and France. The main assumption on which the first MFA was based – that the Community market would continue to expand to make room for the growing exports of Third World producers – did not materialise. The Commission was very slow in taking any action against imports from low-cost producers and almost nothing happened until France and Britain took unilateral measures in the summer of 1976 to protect their industries.

It was, therefore, inevitable that the second MFA would be signed in a very unfavourable climate for Third World producers. The Community made it clear that its agreement to the new MFA signed in 1977 was conditional on the successful negotiation of bilateral agreements with individual countries, which led to the conclusion of stringent agreements with about thirty low-cost exporting countries from the developing world. The whole range of textile and clothing products was divided into six groups, each being subdivided in turn into several categories. A quota system established rigid quantitative limits for each category of 'sensitive' products from those countries that were major suppliers within the product category. A second import regime was also introduced, the so-called 'basket system', which established a threshold level for each product not covered by a quantitative limit for each major supplier. As a result of the MFA and the pressure exercised by the Community on exporting countries for 'voluntary' restraint, global imports of textile and clothing products actually fell in volume by 1977. The MFA agreement expires in 1981 and unless some major readjustment takes place within the Community industry, which seems highly unlikely, there will be renewed pressure for more protection.

Shipbuilding

Between 1960 and 1973 the rapid development of international trade and the constant expansion of fleets provided the European shipyards with fat order books. But the recession of the mid-1970s and its impact on international trade have left the world with a large surplus of tankers. Forecasts made by AWES (Association of West European Shipbuilders, which includes Sweden, Finland, Spain and Portugal, as well as the member countries of the Community) and the Commission suggested that the market would be unable to take up the surplus tonnage before the mid-1980s. The picture drawn for Western European shipyards in the future looked even gloomier because of expectations of an accelerated drift of production to the Far East and Latin America in the 1980s.

The Commission in its Reorganisation Programme of December 1977 argued in favour of a major restructuring operation that would improve the competitiveness of Community industry, reduce productive capacity by 45 per cent and provide new jobs for redundant workers. The cost of the Reorganisation Programme, which would last for a period of five years, would be about 4,650m. units of account in 1977 prices, equivalent to almost a half of an annual Community Budget.

The Commission programme came under severe criticism from member governments and the industry itself. First of all, the accuracy of forecasts based on production figures from the trough of the economic cycle was seriously challenged. In an industry that is subject to large cyclical swings in demand, most people considered the Commission forecasts as overly pessimistic. On the other hand, the Commission proposals were criticised as vague because no attempt was made to indicate how the production cuts would be shared among member countries. This was after all the main political question and the Commission had no easy answer to offer.

These proposals were rejected by the Council of Ministers in July 1978 and member countries continued to subsidise their shipbuilding industry to the order of 30 per cent on contract prices for new ships. But the world market was so depressed that in 1978 the Nine could not even spend the subsidies they had already budgeted for because of the insufficient amount of orders placed with shipyards in Community countries. As far as the shipbuilding industry is concerned, state aids provide a substitute for tariff protection *vis-à-vis* foreign producers. What the Commission has tried to do is to bring about some harmonisation of aids so as to avoid a serious distortion of competition within the Community. In this respect, the Nine have gone much further than OECD members, who have been discussing state aids to the shipbuilding industry within the framework of Working Party Six. Significantly, with the Fourth Directive of April 1978, state aids in the Nine were linked to restructuring measures.

One proposal put forward by the Commission in 1979 is the so-called 'scrap and build' programme. The aim is to stimulate Community output and save an estimated 35,000–40,000 jobs by offering incentives to shipowners to scrap a target figure of 2m. cgrt p.a. and subsidise new building up to 1m. cgrt p.a. The costs would be borne by the Community, possibly through the so-called Ortoli facility. The idea is, after all, not a very novel one; it was tried on a massive scale during the 1930s. As with steel and textiles, we find again the same countries, namely, West Germany, the Netherlands and Denmark, who have been most reluctant to accept the idea of Community subsidies for a declining industry. With the arrival of Conservatives in power, Britain has also joined the ranks of the 'free market' camp.

Some peculiarities of the shipbuilding industry may help to explain the reactions of different governments to the present crisis and the inability of the Community as a whole to adopt some form of common policy. One is the security aspect and the fact that historically the shipbuilding industry is closely related to defence which, in turn, has meant a long history of direct government involvement. The other is the capital-intensive nature of the industry which makes any phasing out of productive capacity a very costly operation. The third is that external protection cannot take the form of tariffs but only of public aids and subsidies. Here government control becomes more difficult because of the extensive use of flags of convenience. Finally, shipbuilding is an oligopolistic market at the world level, with production concentrated in OECD countries, although this seems to be changing rapidly with countries like South Korea, Brazil, Poland and Taiwan entering the market as serious competitors. In 1978, for the first time, shipyards outside Western Europe and Japan took over 30 per cent of new orders.

Conclusions

Falling world demand and rapidly rising costs in Western Europe, combined with serious structural problems in these three sectors, have led to massive overcapacities and big financial and employment losses. In a period of growing unemployment the loss of jobs became the main consideration for all governments concerned. One theoretical solution immediately rejected at the political level, as a result of pressure coming from industrialists and trade unions, was to leave it to the market forces to bring about the necessary adjustment. But once the pure leave-it-to-the market approach was rejected, the question immediately arose whether state intervention would take the form of national protectionist measures, which would mean the end of the common market in those sectors, or the form of Community measures. The second question was whether Community members would try to avoid the burden of adjustment by resorting to purely protectionist measures directed against non-members of the club.

Response has varied from one sector to the other. In the case of steel, the common market has been preserved by the setting-up of a cartel of producers (an anathema to the fathers of the ECSC) and the introduction of strong protectionist measures *vis-à-vis* the outside world. But there is very little agreement about the sharing of the burden of adjustment inside the Community. With very few exceptions, restructuring policies have taken a purely national form and in some cases governments have adopted the easy solution of sitting on the problem and doing nothing. With respect to textiles and clothing, Community policy has been limited to external protectionist measures and little else. Finally, as far as the shipbuilding industry is concerned, the Community's role has so far been virtually non-existent, despite initiatives emanating from Brussels.

The particular characteristics of each sector partly explain the differing responses to the problem of surplus capacity. Significantly, some factors seem to determine whether the Community is able to adopt common policies toward it. It is certainly no coincidence that most of the common measures have been measures of external economic policy. The explanation that it is always easier to pass the burden on to foreigners through protectionist measures, however, is not sufficient – because protection could have been introduced at the national and not at the Community level. It suggests that the existence of a common instrument – the external tariff and the common commercial policy – forced or led member countries to act in unison. The same point seems to be confirmed conversely if one examines the member countries' lack of success in adopting common internal measures in the three sectors. The implementation of the anti-crisis plan cannot be completely unrelated to the legal powers given to the supranational institution by the Treaty of Paris. However, it might be argued that in the present crisis the existence of the Community has facilitated the adoption of external protectionist measures, given the bargaining strength of the European trade bloc in international negotiations. If this is true – and it is impossible to test such a hypothesis – then it is exactly the opposite of the effect that European integration had in the 1960s when it undoubtedly contributed to international trade liberalisation.

Faced with a prolonged recession and major structural problems in industry, the Community was caught completely unprepared. The Treaty of Rome made no provisions for an industrial policy, relying almost entirely on market integration. Since member governments had been deprived of the instrument of tariff protection, they had to resort to other measures, which economists lump together under the name of non-tariff barriers, in order to protect their national industries. The Commission tried to avoid the spreading of uncontrolled state aids and subsidies, which would make nonsense of the Common Market. It also tried to emphasise the need for adjustment and that protectionist measures *vis-à-vis* third countries should be considered only a temporary solution. Commission proposals often reminded one of what has been called in neo-functionalist theory the 'upgrading of common interests'.

It would certainly not be desirable or feasible for the Commission to play an active intervention role in industries with serious structural problems. If state bureaucracies find it extremely difficult to deal with this problem successfully, then it would be nonsensical to ask the Commission to perform such a task. But if some form of co-ordination of national policies is desirable, then common instruments are needed to make this possible. The chances for an effective adjustment policy, which would be part of an overall industrial policy, would be much greater if the Community were to have sufficient financial resources at its disposal for the creation of new jobs and for the retraining of workers made redundant by the closure of uncompetitive firms.

The creation of transnational pressure groups at the European level can only be the result of the realisation by private interests that political power is no longer completely monopolised by the nation-state. Eurofer, Comitextil and AWES have become valuable interlocutors for the European institutions, without implying that their constituent parts have ceased to operate at the national level as well. In contrast, trade unions have not as yet been successful in exerting any real influence on Community decisions. Collaboration within such bodies as the European Trade Union Confederation (ETUC) has been limited and action has concentrated on the national level.

There also exists a more general problem which does not apply only to the Community as such. This is the inability of Western European governments to provide an answer to the crisis of the 1970s. Surplus capacity in declining industrial sectors is closely related to the new political and economic environment in Western Europe, which is the result of a number of structural changes. The growth of specialisation and interdependence, of skill and capital intensity, coupled with the attitudes of organised labour, has created serious rigidities in product and factor markets. At the same time, the increasing openness of national economies and the shift of productive resources to Third World countries where multinational companies can take advantage of low wages and 'social peace', usually at the expense of political freedom, have intensified the need for continuous internal adjustment. Popular expectations for growing incomes, security of jobs and stable prices have been rising while governments have often proved unable to deliver the goods.

The limitations of Keynesian demand management have become all too obvious in recent years and there is growing recognition of the need for structural policies, such as industrial and manpower policies, to bring about the necessary adjustment as effectively as the free market mechanism – but less violently. The question is, first, whether the mixed economy and the welfare system in Europe is adaptable enough to survive in a period of slow, or zero, rates of growth, and secondly, whether it can do so only at the expense of Third World countries. This is a major challenge facing Western European governments.

Note: Chapter 11

This is an abridged version of an article published in *International Organization*, Summer 1980. We would like to thank the editors for permission to reproduce *in extenso* parts of this article.

12

The American Steel Industry and International Competition

STEVEN J. WARNECKE

While OECD nations threatened by steel imports have resorted to the usual armoury of protectionist devices such as subsidies and voluntary export agreements, both the United States and the European Community have introduced complex reference price systems. This chapter will deal with the American variant.

At a minimum, it is valuable to describe the structure of this particular mechanism as well as the administrative and political routes through which it has been implemented. If nothing else, such a description will illustrate the complexity of the system within which US trade law is formulated and implemented, the numerous points through which pressure groups are able to exercise a veto power, and how the system itself may have become an obstacle to solving the problems which led to its establishment.

In broader terms, however, the US reference price system provides an ideal focus for examining the difficulties political leaders face in their efforts to mediate between domestic pressures and international obligations – a function of particular significance in the American case as a result of the central role of the United States in the global economic system.

The American Steel Industry:
Reaction to International Competition

The global recession has precipitated increased restrictions on the operation of the EC's internal market and on imports of steel into the United States. Ideally, from the GATT viewpoint, economic efficiency should be the deciding criterion in resolving disputes among nations. But economics is ahistorical and apolitical. Thus, in addition to the economic issues at stake, there are also political and historical factors which must be taken into account. As a result of Japan's dependence on steel exports, the dual discrimination imposed by the EC and the United States has intensified fears of a Western effort to shift the burden of adjustment to Asia. This is simply a continuation of a pattern which arose during the 1960s. Sectoral problems have been viewed as either involving conflicts between Japan and the other OECD nations, or between the industrialised countries and Third World states. However, a new and more significant pattern has emerged as a result of the intensification of protectionist pressures in the United States. The various efforts to shield American industries from foreign competition are indications that Washington is no longer in a position to be idle in trade conflicts. In the past, presidents could neutralise protectionist pressures through appeals to the US obligation to support GATT fully as part of the Bretton Woods system or to allow a certain degree of trade discrimination against US producers in order to contribute to European integration and the reconstruction of Japanese industry. With the demise of the Bretton Woods system, the failure of the EC to achieve a higher level of political and economic consolidation and the relative decline in the power of the United States, it is no longer possible for Washington to remain entirely deaf to domestic lobbies and to subordinate trade policy to other foreign policy considerations.

Under these circumstances, the steel industry as well as other industries has found it easier to advance arguments for special trade measures. In regard to steel, there have been two manifestations of efforts to foster a more sheltered environment. On the one hand, there has been a general attack on the EC's practice of remitting VAT on exported products, a practice acceptable under GATT. On the other hand, there have been specific attacks on specific foreign steel producers through petitions to the Treasury, the International Trade Commission and the court system. The general approach, if successful, would potentially affect all products exported from the Nine which enjoy such rebates. From the viewpoint of American producers, this practice is *prima facie* evidence of an unfair subsidy, which under US law warrants the imposition of a countervailing duty without the necessity of proving damage has occurred. (As a result of the conclusion of the GATT negotiations US law will probably be amended to require a determination of injury.)

As a result of the pluralistic structure of the American government, domestic industries have been able to bring pressure on the Executive through Congress, the court system, the Treasury Department and the International Trade Commission. While these bodies do not necessarily side automatically with industry demands for relief, the threat or actual implementation of a suit contributes to the pressure which has been brought to bear on the Carter Administration through the GATT negotiations. If such suits continue after the new multilateral trade agreement is ratified, they will undermine the implementation of the accord. Moreover, the random nature of such suits has introduced a large element of uncertainty into the plans of foreign firms and governments, in part because of the importance of the American market for steel exports.

In an effort to quell domestic pressures and suits which threatened the trade negotiations, during 1977 Robert Strauss, the Special Trade Representative, concluded bilateral market-sharing arrangements to limit imports of colour TV sets from Japan and shoes from Taiwan and South Korea. The immediate cause was the necessity of defusing congressional demands for prompt protective action in the form of tariffs and quotas. This was followed by Strauss forcing Japan to agree to modify elements of its trade policy to accommodate political and economic interests. In the course of pursuing these goals, the Special Trade Representative maintained that in order to escape chaos in trade matters he was resorting to bilateral agreements which hopefully would provide an element of control and co-operation. This placed the United States in a rather ambiguous position, since as the guarantor of the rule of law in international trade, it was enforcing exceptions in its own favour.

Although this was done with the intent of improving the environment for the successful conclusion of the multilateral trade negotiations, inevitably, the steel industry would be able to take advantage of the 'temporary' gains of other American industries. In the face of foreign competition, increases in operating costs, a squeeze on profits and huge expenditures to meet new environmental pollution standards the American steel industry did not show a profit in 1975–8. During 1977 more than 30,000 steelworkers were laid off and several million tonnes of production capacity were idle. Having had minimum success in fending off foreign competition through petitions to the International Trade Commission, the industry had introduced an ever-increasing number of suits in the court system as well as turning to the 'steel lobby' in Congress. Foreign producers – both the efficient Japanese and the subsidised Europeans – were the principal targets, and the industry goals were substantially to roll back market penetration by foreign producers and to modernise existing facilities. In regard to the former, imports accounted for about 15 per cent of US demand, with one-half coming from Japan. While it was possible to argue that this was not unusually high and that the American steel industry had failed to invest in modernised facilities to the extent necessary, the American Executive could no longer ignore the problems of the industry. This had as much to do with domestic political and economic reasons as with the pressure on the United States not to appear to do anything significant that would disrupt the trade negotiations.

In late 1977 President Carter established an inter-agency taskforce headed by Anthony Solomon, the Treasury Under Secretary for Monetary Affairs. The committee was charged with preparing a new policy, undoubtedly a difficult task given the number of interests which had to be taken into consideration. Quotas and tariffs could not be used as a result of binding GATT obligations. Whatever measures were devised would have to be linked with the establishment of conditions to force the steel industry to modernise further. Outright protection would have increased the pressures forcing domestic inflation upward, and unleashed a destructive trade war with Japan and the EC. Finally, the administrative method chosen would have to meet both domestic and foreign complaints about the complexity, delays and uncertainties caused by existing remedies open to the American steel industry. The committee's report, released in October 1977, ascribed most of the industry's ills not to the weaknesses of past management, but to unfair practices by foreign competitors and governments. It proposed protection of the American steel industry through the implementation of a reference or 'trigger price' system. In the past, government agencies had only undertaken countervailing duty and dumping investigations after a formal complaint from an industry. The trigger price system would now prompt the Treasury to undertake investigations on its own initiative.

Under this system, foreign producers will not be allowed to sell their steel products below minimum prices based on the production and transportation costs of the world's most efficient producers, the Japanese. Those who do will be disciplined by a fast dumping procedure that will take 60–90 days, instead of the usual one-year delay. This system appears to be preferable to quotas, let alone reserved markets, because it would allow those whose low prices are based on real efficiency to be free to compete in US markets. However, the system also set a minimum price for imported steel, and thus enabled domestic industry to get higher prices for its own products. Whether domestic industry would accept such a system would depend on 'acceptable' and durable profit levels. Even then, as often happens with flexible or temporary protective devices, the industry, having succeeded in obtaining partial shelter, then asks for more. One of the major questions, therefore, is whether US industry would restructure. In order to encourage further rationalisation, the trigger price system was linked to a $100m. government loan guarantee. In addition, the industry would get assistance quite similar to that extended to declining sectors in Europe: faster tax write-offs on capital equipment, partial exemption from Anti-trust Laws, government aid to research and development and changes in environmental laws to cut anti-pollution costs.

The key is the reference price system, since it would be the first part of the package to take effect. If it reduced the pressure of imports, even temporarily, it would relieve pressure on the Carter Administration by robbing the industry of its principal argument for special consideration. Although devised in late 1977, for a number of reasons it was not introduced until April 1978. The first announcement, however, was in January, when the Treasury released most of the minimum prices it had devised to provide an early warning of the illegal dumping of foreign steel at below production costs. In turn, this warning would trigger a Treasury investigation. The average of the separate reference prices established for nearly a score of different steel products was $330 a tonne, $20 (or 5·7 per cent) above the average price of US products in the eastern United States. However, this was decidedly below the $360 a tonne average proposed by the steel industry.

How were these prices calculated? The trigger prices for seventeen types of products were established from cost data supplied by the Japanese government. The US Treasury compared the trigger prices of five major carbon steel categories, plus duties, with present East Coast list prices of domestic manufacturers. For two lines – tin plate and hot-rolled bars – the US price was lower. These are also the two most costly types of steel of the five groups. The three lines for which the US list price exceeded the trigger price plus duty were cold-rolled sheet, hot-rolled sheet and plate. The Japanese cost data came from six major integrated steel companies and some smaller, electric furnace steelmakers. The calculations were based on the assumed operating ratio of 85 per cent in Japan, a figure that reflected experience since 1956. Although the present rate at the time of calculation was only 70 per cent, it was assumed that this was a temporary factor. This difference is important, since higher capacity usage means lower average costs. Using an exchange rate of ¥240 to the dollar, the following factor costs were computed per tonne of finished steel: raw materials $165·19, labour $68·56 and overhead $64·05. To the total production cost of $297·80, the Treasury added $17 for depreciation, $34 for interest and profit and $50·62 for return to capital which was equivalent to 13 per cent of total assets. Then it added average costs for freight to the East Coast, insurance and handling. Similar calculations were made for the West Coast where the Japanese enjoy a shipping advantage. The trigger prices would be increased in those cases where imports included extras such as charges for special sizing and finishes. What remained was the completion of the calculations of prices for wire, tubular products, cold-finished and alloy steels. The final prices do not include the 3–4 per cent mark-up made by domestic importers.

During the release of these reference prices, the Treasury emphasised that the success of the domestic steel industry's effort to recapture a share of the market held by foreign producers depended upon its own price policy. Whether this was a warning not to use the reference price system as a floor price upon which to raise domestic prices was not clear. However, unless the domestic steel industry could increase its profit margins over a sufficiently long period, the entire reference price system would turn out to be useless in so far as encouraging further rationalisation of the American steel industry was concerned.

This is a rather cumbersome system, which has been criticised by producers, importers, users and law-makers. In addition to having to calculate and monitor prices on innumerable products, the reference prices are recalculated on a quarterly basis. This means that the entire system is open to pressure for change from private industry each time the trigger list is revised. Moreover, before a penalty is imposed against foreign firms, two separate findings are required. The Treasury must determine whether dumping has occurred. Then the International Trade Commission must determine whether American industry has been damaged. Furthermore, foreign exporters are burdened with the uncertainty that even though their merchandise has cleared the customs trigger, the Treasury Department can impose penalties retroactively. Finally, the system does not cover that 25 per cent of the market which includes specialty, alloy steels.

In March 1978, United States Steel Corporation withdrew its anti-dumping suit against Japanese firms to allow the Treasury to focus on enforcing the trigger price system. While this was a diplomatic act on the part of the largest steel producer in America, it was also an indication of the potential power of the steel industry to frustrate the trigger price system through a re-imposition of anti-dumping suits and countervailing duty petitions. Moreover, the reference price system must be seen as trying to shift the burden of adjustment not only on to foreign producers, but also on to domestic steel importers and their clients. The reference price system would only be economically justified to the extent it did contribute to a rationalisation of American steel production capacity. Otherwise, it might simply lead to a specific industry protecting itself at the cost of its own economic efficiency and that of its domestic clients. In addition, there was the issue of what constituted an acceptable share of the domestic market for domestic producers. In response to the industry's plight, David Roderick, president of US Steel, had said: 'We are for free fair trade without reverting to government loan subsidies so widely practiced by foreign producers.' But 'free trade' and 'fair trade' are two different things. The latter introduces a political element into the determination of what is an acceptable market share for foreign producers.

The lack of unanimity between American steel producers and domestic steel importing firms was also reflected in the federal government. In addition to the split between Congress and the President on the balance to be struck between GATT obligations and protecting domestic industry, the Federal Trade Commission came out decisively against the reference price system. At the time the first trigger prices were announced in January 1978, the FTC released a study on the domestic and international steel industries, which had been started in 1976. The study challenged most of the key arguments of the domestic steel industry for substantial relief. The FTC asserted that the domestic industry was being undercut, not through dumping, but through the lower production costs of foreign firms. In regard to subsidies, the study found that they constituted less than 1 per cent of the selling price of foreign steel in the United States, with the exception of British Steel. The FTC attacked the reference price system as a pernicious form of trade restriction that would cost consumers 1 billion dollars a year. The study concluded that free market forces would provide appropriate incentives for the long-term development of the domestic steel industry. While this is a politically unrealistic view as a result of the political power of the domestic steel industry, it does suggest basic issues. Under what conditions and through what means could a restructuring of the steel industry be accomplished? To what extent should the domestic steel industry be penalised for its own failures to respond adequately in the past, if this were the case as the FTC maintained? Correspondingly, to what extent should efficient foreign firms be penalised by an effort to revive the US industry so that it could reclaim a third of the market share which had been lost to foreign producers? Or were there a variety of other considerations the US Executive should take into account that might reduce the eagerness of the government to shelter domestic industry, such as the necessity of expanding the market share of steel from the advanced industrialising nations?

The Trigger Price System in Action

The Treasury's announcement of the first reference prices in January 1978 occurred under ominous circumstances. US Steel announced simultaneously that its fourth-quarter earnings in 1977 were the worst in thirty years. Soon thereafter, import figures for December were released indicating that foreign producers had set a record of 24 per cent of the domestic market in that month. April figures indicated a surge in imports to beat the implementation of the trigger price system. The May figures, however, showed a 30 per cent drop in steel imports when compared with those for April and a 16·8 per cent drop when compared with the same month a year ago. By then the steel industry was insisting that the foreign share be reduced to 14 per cent but the Treasury Department quite correctly refused to commit itself to any figure at all. Although the reference price system placed a ceiling on future price increases, the domestic industry began to increase its prices within the parameters set by the ceilings of the different reference prices. And individual producers, discontented with the system, began to initiate anti-dumping and countervailing suits against foreign firms.

How viable has the reference price system been as a basis for reducing conflict between the domestic industry and foreign firms? From the outset it has been surrounded by controversy. The domestic industry has continually emphasised that reference prices are too low. Although many US firms have begun to show profits, the industry leaders have emphasised that unless they can continue for some time, too much should not be read into what may turn out to be a temporary advantage for American producers. The reference price system itself has proved rather shaky, and, as was to be expected, has had undesirable side-effects. For instance, the Treasury has had to lower estimates for Great Lakes freight costs, because carriers in this area were losing business to East and Gulf Coast ports.

More seriously, the basis for calculating the system was called into question. Treasury officials cast doubt on whether Japanese production costs continued to be the lowest as a result of the continued revaluation of the yen. In addition, Japanese steel was continuing to operate at 70 per cent of capacity, meaning its unit costs were higher than the 85 per cent basis used by the Treasury. Furthermore, the heavy debt-financing used by Japanese steel had finally turned on the major producers. During the period of high economic growth, the Japanese debt–equity ratio had grown to 4:1 in contrast to the American industry's ratio of 1:1. This, combined with the industry's precarious short-term liquidity ratio, meant that the companies were extremely vulnerable to a decline in foreign market access.

If Japan continued to be considered the most efficient producer, subsequent reference price quarterly adjustments might make it easier for less efficient producers to sell into the US market. In consequence, by the summer of 1978 the Treasury was considering whether to change the basis for calculating trigger prices, either by focusing on another low-cost producer or by introducing a two-tier system with a set of prices applying specifically to European steel. In August Peter Ehrenhaft, a deputy assistant secretary at the Treasury, was quoted as saying that while European producers were selling above trigger prices in the United States, many did not appear to be selling at fair value – a rather vague concept. If Treasury discussion about revision of calculations was in part a response to methodological difficulties as well as in part an effort to be seen to be responding to industry pressures, intimations that the system might be modified were bound to increase the irritation of foreign governments and the uncertainty of foreign producers. Even then, since the Administration had not committed itself to reducing imports to precise levels, but was more concerned to prevent further injury to the domestic industry through unfair pricing, a firm basis of support among American steel producers had not been forged. This was manifested in September, when steel corporations threatened to re-introduce new anti-dumping suits.

In October the Treasury announced that it was starting its first anti-dumping investigations based on information gathered under the trigger price system. But these were investigations against companies in Spain, Taiwan and Poland, which must be accounted as small exporters of steel to the United States. Their exports constituted less than 3 per cent of

US imports. While the first investigation had a symbolic and political import for the domestic industry, it raised the concern that the Treasury was trying to divert attention from the Japanese and Europeans. By December the stainless steel industry, which had earlier withdrawn complaints when the Treasury had indicated that the reference price system might be extended to specialty steels, now announced that it would press for the extension of steel curbs to cover its products too. The specialty steel industry employs about 65,000 of the 500,000 workers in the steel union. The industry was joined by the United Steelworkers in indicating that pressure would be brought to bear on the administration. In December twenty major US special steel producers backed by the United Steelworkers Union formally requested a further three-year extension of special steel import quotas until mid-1982. Thus the reference price system, which covered carbon steels mainly, was to be reinforced at the specialty steel end. This was followed by a Treasury announcement that it would investigate the complaint of Lukens Steel that carbon steel plate imported from Belgium, France, West Germany, Italy and Britain was being sold in the United States at less than fair value and below the guidance prices set by the European Community itself. The complaint, however, did not allege that the sales were below the producers' costs of production. In early 1979, the Treasury terminated the investigation with a finding that no dumping had occurred.

While the trigger price system seems to have placed a cap upon individual industry suits for relief, thereby serving a political purpose, this accomplishment is only effective in the short run. The year 1978/9 brought into play a pattern which is repeated with each quarter the reference prices are revised. Domestic steel producers protest that they lack adequate protection and insist that more be done to restrict foreign steel exports to the United States. The reference prices are revised, followed soon after by increases in domestic steel prices. At the same time, the steel industry and steelworkers' union keep up pressure with the steel lobby in Congress, the results of which are reflected in such Bills as that submitted by Senators Bayh and Heinz to give American steel products a statutory preference over imports when they compete for federal contracts. Obviously, this conflicts with one of the major goals of the United States within the MTNs of opening up government purchasing to foreign producers. Monthly statistics indicating a decline in foreign imports coupled with quarterly announcements from many domestic steel firms of profits are received by the steel industry with extremely conservative optimism. At best, then, the reference price system has defused some of the steel industry's demands for protection, and in the course of time may bring about some rationalisation without the industry being able to ask for more protection. But in the short run, attention is focused on monthly import statistics, the activity or lack thereof of the Treasury Department and quarterly reports on production and earnings. Within this framework, there are still too many opportunities for a determined and organised industry to impose economic costs on the rest of the American economy as well as threaten a new trade agreement.

The real questions require stepping beyond monthly statistics and inquiring about (1) what conditions would make further rationalisation palatable to the steel industry and the unions, (2) what mechanisms would be the most effective and (3) what should be the bases for international comparison to determine who should bear the cost of adjustment, especially in a period of economic recession and overcapacity. To introduce this subject, a few paragraphs are necessary on the competitiveness of the US industry.

The Efficiency of US Steel Firms

What arguments are relevant for determining the conditions under which imports should be allowed? The US steel industry, in part, has been the victim of its disproportionate role after 1945 as a result of the decline of production in Japan and Europe. Although the industry is not averse to referring to its historical market share, this argument refers to an atypical period. More important is whether the industry has kept pace with changing patterns of competition and production efficiency. The recent past has been filled with record financial losses, plant closures and companies close to failure. Many sections of the industry are badly in need of modernisation, and even though it is showing some quarterly profits now, the industry is not earning a sufficient return to generate the funds needed for both capital investment and anti-pollution and other environmental measures. The average age of US Steel Corporation plants is estimated at eighteen years, Kaiser Steel at seventeen, Wheeling Pittsburgh at sixteen and Bethlehem at eleven.

Some rationalisation has taken place. Bethlehem closed its large Johnston, Pennsylvania, and Lackawanna, New York, plants, after the largest corporate loss in US history. And in 1977 7·5m. tonnes of unproductive capacity were shut down. The Jones and Laughlin merger with Youngstown Sheet and Tube comes after one of the most significant examples of conglomerate mismanagement of acquisitions. In the 1960s LTV bought Jones and Laughlin – the seventh largest producers – and Lykes acquired Youngstown – the eighth largest. By 1977 both the conglomerate parents and their steel subsidiaries were running in the red and their financial structures were in a shambles.

In contrast, all increases in Japanese production until 1955 were due to modernisation of existing facilities. No new plants were built. The ten-year delay was crucial, because of the development of the basic oxygen furnace. Ninety-three per cent of current Japanese steel manufacturing capacity was built after 1955, while the corresponding figure for the United States is 32 per cent. In 1979 the BOF process accounted for 80 per cent of Japanese production and for only 62·5 per cent of US production. If the American steel industry can complain about foreign dumping and subsidy practices, in turn, the more efficient producers can point to the failure of US management to invest in new processes and plants at a time when American firms had a competitive advantage.

The Future

Although the protection offered American industry through the trigger price system has been combined with an incentive to contract, the industry is not obligated by law to take advantage of the government loan guarantee. Moreover, the other measures such as partial exemption from the Anti-trust Laws and modifications in pollution standards are not iron-clad guarantees steel firms can depend on. While the federal government has meant such proposals to be a support for the industry in a time of adversity, anti-trust exemptions and efforts to modify environmental laws could get specific producers enmeshed in the court system for years. At heart, then, the incentives to restructure are neither mandatory nor enforceable. The Executive has acceded to the industry's view on the proper relationship between government and the private sector in so far as rationalisation of capacity is concerned. While European governments have not had notable successes in trimming back the size of their steel sectors, the effort to strike a different balance with the private sector stands in contrast to American practice. The emphasis, then, in the American approach is in favour of a system of creeping reference prices, which are no guarantee that the industry will attain and maintain profit margins necessary for restructuring.

There will be some change in the tactical position of the industry if the new MTN agreement is ratified by Congress. In the future, countervailing duty suits would have to be based on a demonstration of injury. If the steel as well as other American industries can no longer hide behind the more lenient US provisions on subsidies and CDs they will turn their lobbying efforts to Congress. Consequently, a long-range solution involves not only finding internationally acceptable standards for determining what constitutes fair competition, but facilitating at least a partial restructuring of the US steel industry. However, the protectionist view of this industry is, as in other cases, a manifestation of rather deep structural problems. The nature of these problems has fundamentally transformed the nature and implication of trade conflicts between the United States and other industrialised states.

Many of the petitions for relief come from companies located in the 'declining' north-east. Thus one reason for the virulence of these petitions is an internal conflict between a 'declining' region and other sections of the United States, a conflict in which threatened corporations refuse to allow a new distribution of production either domestically or internationally. But this regional problem is all the more serious because it is closely tied to a basic reversal of the previously liberal approach of organised labour in the United States.

At the AFL/CIO annual convention in late 1977, George Meany, the president, called for a new foreign trade policy which would recognise that free trade is a 'joke and a myth', and which would regulate imports and provide sterner enforcement of laws against foreign dumping and the erosion of domestic jobs. Although this strong position was reminiscent of the Burke/Hartke Bill, by February 1978 the AFL/CIO had abandoned its advocacy of a comprehensive protectionist Trade Bill. Instead it called for a series of legislative steps to shield American workers from foreign competition and establish fair trade. Among the fourteen points it proposed were: fair trade legislation to regulate imports, presumably through quotas and other means; bilateral agreements for textile and garment-producing nations to supplement the Multi-Fibre Agreement and reduce the flow of imports into the United States; requirements that tariff-cutting accords reached in the Tokyo Round be subjected to specific congressional approval; fair labour standards tied to the acceptance of imports; repeal of tax provisions that encourage US firms to locate abroad; and improved anti-dumping procedures.

This position not only reflects unemployment rates, the trouble with the dollar and low domestic investment rates, but, even more ominously, that many basic industries have plants that are worn out or obsolete. This applies particularly to the industrial belt that stretches from New England in the north-east through Pennsylvania to the manufacturing mid-west states of Wisconsin and Illinois. This was the seat of the US industrial revolution which now has problems similar to those of the midlands in the UK. Particularly striking is that as this decline has occurred corporate managers and labour leaders have banded together to go to Washington for protection. Typical is *Compact,* the acronym for the Committee to Preserve American Color Television. Its co-chairmen are an executive from Corning Glass and an AFL/CIO official.

If one can argue that neither management nor labour in the steel industry should be able to use protectionist positions to hide poor decisions of the former and unrealistic wage demands of the latter, this is only part of a new approach to a sectoral problem. There would have to be a powerful branch of the federal government which could consistently and persistently expose industry and labour views to critical scrutiny. If this is improbable, given the degree to which groups and lobbies are able to capture parts of the government process in a pluralistic and democratic system, there is a further dimension to this issue. In the past, as a result of the prevailing market ideology, both government and the private sector were not accustomed to viewing problems in the regional and industrial terms prevalent in Western Europe. Instead, market forces were allowed to prevail, counterbalanced to some extent through competition among lobbies from different regions and competing industries. Neither business nor government has ever had to give much thought to the structure or distribution of industry in the United States, much less how it relates to the worldwide structure and distribution of specific sectors. While US industries such as steel or shipbuilding are now keenly concerned about the international distribution of industry, they still must make a giant conceptual, much less policy-oriented, step to a new perspective on the structure and distribution of domestic industries. An insistence on maintaining things as they are will not only further affect inefficiency domestically, but also affect the global economic system.

13

Responses of a Multinational Corporation to the Problem of Surplus Capacity

ANTHONY LOWE

It is difficult to generalise about the responses of the multinational corporation (MNC) to the problems of surplus capacity. One can well conceive that the responses of, say, a multinational mining corporation could be very different from those of a multinational car manufacturer, whose responses in turn could be expected to differ very much from those of a multinational petrochemicals producer. The petrochemicals industry is the concern and field of expertise, such as it is, of the present writer, and some of the subsequent discussion will be made with the petrochemicals industry in particular in mind.

The important feature of highly capital-intensive continuous-process industries such as the petrochemicals industry is that their fixed costs – mainly shift and maintenance labour – are insensitive to the level of plant occupancy. As a consequence, operation of plant at reduced throughput as one immediate response to the problem of overcapacity cannot be regarded as a solution, since the plant must still continue to carry the same financial burden of shift and maintenance labour, to say nothing of management and other general overheads, as would that plant operating at full capacity.

Before, however, discussing responses which might offer some solution to the problem of surplus capacity, one should inquire whether the response of a MNC could be expected to be different from that of the corporation operating within the national borders of a single sovereign state. After all, one of the charges sometimes made about the multinational corporation is that it has the ability to shift production from one country to another in order to take advantage of the most favourable tax or subsidy regime, or, when confronted with surplus capacity in the totality of its operations, to shut down its least profitable operation, and instead to concentrate production at its most efficient plants, wherever they may be located.

In practice, however, it is arguable that the MNC will experience greater difficulty than the purely national company in adopting this response. Certainly there have been some spectacular examples in the past decade or so of MNCs in the textile and man-made fibres industries which have, perforce, been constrained by political pressures to concentrate their operations in their *least* efficient plants in one country while shutting down more efficient, and in some cases newly constructed, ultra-efficient plants in another country.

In fact, however, multinational corporations operate in a world in which they well recognise and fully accept that they are particularly subject not only to the legal requirements but also to the political constraints of the sovereign states in which they operate. Furthermore, MNCs will generally have as an objective *long-term continuity* of operation in any country with good market prospects and a secure industrial infrastructure. They will therefore be reluctant to solve the problem of surplus capacity by closing completely operations in one country, while at the same time concentrating the remainder of their production in plants in another country, despite the *short-term relief* to cash flow problems which might be available following this course of action.

Further, within an MNC, the management (themselves salaried employees) will recognise, first, that the employees do not, and perhaps should not, be expected to bear the whole burden of hard times in situations of overcapacity; secondly, that a skilled workforce once dispersed cannot easily be reconstituted when it is desired to resume operations at a later date. This is particularly the case in a high-technology industry such as the petrochemical industry where, typically, 10 per cent of the industry's workforce are graduates, 70 per cent are skilled craftsmen, 20 per cent are classified as semi-skilled and virtually none are categorised as unskilled.

On an equally pragmatic level, shutting down a plant and laying off the staff is becoming a costly exercise for corporations, either because of the corporation's own remuneration policies or because of the need to comply with legislation regarding compensation on redundancy. In Britain, which is a relatively low-wage country with correspondingly low norms of compensation for loss of job, it can easily cost $50,000 in severance payments to a skilled craftsman, aged 50, in the petrochemical industry, with twenty years' service behind him. Fifty thousand dollars may not seem a particularly large sum in absolute terms, although it may be seen in better perspective when it is realised that the average net profit per employee in the British chemical industry in recent years has been less than $4,000 a year.

So far attention has been drawn to the view that the response to surplus capacity which Adam Smith might have recommended, and the response which the detractors of the multinational companies often allege to be the preferred course of action by the MNCs, is not a practical solution for a corporation which is making profits overall.

Clearly, however, other considerations supervene when a large MNC is not making profits overall, as illustrated recently by some companies in the car industry which face bankruptcy; closure of plants as a response to surplus capacity in these cases is not a matter of choice or judgement, but is forced upon the corporation by dire necessity.

Some of the other possible responses to the problem of surplus capacity, which have been referred to in other chapters in this volume, such as stimulation of demand in the LDCs by means of aid schemes or by massive transfer of resources, lie outside the field of potential responses by an MNC. Even though they may be very large in their own industrial context, the individual MNC is of itself unable to initiate political action of the sort that could stimulate world economic expansion.

Conversely, and unfortunately, industrial corporations, probably more so in the case of national rather than multinational corporations, are likely to have more influence in *restricting* world trade by means of appeals to their national governments or to bodies such as the European Commission for 'interim' protection in order to reduce imports, and thereby to enable operation of national plants at higher rates of occupancy during a period of surplus capacity. The MNC with, by definition, manufacturing and marketing interests in many countries is more likely than a purely national operation to see the folly of protection measures designed to enable a national industry to withstand 'unfair' competition during a period of 'temporary' overcapacity. The management of an MNC, with a more global perspective, is likely to view protection as the beginning of the slippery slope to the abyss of constricted world trade, and as a fossilisation of resources in the bedrock of past industrial history, at precisely the moment when the situation calls for the redeployment of resources in the interests both of creation of high-grade new employment and the satisfaction of the consumers' needs at prices that they can afford to pay.

Similar considerations will apply to the formation of production or market-sharing cartels, necessarily under the supervision of governments in most of the industrialised countries of the world. The objections to cartels, such as featherbedding of the least efficient producers, are well known. They have been well illustrated in the case of the European Steel Community and the Multi-Fibre Agreement. It was probably on this basis, coupled with the view that cartels represent an outstandingly undesirable interference with the market system, that the majority of European petrochemical producers rejected the tentative initiative by the European Commission to establish production and market-sharing agreements in certain hard-pressed sectors of the petrochemical industry, such as plastics, early in 1978.

What, then, can be the response of the management of the MNCs in a process industry such as the petrochemical industry to the problem of surplus capacity? Managements will, of course, flex every muscle towards the improvement of the competitivity of their companies, and hence the enlargement of market share and plant occupancy at the expense of less capable competitors. It has, however, to be recognised that while this response is logical for the individual corporation, in total industry terms it represents no more than the transfer of the problem of surplus capacity, not its solution.

To some extent, within the political constraints discussed earlier and in line with its own generally self-imposed view of its obligations to its employees as well as to its shareholders, the MNC will probably attempt to rationalise production as between its manufacturing facilities; in practical terms, the room for manoeuvre in this direction is likely to be limited.

In the final analysis, however, these measures are likely to amount to no more than tapping the barometer rather than changing the weather. Many managements will recognise that there is very little that they can do to respond to the root causes of the problem of surplus capacity during a period of worldwide economic contraction (or, to be more precise, in a world that has become accustomed to high growth expectations, during a period of very low growth).

The primary responses of many managements of MNCs, therefore, is likely to be one of shelving plans for future capital expenditure, of gritting teeth and, like fishermen's wives on the night of the storm, watching for the dawn of economic recovery, and praying that they will not be widowed before the warm sun of industrial prosperity finally returns.

Part Five: Policy Options

14

American Views and Choices

WILLIAM DIEBOLD, Jr

'The management of surplus capacity' does not describe the complex of problems that most Americans think they are facing at the end of the 1970s and the beginning of the 1980s. Even the *avant-garde* of industrial policy does not think in these terms. If the term 'excess capacity' is heard at all, it refers to specific cases (and not too many of them) and is not a rather general description of the situation, as often seems to be the case in Europe. Naturally, Americans are not blind to the fact that in recession there is excess capacity in the economy but this does not greatly influence such discussion as there is about future industrial policy. The difference does not seem to be just a matter of words; I can find no American terminology into which the European preoccupation with surplus capacity can be translated.

Part of the explanation may lie in the past. Americans have been what one historian called a 'people of plenty'. The ideals of liberty and equality, he pointed out, instead of clashing with one another, became 'almost synonymous . . . meaning "freedom to grasp opportunity" '. To make that possible, it was necessary to remove 'certain negative impediments to success, and then our positive access to a larger measure of abundance permits fulfilment of the success promise' (Potter, 1954, pp. 92–3). To have excess land was good, not bad. To restrain a person from adding to the economic capacity of the country was hardly an issue. The 'excess' population of Europe became the relatively scarce labour supply of the United States.

Monopoly and the restriction of production and sales associated with it have always been highly unpopular in the United States. At first monopolies were privileges created by the British Crown; then they were creations of native industrialists and financiers. The Anti-trust Laws aimed to prevent the concentration of power and promote competition but to do that they had to make it easier for new producers to enter a market and for all to add to capacity. There was a better chance of keeping people from cornering a market or fixing prices if the supply was large rather than small. National expansion and the satisfaction of demand required mass production and products that were cheap and plentiful rather than dear and scarce. Hand-wrought goods might have a snob value but 'machine-made goods . . . are a more perfect product – show a more perfect adaption of means to end'. It was Thorstein Veblen who said that, not Henry Ford (Veblen, 1899, p. 159). It would be an exaggeration to say that it was the national purpose of the United States to create excess capacity but there does seem to be a case for believing that the American experience strongly supports expansion not contraction. Anyone who argues that the trouble with the economy is that productive capacity is too large is likely to be regarded with some suspicion, even if he can show that he is not trying to serve his own interests by raising prices.

Naturally, the Great Depression challenged the older attitude. The American economic system seemed to have broken down; maybe being geared to abundance was part of the trouble. There was no denying that excess capacity was a dominant depressing fact. Some advocates of planning spoke as if the main reason for it was to keep businessmen from producing surpluses and throwing them on the market. The government should work out the real needs of the country and set a ceiling on output. Businessmen said the problem was low prices and excessive competition. They were divided as to what should be done but usually hoped the government would let them work things out rather than trying to take control itself. They were proud of what Americans had done for the technical rationalisation of industry but when they looked at 'economic rationalisation, in the sense in which it is understood abroad' their tone became wistful. 'With legal sanctions, rather than hindrance, it has created organs of control which for better or worse direct the destinies of great industries' (National Industrial Conference Board, 1931, p. vi). The industry codes worked out under the National Industrial Recovery Act reflected these new and somewhat conflicting forces. Official rules aimed at limiting competition and raising prices were often largely written by trade associations. The coalminers wanted limits on production but the Bituminous Coal Conservation Act of 1935 reflected the operators' preference for relying on price and marketing arrangements. In agriculture highly visible surpluses were simply destroyed and the prospect of future excess was throttled by limits on output. To deal with the excess supply of labour, unions in a number of industries supported 'spread the work' movements on the principle that it was better to have more people working shorter hours than fewer working full-time.

This attack on excess capacity did not last very long. The NRA was declared unconstitutional. There was not very much planning. Remunerative farm prices produced surpluses and although Henry Wallace later was accused of unrealistic expansionism when he spoke of 60 million postwar jobs he never entirely lived down the folk-memory that it was he who ordered the wholesale slaughter of little pigs. Restrictions on production continued to be a feature of American agriculture but did not succeed in preventing surpluses. Even so there has always been an underlying uneasiness in America about paying people not to produce. Partly because there were no restrictions on production, the price and marketing arrangements in bituminous coal were never very successful and the biggest contribution to the industry's problems came through collective bargaining – an arrangement which enhanced job stability and imposed financial benefits for the United Mine Workers in return for their acceptance of extensive mechanisation.

By the late 1930s there was a new kind of concern about excess capacity, especially in intellectual circles. This was the stagnation theory championed especially by Alvin Hansen, the leading American Keynesian. The analysis was that the United States had become a mature economy which could no longer grow as rapidly as in the past; there would be fewer opportunities for new investment and that in itself would contribute to slower growth. By implication, excess capacity would be a problem – but only temporarily, until existing plant contracted to the new levels of demand. There was an adjustment problem which could be solved but might give trouble later on. It was all rather like the sort of talk often heard at the OECD today. Even so, the dominant purpose of the Temporary National Economic Committee (TNEC) which undertook a massive inquiry ending in 1941 was to uncover restraints on competition that might be holding up prices and preventing the full use of resources.

The stagnation theory did not last any longer than the stagnation. The war brought expansion and the capacity question quickly became the opposite one of breaking bottlenecks and learning to do things more quickly so as to increase productive capacity ahead of demand.

At the end of the war the country was naturally left with surplus capacity in arms production and a number of other items. The artificial rubber industry was accorded a transitional period after which it had to process the natural product, which it did successfully. The aluminium expansion had been so handled as to increase and encourage postwar competition. The Committee for Economic Development founded in 1942 did much to assure a high level of postwar employment by preparing business for a good bit of the transition. Some of the alarmist talk about excess capacity – by Henry Wallace, for instance – turned out to be false. The feared repetition of the post-First World War recession did not take place (Wallace, 1946). Loans to allies and expenditures in the occupied territories helped keep up exports (but the need for them to maintain full use of capacity was exaggerated by businessmen and led to some misunderstandings in Moscow as well as Washington). By the time of the Marshall Plan there were some significant shortages. Only agriculture continued to be treated as if it presented a permanent, structural problem of excess capacity.

The American bias against restriction – if that is what it is – applies to the rest of the world. Given what was being done in American farm policy, it was not surprising that there was an effort to work out international commodity agreements for some products. The *mot* in the State Department in the late 1940s was that 'a commodity agreement is a cartel approved by the Department of Agriculture'. While the proposed chapter of the ITO allowed for such agreements, its aim was to insure that consumers had a share in running them and that they were not too restrictive. 'Cartels' have always been in bad odour in the United States, whether the target was the British and Dutch raw materials arrangements fought by Herbert Hoover when he was Secretary of Commerce or the German-dominated international business arrangements associated with the spread of Nazism (especially I. G. Farben, not a cartel). Thus, OPEC confirms the common American verdict that cartels are alien and undesirable. Suspicion almost certainly outweighs approval in the reactions of most Americans to the restrictive arrangements now being discussed or established in Europe for shipbuilding, the petrochemicals industry and steel manufacture.

All this does not mean that concerns about excess capacity are totally absent in the United States. After all, business investments are much affected by views of the matter (and sometimes irrationally when a depressed current market affects action that should be based on the long-run need for raw materials). The percentage use of capacity is recognised as a key factor in profitability and costs (though a badly measured one). It even finds a place in the calculation of Japanese costs for the trigger price scheme in steel. There is more tolerance of international shipping conferences than of other forms of restriction. Control of capacity is part of the aim of many international regimes supported by the United States, notably in aviation and trucking; the current popularity of de-regulation stems largely from belief in the virtues of price competition but there is a direct connection with easier entry of new competition and the capacity of the industry. The effect of changes in defence spending in creating excess capacity in industries and firms is recognised and, to a degree, compensated for by policy measures. In the 1950s and 1960s the Texas Railroad Commission's pre-rationing of oil production affected other states as well, while import quotas insured that domestic oil would be used at a faster rate than otherwise. Nowadays though the objective of energy policy – however falteringly pursued – is to enlarge the domestic production of capacity. There is also a somewhat diffused belief that in other policies, too, the government will have to be concerned in the coming decades with 'the supply side' of the economy – but more to expand than to contract capacity.

Perhaps the historical elements are not as important as recent experience in explaining why Americans are not as preoccupied as

Europeans with excess capacity. The United States grew more rapidly than Europe after the recession of the mid-1970s; it was used to a lower rate of growth than Europe and Japan in the 1950s and 1960s; it lives with a rate of unemployment which (even after allowing for statistical differences) is far higher than is acceptable in Europe (not that it should). Whatever the explanation, I do not find in the United States the pessimism about the economic future that is so pervasive in Europe. and that seems to underlie the preoccupation with excess capacity. Perhaps, if the recession of 1979–80 proves severe, there will be significant shifts in American attitudes. Without that eventuality, however – and regardless of how much influence should be ascribed to the historical factors sketched – it is hard to believe that the American approach to issues of structural change will give prime consideration to the management of surplus capacity, international or national.

The Trade Policy Alternative

One possible rejoinder to this last contention might well be the fact that there is substantially no appreciation of a problem of surplus capacity and therefore no discussion of policies for structural change in the United States, but this does not necessarily mean that the problem does not exist. When they overcome their lag and become aware of the problems facing them, it could be argued, the Americans will come to see these things in much the same terms as the Europeans. That American thinking does lag in these matters is clear (but partly because it still takes expansion as the norm and expects it to come about largely through private initiative not state intervention). That a change is taking place and is likely to continue will be argued below. But it does not follow logically that the emphasis will then shift to excess capacity. The burden of proof is on those who predict a reversal of the historical bias.

In the one sector besides energy in which American discussion begins to adumbrate something like a true industrial policy – that is, steel – a significant difference between American and European measures is that there is an almost complete absence of discussion about the desirable size of the US steel industry in the future. The emphasis is all on price, investment, efficiency and fair competition – as if competition were going to be allowed to determine how much steel the United States produced in the future. Perhaps it is, but if imports rise that is taken as a sign that something is wrong with the trigger price system and other measures to ensure fair competition and that consequently obstacles are being put in the way of the other goals since prices, investment and efficiency are linked in a direct chain. At least that is how the industry seems to argue and as yet (this is being written in October 1979) there is no serious challenge to the view from the government or the rest of

American business. This does not necessarily mean that maintaining something like 85 per cent self-sufficiency will in fact become public policy, but it is the nearest thing to a target yet in sight.

The steel example points to a second explanation of why the United States differs from Europe in not being unduly concerned about excess capacity: the United States deals with the issue by its trade policies – it is able to avoid excess capacity at home by keeping it abroad. This argument is far more plausible than the first and there is more evidence to support it. The 'people of plenty' lived behind high industrial tariffs; when support measures raised agricultural costs, farmers, too, were given protection and exports were subsidised. It follows, if you take this line of argument, that where world excess capacity is greatest US import restraints will be strongest, and that view can certainly be supported by looking at textiles, clothing, shoes and, to a degree, chemicals as well as steel. (Whether electronics should be seen in the light of global capacity or the rapid shifting of comparative advantage is a separate matter.) To the extent that other countries bring a halt to excess capacity, the United States does not need to raise import barriers; to the extent that the others fail to do this, or even push products toward the American market, they will meet resistance.

There is some basis for this argument but it needs to be put in a slightly different light. The United States is not alone in its response; other industrial countries do exactly the same thing. All have recognised, however, that they are not free agents in these matters. The obverse of reciprocity is retaliation and to beggar your neighbour may reduce your own estate. The use of import barriers to sustain national industrial policy measures or to keep out foreign 'surpluses' comes to very much the same thing. The use of non-tariff barriers for these purposes is now putting so great a strain on co-operation that it is jeopardising past accomplishments in international trade liberalisation and for this reason should be given priority attention by Europe and Japan as well as the United States (see Diebold, 1979). There is no evidence that the United States is more protectionist than the European Community and Japan. (A contrary argument could be made, but there is no room here to present all the evidence and without it words remain words. Such data as there are are not likely to be conclusive.) What is more pertinent is to ask whether, quite apart from the surplus capacity question, trade policy issues may lead the United States to a more explicit focus on industrial policy questions. There are at least half a dozen quite concrete ways in which this seems likely to happen.

Though no one could be entirely sure at the time, the passage of the Trade Agreements Act in 1934 was a turning point in the history of American trade policy. Unlike all attempts to lower tariffs in the previous 145 years, it did not peter out to be replaced by higher rates of duties. GATT is, in a way, the internationalisation of that aim and method. Although there have been several occasions when the survival of this American policy was in doubt, it has each time come through in recognisable – and sometimes strengthened – form. While a forty-five year record does not guarantee continuation, it would seem to be more than a string of happenstances. Therefore it is reasonable to ask what the United States policy will have to be if it wishes to continue to bring about at least some further liberalisation of international trade.

'Use the MTN' is one obvious answer, because otherwise the inability of the GATT system to deal with non-tariff barriers would undermine the value of past tariff reductions and lead to an increasing disregard of rules. To use the MTN codes, notably those on subsidies and government procurement, countries will have to negotiate around some of their major industrial policy instruments and therefore the reasons for their use. Whether the emphasis is on removing specific barriers or establishing standards of 'fair trade' in various fields, industrial policy issues will be on the international agenda. Nothing in this process requires the United States either to adopt a comprehensive industrial policy or to take specific partial measures. It will, however, have to examine its own practices when they are challenged by foreigners in ways that will raise questions concerning industrial structure. And when it is challenging the practices of others with the aim of making them open their markets to its exports, the results – successes, failures, compromises – will begin to define, in trade policy terms, acceptable international dimensions of national industrial policies. It would be an odd world in which American businessmen, labour unions and perhaps consumers did not then ask their government to do for them what was permitted for others. Whether that would be sensible or not cannot be determined without the kind of structural thinking that has sometimes been an element in past trade policy, but usually not.

Sometimes the result may not be an agreement on the rules of fair trade, or a total failure to agree, but some kind of special arrangement that will appear to balance the interests of a number of countries in a particular sector – as in steel, textiles and the new civil aviation agreement. To make sense of this, Americans will again have to question both the long-term structure of their economy and the devices that may produce the results they want. Again there will be domestic pressures to take certain kinds of action to make the new arrangements, whatever they are, work to American advantage. Textiles and steel will presumably not be the last hard cases. To deal with them, three courses of action are possible: orderly marketing agreements imposed by the main consumers; unilateral action under a version of GATT rules on safeguards that permits self-determination of restraints; or ways of making settlements involving a number of interested countries (including NICs as well as older industrial centres), which may be safeguards employing international surveillance or new kinds of understandings.

Not just trade policy measures but subsidies to investment will come into question. The widespread practice of inducing foreign investment by tax and other incentives and fostering exports is increasingly seen as a trade distortion that might be challenged through the MTN. Thus, whether through that channel, or by more direct bilateral confrontations between home and host government, yet another industrial policy question will be forced on the Americans. As American states also engage in the solicitation of foreign investment, this kind of negotiation will become a two-way street. It is also possible – though at the moment it does not seem too likely – that the increase in foreign investment in the United States will generate reactions that will pose international issues and raise domestic questions that can only be dealt with sensibly against a background of some idea of what the future structure of the American economy ought to be.

Even if the climate for further trade liberalisation proves to be better than now seems likely, it is doubtful if the United States can go along as before. From 1934 to 1962 the professed policy of the United States was to reduce import barriers while avoiding injury to domestic industry by selective tariff reduction. That possibility disappeared when the Trade Expansion Act of 1962 provided for across-the-board tariff cuts. The new approach was a programme for adjustment assistance to industries (and especially workers) affected by imports. But the machinery did not work and only by the early 1970s could much be done in this field. The Trade Act of 1974 provided more practicable arrangements and further steps may be taken to increase the possibilities of taking effective adjustment measures. This is no assurance that trade liberalisation will take place in difficult sectors, especially when alternative jobs and activities are not obviously in sight. However, without a better adjustment mechanism than has existed in the past there can hardly be any further liberalisation. To make sense of adjustment it is necessary to make a decision both about the future of the industry being 'adjusted' and, usually, about the alternative activities being encouraged to take its place when it is contracted. Here the question of 'excess capacity', at home or abroad, comes very centrally into the picture.

International Competitiveness

Behind decisions on trade policy lie judgements about the ability of an economy to compete with the rest of the world – or the part of it that matters most. Whether the focus is on imports or exports, the issue is crucial. Americans know that but are far from clear what they have to do about it. They are used to having the issue take care of itself – usually, they thought, because their system favoured capital-intensive methods or provided other technological advantages that enabled it to overcome higher labour costs, more leisure, lower investment rates and various other disabilities. At the turn of the decade there was concern whether the American ability to compete had dwindled to the areas of agriculture, coal and a narrowing band of high-technology industries. The devaluation of the dollar seemed to indicate that simpler and more classical explanations were sufficient. Then, by the late 1970s, the spectre of the inability to compete was back once more. The exchange-rate solution might have worked again, but no one seemed willing to see the dollar go low enough to try. A cut in American inflation below that of some other countries would have helped, but the possibility was elusive. Export promotion by credit, trade fairs, salesmanship, tax relief, government help to business, and so on, could no doubt contribute something, but not a great deal if there were not enough American products that were better than, cheaper than, or completely different from what others had to offer.

Thus one more set of pressures has been generated that forces Americans at least to look at industrial policy measures, if not to indulge in them. But where should the emphasis be put? Productivity ranks high; protection and subsidy have to be limited to transitional periods or there will be no real gains. Policy has to be directed not only at industries that are themselves significant exporters but at their suppliers and all who affect their costs. Thus export promotion comes to have implications for the whole economy, including imports, and in principle could lead to an industrial policy which puts a high value on efficiency.

A likely starting point will be a focus on productivity and the government's role in stimulating research and development. Americans have usually resisted foreign interpretations of space, the moon, defence, and so on, as major elements of industrial policy because of the resulting stimulus to technological innovation, the government financing of R & D, and the implicit subsidy to private exploitation resulting from the government's absorption of development costs. However, an indirect acknowledgement of the validity of this foreign view might be read into the increasing American agitation for more government spending on R & D stimulated by worry over productivity and competitiveness. The correct methods and proper targets are much in dispute. Should the government itself spend more on R & D or simply encourage private business to do so? (It would amount to a subsidy since full tax write-offs for such expenditures already exist.) What should the balance be between, for example, Lord Rothschild's preference for giving money to those who agree to work on specific problems and the more traditional broader support of scientists? One big project or many small ones? Academic, business or government laboratories? The emphasis on basic or applied research? All the familiar alternatives have to be considered. And then questions will arise about the disposition of technology that is produced with government financial help. Should it be available to all who pay the licence fee or ought companies that played a part have exclusive proprietary rights for a time? Are patents and knowhow to be sold abroad as freely as at home or does there have to be some kind of showing as to the effect of technology exports on jobs, exports of goods, the position of American firms in foreign markets and matters of that sort (not to mention security)? It is but a step to further questions about American participation – public or private – in international arrangements for research, development and the combined production of expensive technology.

A comparable course can be traced in other fields. If new technology means fewer jobs for the same output, what arrangements will permit its orderly introduction without throwing people out of work – or at least giving them a cushion to land on? There are some good examples of how this can be done and some very bad ones. Related questions apply to how a firm treats its American employees when it shifts operations abroad. Little or nothing remains of the sweeping approach of the Burke–Hartke Bill that would have made it difficult for any company to 'export jobs', but if too many companies are too callous about the matter there may well be a new reaction. It should not be too hard, through prudent management, collective bargaining and possibly the extension of the concept of federal adjustment assistance to mitigate this kind of problem. The United States is certainly not about to adopt a variant of Japanese lifetime employment (though IBM has something like that) and is unlikely to go as far as some European countries in making layoffs almost prohibitively costly, but unless it does something to combine job and income security with increased flexibility in the use of labour, it is unlikely to overcome its lack of competitiveness. The structure of the labour supply is itself a part of the American problem, with high unemployment among young people and blacks persisting even though shortages of skilled labour appear whenever the economy hits a certain level of activity. The American version of Europe's foreign workers problem is an internal one that includes Puerto Rican and continental migration and black urban concentrations as well. Thus adjustment through immigration policy is limited and the question arises whether the protection of low-productivity jobs contributes to the national economic and social welfare if they are the only jobs these workers can do.

In quite a different field – Anti-trust Law – international competitiveness and concepts of industrial policy cast some new light on old debates. But the picture is still very disorderly. Law is law but competition, restraint of trade, monopolistic practices and the like are economic and behavioural facts whose existence and meaning depend in part on circumstances. This is recognised in the way the Department of Justice, prosecuting attorneys, defendants, judges and sometimes juries act; they make judgements about markets, acquisition, divestiture, size, intentions, effects, and the like, in terms of the situation presented to them and the precedents relevant to a particular part of the law. Inevitably there are discrepancies in concept, standards and results. An industrial policy that provided guidelines may be too disturbing a thought to have much of a future but it is hardly unreasonable to suggest that some consistent framework would be desirable. That may not be enough if, for example, the size that is necessary for competition on a global scale would spell dominance of the domestic market. But such a size suggests a global oligopoly which would bring foreign competition into the American market. In other sectors it could well be argued that only strong competition at home would ensure the ability of American firms to compete successfully abroad. Whatever the merits of any of these arguments, the point is that the arguments are not being made nor the debate conducted – and it would be more sensible if they were.

Productivity, technology, labour, anti-trust – it is obvious that American attention to such matters cannot be confined to their bearing on international competition. Foreign trade is about twice as large in relation to the GNP of the United States as it was a decade or two ago and the economy is being internationalised in other ways as well. Still, it is the overall performance of the economy – and especially its non-performance – that should be the focus of policy. One can no longer treat the international results as by-products, as was often done in the past when it was said that if the United States kept its house in order, the balance of payments, exports and many other things would take care of themselves. They will not, but they cannot be taken care of unless something is done about the economy as a whole. If the past were a reliable guide, one might surmise that Americans were more likely to think hard about what was wrong with their economy and do uncomfortable things to correct it because of what they saw at home rather than because they were told their behaviour was causing trouble to the rest of the world. They are not alone in that characteristic as the OECD orientations recognise when they tell each country that it should adapt to structural change abroad in its own interest and in order to make better use of its own resources, not in order to be a better international citizen. Still, as the last few paragraphs have shown (and more cases could be added), there is a string of stimuli emanating from worries about international competitiveness and these may be easier to identify than the manifestations of the same troubles diffused through the economy.

Whichever stimulus brings action, a key question is whether the response will emphasise the need to adapt to structural change – that is, make for more efficiency – or whether it will be to try to find a way to keep alive certain industries that cannot meet the test of international competition – agriculture for many years, textiles for a long time, now perhaps steel. Every country has similar cases and therefore faces these questions.

(1)   How can these other purposes be served at the least cost, whether

the emphasis is on jobs, stability, security of supply, or whatever? If being a great power means providing at least 80 per cent or so of one's own steel, how is the sheltered industry to be kept efficient? If it is not, the steel-using industries will also be non-competitive.

(2)   How much cumulative burden from such 'special cases' can the economy bear if it is also to serve other needs of the electorate and compete efficiently abroad? Waste and inefficiencies that could be borne without too much trouble when the going was good, and everyone was richer each year than the year before, become a serious burden when growth slows, unemployment stays high and the main expectation is of more inflation.

(3)   How are these national choices to be accommodated internationally? Other countries will strike their own balance. No one can expect to get all his wishes fulfilled, to be allowed to compete in some fields while keeping other countries from competing in different fields. There will have to be some compromises – matching the choices of one with the different choices of other countries. Without accommodation there will be not only friction but a further accumulation of inefficiencies in the international system as a whole.

There are not too many Americans thinking along these lines at present. But it seems likely that it is in these national and domestic terms that some important choices in industrial policy will present themselves, rather than in terms of an international problem of the managing of surplus capacity. Whether you think that is good or bad depends on what you think the real problems are.

References: Chapter 14

Diebold, W., Jr, (1979), *Industrial Policy as an International Issue* (New York: McGraw-Hill).
National Industrial Conference Board (1931).
Potter, D.M. (1954), *People of Plenty* (Chicago: University of Chicago Press).
Veblen, T. (1899), *The Theory of the Leisure Class* (London: Allen & Unwin).
Wallace, H. (1946), *Sixty Million Jobs* (London: Heinemann).

15

Prospects for the 1980s
– a Japanese View

TADASHI NAKAMAE

This chapter begins by making five points.

The first is that the United States is not a declining economic power plagued by a secular fall in productivity. This widely held view seems to be supported by the long-term downward trend of total US output figures (GNP) divided by the number employed. But figures for the manufacturing sector of the American economy tell a different story. While productivity in the US economy as a whole at the beginning of 1979 was little changed from its 1973 level, productivity in the manufacturing sector increased by over 10 per cent. This increase is important because the manufacturing sector is the producer of real wealth in modern industrial societies and because it is basically the only internationally competitive sector. And it directly challenges the currently popular belief that America is a declining world economic force and supports the view that in the 1980s American goods will become increasingly more competitive in international markets.

The second point concerns a significant paradox in Japanese inflation statistics for the 1960s. The explanation for this paradox is a further illustration of the point made in the previous example: the manufacturing sector is not only far more capable of increasing productivity than the other sectors of the economy but is also the basis of a nation's real wealth.

During the 1960s Japanese inflation was characterised by two different and anomalous trends. The consumer price index (CPI) rose at the average annual rate of 7 per cent while the wholesale price index (WPI) rose at an annual rate of 1 per cent. This relationship looks even more peculiar since the Japanese CPI was the highest among the industrial nations and its WPI was the lowest. The gap between the two rates of inflation can be explained as follows. In the 1960s Japanese economic growth was almost totally based on capital investment. Correspondingly, due to this increase in capital formation, productivity in the manufacturing sector of the economy increased at an annual rate of over 10 per cent. During this period manufacturing industry could afford to pay annual wage increases of more than 10 per cent without causing an increase in industrial prices (which conceptually correspond to the WPI).

However, while wage increases in manufacturing reflect industry's ability to pay through increased productivity, wage increases in other sectors depend rather more on the political and social influence of the sector's workers than on the ability of that sector to pay those increases. Japanese workers employed by the service sectors sought and received wage increases in the 1960s comparable to those achieved in the manufacturing sector. However, and this point must be emphasised, the service sector in Japan during the 1960s did not, and as a rule does not, experience the same increases in productivity which characterise the manufacturing sector. The result in Japan during the 1960s was a rate of consumer-price inflation totally out of line with wholesale-price rises.

The next two points concern the comparative record of the industrial countries in the years after 1973, and deal with the problems of inflation and unemployment in those years. First some misapprehensions must be corrected. One is that Japan suffered only mild unemployment, because official statistics showed only a modest rise in the unemployment rate. However, closer examination of the statistics shows that employment in the manufacturing sector – the sector in the economy which generates real wealth – experienced a 12 per cent drop over the six-year period. This decline was the most serious among industrial countries.

The second misapprehension is that growth rates for the industrialised countries have slowed down sharply since 1973. This is certainly true for Europe and perhaps for Japan, but it is not true for the United States. The real growth of non-residential fixed investment – an important indicator for the future dynamism and productivity of the manufacturing sector – has increased at a constant and steady pace. As Table 15.1 shows, the ratio of non-residential investment to GNP in America has made a steady recovery while the European ratios have been very sluggish. Only Japan has started to recover since 1978.

Table 15.1   *The ratio of private non-residential investment to GNP (percentages)*

	73	75	76	77	78	79[a]
Japan	18·9	14·2	13·4	13·5	13·1	15·2
Germany	14·8	12·7	11·4	11·7	11·9	12·5
France	12·9	9·6	10·1	9·4	9·0	8·9
USA	10·6	9·7	9·5	10·1	10·4	10·7
UK	9·3	9·2	9·0	10·0	10·5	10·6
Italy	9·0	9·3	9·0	9·3	9·2	9·7

[a]Estimate.
Source: OECD, *Economic Outlook, 1979* (Paris: OECD, 1979).

A third misapprehension is that all the industrial countries have suffered throughout the 1970s from stagflation – and are still suffering from it. The neologism, stagflation, describes the stagnation of the economy simultaneous with inflation. More precisely defined, it is a situation marked by declining profitability with rising prices. By contrast, classic inflation is accompanied by increasing profitability. During stagflation the equity market is very weak while during classic inflation the equity market performs very well. Recently, the performance of Wall Street and the profitability of American corporations since 1975 suggests that the United States is experiencing a period of business profitability, reflected in a marked improvement in the equity market. This surely suggests that the nature of inflation in America has changed from stagflation to classic inflation. Too often academic economists in the past have regarded the performance of the equity market as peripheral to the performance of the economy. They tended to ignore the market because they did not understand how it worked. But equity markets remain the most important indicator of the future of the economy.

These three points must surely affect our analysis of how, since 1973, the industrialised countries of the world have faced the problem of balancing a high rate of employment with a low rate of inflation. They have done so by using entirely different economic policies. To some extent the choice between which goal to pursue was determined by historical memories.

In Britain, which suffered from very serious unemployment problems in the 1930s, the government desperately tried to achieve a high employment rate, while in Germany, which suffered from very high inflation during the 1920s and 1930s, policy-makers tried very hard to maintain price stability. But the other deciding factor seemed to be the strength or weakness of the currency.

Basically the adjustment processes of the industrial countries fell into two categories, strong and weak, with the United States occupying a position and pursuing an adjustment policy somewhat elusive of this precise classification. The strong countries, for example, Germany, Switzerland and the Netherlands, were generally characterised by a surplus in their balance of payments, a low inflation rate, an increase in the value of their currency since 1973 and a general decline in both production and employment since 1973. Conversely, the weak industrial countries' performance post-1973 has been a mirror image characterised by balance-of-payments deficits, a high inflation rate, a decline in the value of their currencies and attempts at increasing or at least maintaining pre-1973 employment levels. The weak countries pursued a strategy of 'high employment' while the strong countries pursued a strategy of 'low inflation'.

Theoretically speaking, under the sluggish economic conditions that

Table 15.2 The pattern of inflation

Wholesale prices (% increase over the preceding year)

	1973	1974	1975	1976	1977	1978	1979
Switzerland	10.7	16.2	−2.3	−0.7	−0.8	3.8	3.0
West Germany	6.6	13.4	4.7	3.9	1.5	2.6	1.1
Netherlands	7.3	9.3	7.0	6.5	6.1	4.1	4.2
Japan	15.9	31.3	3.0	5.5	0.1	3.8	3.5
UK	7.3	23.4	24.1	16.4	17.8	8.3	13.4
Italy	17.0	40.7	8.6	22.9	14.3	12.1	14.8
France	14.7	29.1	−6.7	7.4	2.1	9.1	10.7
USA	13.1	18.9	9.2	4.7	6.0	7.5	11.3

Consumer price index (% increase over the preceding year)

	1973	1974	1975	1976	1977	1978	1979
Switzerland	8.7	9.8	6.7	1.7	1.6	−0.1	2.0
West Germany	6.9	7.0	6.0	4.5	3.8	1.3	5.0
Netherlands	8.0	9.7	10.2	8.8	5.4	1.7	3.2
Japan	11.7	22.7	12.1	9.6	7.6	−2.5	7.3
UK	9.1	16.0	24.3	16.6	15.0	9.1	12.2
Italy	10.8	19.1	17.0	16.8	16.6	8.4	15.5
France	7.3	13.7	11.8	9.2	9.5	4.3	13.3
USA	6.2	11.0	9.1	5.8	6.5	7.8	12.5

Source: International Financial Statistics (IMF).

Table 15.3   *Employment in the manufacturing sector (1973 = 100)*

	1975	1976	1977
Switzerland	90·7	84·3	84·5
West Germany	90·8	88·6	88·8
Netherlands	95·7	91·4	90·3
Japan	94·3	91·7	89·2
UK	95·7	93·1	94·9
Italy	104·2	104·5	97·6
France	98·2	971·1	96·6
USA	91·4	94·5	98·0

Source: OECD, *Economic Outlook, 1978* (Paris: OECD, 1978).

have characterised the world since 1973, productivity can best be increased, wage costs kept down and international competitiveness maintained or improved by shedding labour. The result should be export expansion and, in the long run, a return to full employment. However, it proved far easier for Switzerland and West Germany with a high percentage of foreign workers in the labour force to do this. Foreign workers often worked on short-term contracts and enjoyed very little political or social power in their host countries. By contrast, the Italian government had to cope with Italian workers returning home from Germany, Switzerland and elsewhere and had no foreign workers to send home. Moreover, the domestic political situation in Italy was such that the cutbacks in employment, which the successful pursuit of a low inflation strategy would have entailed, were quite unacceptable to already restive and militantly led trade unions. To a lesser extent both the UK and France, because of the political unpopularity of high unemployment, found themselves committed to the same high employment policies as Italy.

But hanging on to workers in times of sluggish demand and low investment only lowers international competitiveness – a decline clearly reflected in the balance-of-payments deficits of the UK, France and Italy. However, the most damaging result of this commitment to high employment policies has been a high inflation rate. High and persistent inflation rates cannot for long remain politically tenable and the weaker economies after 1975 were forced to adopt similar low inflation policies to the stronger economies. By 1977–8 their inflation rate and balance-of-payments situation had improved but only at the cost of a worsening employment situation.

Thus the policies of the 'low inflation' countries were forced on the 'high employment' countries because over time a low inflation policy, due to its greater competitiveness, tends to displace the products of high employment countries in both foreign and domestic markets. Therefore a high employment country would not be able to maintain its level of employment because a low inflation country would be capturing its markets. Thus in the conflict between low inflation countries and high employment countries, in an open world economy, it seems that the low inflation countries will prevail. But the victory of low inflation countries was achieved only because high employment countries by and large stuck by international trade rules and did not resort to such protectionist measures as import quotas, voluntary export restrictions, or large currency depreciations. And in part it was done by maintaining their international competitiveness (at least in the short term) by reducing employment in their manufacturing sectors.

The United States, however, has been unique in being able to persist with high employment policies since 1975 by ignoring international trade rules. Mainly through dollar devaluations, the United States was able, first, to barricade its economy against competition from low inflation countries and, secondly, to improve its export competitiveness and profitability – thus providing the basis for new investment in the manufacturing industry. The significance of America's increase in capital investment is shown by the narrowing gap between what the United States and the other main industrial countries devoted to investment. For example, the difference between Japan and the United States narrowed from over 8 per cent in 1973 to just over 4 per cent in 1979 and with Germany from over 4 per cent in 1973 to under 2 per cent in 1979. This makes the United States the only economy which has literally invested in the future. Therefore the ground for future American exports has already been prepared, and the United States has, in fact, wrested a long-term advantage for the next phase of world economic growth.

Meanwhile, the low inflation countries by their victory over the high employment countries have succeeded in depressing profitability and manufacturing investment throughout Europe. The future of European industry, when faced with the resurgence of American manufacturing power, looks very bleak. By devaluing the US dollar and by cheapening the international price of labour, the profitability of US industry has been stimulated. The higher profitability of US industry has led to increased manufacturing investment. This automatically strengthens its international competitiveness and increases its share of exports. In Europe, and Japan, many industries are already worried about the prospect of very serious future competition from US manufacturers.

America's relatively smaller dependence on imports combined with the dollar's status as a reserve currency lessened and delayed the inflationary effects of a high employment policy; whereas when the 'weak currency' European countries pursued their high employment policies, the financial side of their economies deteriorated sufficiently to challenge the social and political structure of the state. A declining currency pushed up imported inflation, further depressing their currency in a vicious downward spiral.

One major effect of a change in the exchange rate is a change in the international price of labour. Therefore if the dollar declines, American wage costs compared to the international market decline, thus increasing the profitability of US industries. If the profitability of industry increases, the industry has the incentive and ability to increase capital investment. The above-mentioned process explains the increase in American capital investment under a high employment policy and a weakening dollar. But this combination constitutes a long-term cure for the basic economic problems of the United States (the dollar's weakness and high inflation) — the improvement in productivity by increasing capital investment. For, though in the short term an increase in capital investment creates more inflation, in the long term the problem of competitiveness is solved. This is the explicit American policy as stated repeatedly by William Miller when he was chairman of the Fed.

The result, at any rate, has been a dramatic improvement in the competitiveness of American industry. From mid-1974 to the end of 1977, American export volume was essentially steady, but from the beginning of 1978 there was a rise in export volume that was steep and unquestionable, suggesting that the benefits of the capital investment programme initiated in 1975 had started to take effect in world markets. Further evidence can be found in the greater confidence of American foreign economic policy since 1977. Up to then, American trade policy towards Japan was designed to restrict Japanese exports into the US market. But since 1978 American trade strategy has gradually changed its emphasis to the point where America is now pushing for Japan to open its market to American exports rather than restricting the entry of Japanese products into the United States. A similar shift can be seen in American policy towards China. Taiwan has traditionally been a home for American capital and a supplier of consumer goods to the United States. However, mainland China is a potential supplier of raw materials including oil and also offers the United States a large market for its manufactured goods. Apart from the military and political implications, there was a strong commercial incentive to America's recognition of the People's Republic. The economic motivation behind America's policy shift is obvious. US industry needs more markets.

Current forecasts of a rapid improvement in the American balance of payments after 1978 tell the same story. A forecast prepared by Morgan Guaranty Trust in July 1979 predicted an improvement in the US current account from the deficit of $13·9b. in 1978 to a $7·5b. deficit in 1979 with a deficit no larger for 1980 despite prospective increases in the oil bill. It attributed most of the improvement to a sharp turnaround of trade in manufactured goods from a $4·8b. deficit in 1978 to $8b. surplus in 1979 to a $20b. surplus forecast for 1980.

If indeed this is the basic trend of the American real economy, the response of Europe remains an important question. From a standpoint of competitiveness Europe has been surpassed and does not seem likely to overcome this gap within the next five years. This situation will automatically force Europe to seek protectionism or economic blocs. The formation of economic blocs denies international competition between the industrial nations and will therefore lead to increased competition for Third World markets, especially in the Middle East. The Middle East will be important for three reasons: (1) as a market for manufactured goods; (2) as a supplier of oil; and (3) as a source of financial capital. The second and third require that Europe should maintain the value of its currency. Since the value of Europe's currency is not based on industrial competitiveness Europe must return to the gold standard. These two main trends in Europe – the formation of an economic bloc and a return to the gold standard – will become the backbone of the European Monetary System. Many Europeans insist upon the necessity of the EMS as an alternative reserve currency to the dollar because of the weakness of the American economy and the unreliability of American leadership. This chapter has tried to demonstrate that these are misperceptions of the real situation. The world is currently witnessing a resurgence in US economic power. To survive, the Europeans must form trade and currency blocs. The creation of a major conflict in the relations between Europe and the United States in the 1980s seems to be in the making.

During the decades of the 1950s and 1960s Japan became a leading trading nation whose economy grew twice as fast as world trade. World trade grew at an annual rate of 7 per cent and Japanese exports at 15 per cent. Japanese exports' share of manufactured goods in the world market increased from about 3 per cent to over 12 per cent in 1973. Private capital investment during this period averaged more than 20 per cent of GNP compared with about 15 per cent in Germany and 10 per cent in the United States. But on entering the 1970s, Japan's problem was that just as world economic growth began to slow down, its share of world export markets reached the point where any increase would produce serious conflict. With world trade growth falling from 7 per cent to 3 per cent, Japanese export growth logically had to fall from 15 per cent to 3 per cent. The deflationary implications were substantial. Whereas the growth rate in all other countries could be expected to fall from 7 per cent to 3 per cent, Japanese growth had to suffer a thumping fall from 15 per cent to 3 per cent. Consequently, despite government efforts there was no economic incentive for Japanese industry to maintain its high rate of domestic capital investment. The ratio of private capital investment to GNP declined from more than 20 per cent to less than 14 per cent in 1976. The irony for the Japanese economy was that the actual impact of domestic deflation, due to the fall in private investment, led Japanese industry into increasing its exports (and its Asian investments) in order to maintain its economic viability in the face of declining domestic demand.

Japanese industry also went in for dramatic cost-cutting to maintain competitiveness. Big enterprises reduced the employment of part-timers and demanded that subcontractors cut their costs. This was the counterpart of the labour-force reduction practised by Germany and Switzerland.

Contrary to popular belief, the structure of the Japanese labour force made this a relatively easy option. Only about a quarter of the Japanese labour force is covered by the well-known system of 'life-employment'. The remaining majority is either employed 'part-time' and without benefit of a lifetime contract by one of the large enterprises, or is employed in small subcontracting business where labour mobility is high, job security low and competition very keen. Japanese industries could cut costs and increase their efficiency at the expense of the workers in this sector because the subcontractors could easily reduce their labour force. The official unemployment figures do not cover a large part of the labour force, and hidden unemployment among those workers covered by the life-employment system who were still nominally employed amounted to at least 10 per cent. A more realistic figure for the Japanese unemployment rate immediately following the oil crisis, therefore, would probably be over 6 per cent.

However, under the pressures of the employment situation economic and social strains began to show. The society was becoming divided. On the one hand, there were those working at secure well-paid jobs in big enterprises, while, on the other hand, many more were being increasingly employed in low-paid, over-manned and less pleasant jobs with no prospect of job security. The Japanese social system was beginning to revert dangerously to the 'duality' that existed before the Pacific War. It was this discarded labour from industry during periods of recession that spawned the 'young Turks' of the Japanese army who led the country into an invasion of Manchuria and the Second World War. With the tragedies of that period still fresh in the Japanese mind, this situation of high unemployment and low inflation could not continue. Japan could not compete *ad infinitum* by reducing employment and increasing hidden unemployment.

The pressures exerted by the Western economies were successful in reversing Japan's balance-of-payments surplus but the health of the domestic economy and the stability of Japanese society required that Japan maintain its international competitiveness by returning to its former path of high capital investment. During 1979 Japan has witnessed an increase in capital spending, a decline in the yen and signs of an increase in employment in the manufacturing sector – a position parallel to America's since 1976. Moreover it has become clear in 1979 that Japan, like the United States, is returning to its long-term capital investment trend. Japan has been pushed to this path because the energy crisis has forced changes in its industrial structure towards conserving energy and developing alternatives to traditional energy sources. So the Japanese position will become increasingly like that of America. The two countries will find themselves in a similar position *vis-à-vis* a Europe moving towards economic blocs and protectionism. Japan will be forced to increase its ties with the United States. Considering the Japanese role in the world economy, it is inevitable that Japan will become involved in the coming conflict between the United States and Europe – and not on the European side.

Part Six: Prescriptions

16

An Alternative to Market-Sharing

KAZUO NAKAZAWA

The Bonn Summit in July 1978 brushed aside conflicts with German efficiency, creating the semblance of accord among the Western powers by focusing only on short-term adjustments, and the Tokyo Summit in June 1979 did not really face the fundamental problems of worldwide unemployment and excessive production capacity (see Tables 16.1 and 16.2). The suffocating atmosphere that hangs over world trade today is due, in large measure, to the slowdown in the development of a really novel wave of a group of products (such as television or electronic calculators). The invention of television created a vast number of jobs, at different stages – in manufacturing, distribution and sales, telecasting, performing talents and advertising. Now, the world is eagerly awaiting new technological breakthroughs of this kind. If the advanced industrialised countries fail to achieve the 'upper exit' of shifting to new and sophisticated industrial activities, they will perforce stick to traditional, labour-intensive industries and block the road for their own advance and that of the developing countries.

Table 16.1   *Unemployment rates (%)[a]*

Country	1957–73 average	August 1978
USA	5·0	5·9
Japan	1·1	2·3
West Germany	1·4	4·4
France	1·6	5·8
UK	2·2	5·8

[a]As a percentage of the civilian labour force.
Source: International Economic Indicators, December 1978, US Commerce Department.

Table 16.2   *Industrial capacity utilisation ratios*

Country	1977
US FRB Series	82·4
Comm. Dept Series	83
Wharton Series	90·2
Japan	76·8
West Germany	86·2
France	84·1
UK	87·0

Source: International Economic Indicators, December 1978, US Commerce Department.

In a world of deeper and deeper interdependence, job-defensive measures taken by one country are necessarily contagious. Global expansion of job opportunities is required and this hinges upon technological breakthroughs. The NICs (newly industrialising countries) are experiencing a technological innovation process by simply introducing existing knowhow from advanced nations. The advanced countries have to break new technological ground to achieve the same tempo of innovation but this is not being done. Hence the current impasse in world trade. But we are also faced with an important challenge arising from another round of price hikes in oil, due largely to depreciation of the dollar. The oil price hikes are now the most important damper to further expansion of the world economy and global employment. We are in acute need of developments in new technologies for energy conservation or for the creation of alternative resources. And while the development of these new products should fall within the realm of private industry, the more fundamental technological breakthroughs, as in the energy field, will require public sector support, and joint international efforts by advanced industrialised countries.

An economic and technological breakthrough is required to free from the current state of affairs advanced countries tempted to take defensive actions in trade against the inroad by the NICs, and at the same time to stem the tide of inflation. That the various arrangements discussed at UNCTAD and elsewhere for a more globally equal and fair distribution of income and assets will achieve this end is highly unlikely, as it does not achieve the very end of income equalisation itself (Cline, 1978). The world is in need of a bolder initiative that would expand employment but would not lead to inflation in the long run.

Modern capitalism has, either intentionally or unintentionally, solved the problem of excessive production capacity by physical destruction. Wars have also accelerated the tempo of technological innovation. War in the nuclear age, however, is absolute anathema to everyone. What is needed now is a peace-economy substitute for war which could create demand but not waste, help industrial countries as well as poorer countries, stop the further increase in global unemployment, thereby reducing the risk of trade wars, and deepen economic interdependence among economies (see Sewell, 1978). All of this could also discourage the aggressive deployment of military resources.

This is the eco-political background for another New Deal or a new Marshall Plan. While the New Deal was essentially a 'one-country Keynesian' policy measure, the Marshall Plan, though its original intent was more humane (and later strategic) than economic, proved to be a wise Keynesian policy on an international scale which facilitated the shift from wartime economy to peacetime economy. In view of the fact that the world economy is suffering from a scarcity of natural resources, the Keynesian policy for merely expanding consumption will compound the dilemma in the future. What is needed is a stepping-up of international investments in infrastructure (such as power stations, mass transportation systems, etc.), which will enhance the productivity of the world economy in the future.

Specific proposals on these lines have already been raised. US Senator Javits, for example, has called for Japanese support for a new worldwide Marshall Plan. The plan, as he explained to the Japanese government and business community during his trip to Japan in late November 1977, should be funded by advanced countries (United States, Japan, Germany) and the OPEC countries. The proposed size of the fund would be approximately $25b. According to the senator's explanation of the 'New Marshall Fund', the fund should be directed to investments within the LDCs where such are welcomed. Shortly following this, the International Development Centre of Japan came out with a proposal for a special contribution by Japan of $3b. to international development finance institutions. The predominant concern behind this move, of course, was to reduce the embarrassingly expanding foreign exchange reserves of Japan.

Mr Masaki Nakajima, president of Mitsubishi Research Institute (MRI), publicly proposed the establishment of a 'Global Infrastructure Fund' (MRI, 1977; see also Muller and Everett, 1979). The fund would have annual contributions of $5b. from the United States, West Germany, Japan and Canada, $3b. from other advanced countries and an additional $5b. from OPEC. With loans and grants in addition to the fund's own money of $13b., the fund is to spend $25b. annually, with the total amount of fund outlays by the end of this century equalling roughly the US military outlays during the Second World War – $288b. (equivalent to $530b. in 1975 prices). His list of possible infrastructure investment includes those given in Table 16.3. Some of those ideas may sound extremely unrealistic technically and politically impossible. But there is concurrent thought within Japan and elsewhere.

Table 16.3   *Mitsubishi Research Institute – a global infrastructure fund*

Name	Nations (Areas)	Outline
1 Greening of deserts	North African nations	Greening of the deserts of the Sahara, the Sinai and the Arabian peninsula
2 Collection station for solar heat		Erect a large-scale installation for collection of solar energy in a remote part of the world; total investment in land, pipelines, and accessory equipment would reach $20 to $50 trillion; its total annual energy output would be equivalent to 200b. barrels of oil
3 Second Panama Canal	USA Nicaragua, Panama	Construction in Nicaragua of a large canal linking the Atlantic and Pacific Oceans
4 Kra Isthmus Canal	Thailand, Malaysia, Singapore	A 170km-long canal linking Phangnga Bay on the west coast to the Gulf of Siam on the east coast; would shorten by 2,400 km the sailing distance to and from the Indian Ocean
5 Electric power generation using sea currents		There are twelve promising areas along underdeveloped ocean shores extending from the equator to the temperate zones; maximum generating potential of one area, 35m. kW; total for 12 areas about 200m. kW
6 Himalayan hydro electric project	India, China	Damming of the Sanpo River on the upper reaches of the Brahmaputra in the frontier area between China and the

		Indian province of Assam to make it flow into India through a tunnel across the Himalayas; potential generating capacity 50m. kW, maximum 37m. kW on average; annual generating capacity 240b. to 330b. kWh
7 Control of sea currents in Bering Strait	USA USSR	Construct a dam across Bering Strait at its narrowest point (85 km wide, 45 m deep) and control the sea currents flowing from the Arctic Ocean; this would alter atmospheric conditions in the North Pacific and make the climate more temperate
8 African central lake	Central African nations	Control the flow of the Congo River by building a dam to create a vast lake in the Congo and Chad regions of central Africa to improve natural conditions in the area

Dr Sakuro Okita, former head of the Overseas Economic Co-operation Fund (OECF) which administers Japan's official foreign aid, and his associate (then) at the OECF, Dr Kunio Takase, are promoting a somewhat different idea based on the same philosophy: the Asian Rice Production Redoubling Plan. The estimated cost is $54b. over fifteen years. (This plan was taken up by the Trilateral Commission; *Nihan Keijai Shimbun*, 1976.) Finally, various proposals have also been made outside Japan.

The Princeton meeting of September 1978, sponsored by the Overseas Development Council, took up the massive resource transfers as a part of the agenda. The summary report rounded up the atmosphere of the meeting on this issue as 'general scepticism' (ODC, 1978) though the author of this chapter has certain reservations about this expression. Specific objections, according to the summary, were the following, and I will comment on them one by one.

(1) *'The programme may be inflationary.'* Granted that the transfers would be, generally speaking, inflationary but so are most welfare

programmes within the industrial democracies. However, the point is whether they are really inflationary in the long run or not. All of the proposed projects have the long-term effect of the creation of alternative sources of energy, or massive energy saving (e.g. second Panama Canal).

In most of the industrialised democracies, the unemployed are fed, clothed and housed by the government without any productive contribution and the budget for this type of welfare is much more inflationary in the long run than a job-creating programme. Although existing job-creating programmes within Japan, the United States or elsewhere may be resource-wasteful, the proposed projects are entirely different in nature.

(2)　*'The proposal may lower the volume of concessional transfers to the extent that new capital transfers are not additional to existing flows.'* The proposal is based upon the belief that we face a liquidity surplus today. Capital as a whole is in glut. How much of the capital can be anchored to long-term projects depends upon political will, diplomatic skills and financial engineering of private and official international financial institutions.

(3)　*'The absorptive capacity of many LDCs for more foreign capital is low.'* A planning and designing capability, feasibility study, capacity and other elements of absorptive capacity are lacking in LDCs. International financial institutions have been created for this purpose. They should work harder and extend any help the LDCs need in this area.

(4)　*'Likely LDCs are already heavily in debt.'* The Nokajima proposal does not necessarily include such countries as Brazil, Mexico, etc., who are already heavily in debt. Even where such heavy debtor countries are actually involved, an autonomous account can be created in regard to the proposed projects to avoid further deterioration of their debt–service ratios.

(5)　*'Long-term borrowing by the LDCs may be no easier to service than shorter-term borrowing.'* Some products of the proposal can be sold internationally. Solar energy can easily be sold as hydrogen fuel to run future vehicles (the only non-pollutive engine, as it emits only water). A second Panama Canal would actually produce income.

(6)　*'There are no foreseeable bottlenecks on the supply side.'* Granted that technological breakthroughs and the exploration of alternative resources will eliminate supply bottlenecks, *but* these breakthroughs come more often as by-products of massive human endeavour such as are included in the proposal. Exploration within advanced countries is depleted. Rather than corroborating the law of diminishing returns by exploring near-dry wells or old mines, efforts should be directed to projects in the south. An egalitarian purpose will then also be achieved.

(7) *'Let us use money in Newark rather than in LDCs.'* Aside from an egalitarian standpoint, a 1 billion dollar oil-burning power station in Newark would generate less employment and require less electric machinery than an electric power plant in Korea, as two plants can be built in Korea with the same amount of money. If the money is spent on a water power plant in a LDC, the country's oil import bill will be smaller thereafter, the economy will expand and imports from the United States can increase. A Newark station will increase the US oil import bill. In a word, the bottom-line is whether a Newark project leads to more global economic expansion, more resource saving, or is more energy creative than a project elsewhere. (Also, OPEC deposits at US banks do not represent US savings. To the extent that these external savings are used to finance these proposals, the domestic political problem will be lessened.)

Fundamentally, there is a lingering scepticism as to whether the current stagnation of the OECD economies is cyclical or not. A prudent policy-maker should be prepared to deal with structural problems. Even if the current stagnation should prove to be cyclical, there would not be much labour lost.

In conclusion, and as I have stressed, the criteria for selection of appropriate projects might be the following.

(1) The project should create jobs globally.
(2) The project should increase purchasing power in poorer countries (preferably directly).
(3) The project should lead, in the long run, to resource conservation by saving the cost of transportation or creating new substitutes for natural resources.

Free marketeers might argue that the current economic setbacks are cyclical and therefore we do not have to do anything about depression or the plights of poorer nations as a sound market-economy logic will lead in the long run to more even distribution of income, domestically, and through trade and investment, internationally. But the world can ill afford the social and political costs of the 'wait and see' prescription. Moreover, the private sector lacks the capacity to undertake through market mechanisms the large infrastructure projects that are required to sustain global economic development. Even where low-interest rate capital is available, either due to international political implications of the sensitive location involved or to the requirement of too large an amount of risk money, the private sector alone will never be able to embark on such a venture.

Ecologists may criticise the adverse environmental impact of large infrastructural undertakings. But, properly designed, such projects can minimise environmental hazards and may even have favourable environmental impacts. Some infrastructural projects will greatly reduce the cost of transportation (and any environmental pollution related to it) or might encourage a shift from gasoline-engined cars to hydrogen-run cars. The pluses and minuses of new projects should always be carefully weighed and if the adverse effects are remediable, precautionary measures should be taken. Also, ecologists should be encouraged to offer viable and constructive alternatives.

Politicians will naturally be cautious when negotiating with foreign governments for any major alteration of their local landscape. Needless to say, any large-scale project cannot and should not be carried out without a clear and positive political will of the particular government involved. On the other hand, a private and carefully constituted independent organisation, free of political constraints or the endless red tape of international or national bureaucracies, might play a major role in generating international support for such unprecedented global co-operation.

Conceivably, there might be a 'Proposition 13' type of reaction to a huge international outlay and I share the strong antipathy against big government. However, as long as we have government, full employment is the primary objective of economic policy of the modern state. And, given the international interaction of economies, if we do not raise our eyes and see beyond the 'one-country full employment' model of today, liberal trade will not last long. The matter depends partly on the enlightenment of the voting public and partly on the nature and appeal of specific projects, because the proposal is *not* aid. It is a self-help for the industrialised democracies, serving, at the same time, the international egalitarian cause.

Today's frontier is beyond the national border and awaits joint endeavours by industrial democracies.

References: Chapter 16

Cline, W. R. (1978), *Trade Negotiations in the Tokyo Round: A Quantitative Assessment* (Washington, DC: Brookings Institution).

Mitsubishi Economic Research Institute (1977), *Proceedings*, December.

Muller, E. R., and Everett, M. E. (1979), 'Needed: A Global Marshall Plan', *Washington Post*, 7 January.

Overseas Development Council (1978), *Massive Resource Transfers* (Washington, DC: ODC), August.

Sewell, J. W. (1978), *Can the Rich Prosper without Progress by the Poor?* (Washington, DC: ODC), July.

17

Restructuring out of Recession

RICHARD JOLLY

The Brandt Report (1980 is the latest of a number of analyses and policy documents to propose an increased transfer of additional resources from developed to developing countries as a key element in a global programme for restoring long-run dynamism to the world economy and ending the widespread under-utilisation of capital and labour. In the Brandt Report, the large-scale transfer of resources to developing countries would be part of an integrated emergency programme along with three other components: an international energy strategy; a global food programme; and a start on some major reforms in the international economic system. The transfers would have as their most urgent objectives assistance to the poorest countries and regions most seriously threatened by the current economic crisis and provision for financing the debts and deficits of middle-income countries.

The Brandt proposal is clearly focused on the most important and immediate of the structural imbalances within the world economy today – energy, finance and the weaknesses of international economic institutions. The magnitude of its proposed transfers – an additional $30b. in aid by 1985 and an equivalent volume of additional transfers from various non-government financial sources – is on a sufficient scale to make a serious impact on current levels of capital under-utilisation and unemployment. Nevertheless, the Brandt emergency programme is obviously only one of a series of possible proposals for 'restructuring out of recession'. As a background for considering some of the possible international variations of policy which might be adopted in response to under-utilisation of capital, it may be useful to document more systematically the types and extent of the impact which might be expected from additional transfers. This is a key purpose of this chapter, to present the general evidence of the benefits to be expected from such transfers rather than analyses of the Brandt proposals as such. Over the last few years, a major recycling of financial surpluses to developing countries has in fact sustained economic activity in the developed countries and held the line against further deterioration in respect of unemployment, under-utilisation of capacity and even inflation. The European Community, for example, estimates that there would be 3 million more persons unemployed if the non-oil developing countries had cut their manufactured imports to meet the increased oil prices of 1973–4 rather than borrowing to maintain their level. By borrowing, their purchasing power has risen to account for 25 per cent of US exports and 20 per cent of EC exports. As a result, trade in manufactured goods with the newly industrialising countries alone has been found by the OECD to have created an average net gain of 900,000 jobs for the developed economies in each of the years 1973–7.

Nevertheless, the ability of this process to continue is far from certain. The EC Commission's Annual Report of October 1978 summarised the position as follows:

> The present equilibrium of the world economy depends to a considerable degree on a continuing flow of private lending to the non-oil producing developing countries (and to the Soviet Union and Eastern Europe) on a scale unheard of before 1974 and *would be called in question by any impediment to that flow.*

It is against this wider background that the world economy is now being called upon to adjust to a further increase in the price of oil. It is far from clear that the same recycling mechanisms will be able to operate for a further five years, starting as they do this time with the structure of international debt already considerably extended. Total outstanding debt of developing countries at the end of 1979 will already be some US$300b., and current account deficits of non-oil developing countries in this year alone are estimated to reach a new peak of at least US$50b. This deficit could be met by increased exports and/or increased financial transfers – or it could lead to a reduced level of economic activity and growth. Again we have an estimate based on past experience.

Holsen and Waelbroeck estimated that balance-of-payments borrowing by developing countries in 1975 and 1976, to a value of $8b. and $11b. respectively, avoided the need for a fall in the GNP of the LDCs by 5·0 and 6·9 per cent in these two years and thereby contributed 0·4 per cent and 0·6 per cent to the aggregative demand sustaining the GNPs of the developed countries. They added (Holsen and Waelbroeck, 1976, pp. 171–6):

> It is not usual in analysing business cycle developments to think of developing countries as capable of affecting aggregate demand. This is because they are thought of as adjusting their purchases passively to the level permitted by their foreign exchange earnings. This assumption is not correct any more. Less developed countries' import policies influence demand today in the same way as the US deficit of the late 1960s and early 1970s, and the OPEC balance-of-payments surplus.

Calculations made for UNCTAD by the University of Pennsylvania using the link econometric model of the world economy suggested that an increase of the growth rate by 3 percentage points in the non-oil developing countries would result in an increase of the growth rate by 1 percentage point in the OECD countries (UNCTAD, 1976, p. 39). Since then more disaggregated analyses on alternative hypotheses have been undertaken by various groups. The results of the simulations undertaken by the US Bureau of Intelligence and Research, summarised in Table 17.1, make clear some of the issues.

Table 17.1   *Transfer of $20b. per year to non-OPEC developing regions, maintained for three years (percentage increase)*[a]

Effect on		Year of Transfer		
		First	Second	Third
World Exports	($)	2·6	2·6	2·0
World Exports	(Volume)	3·0	2·8	1·8
OECD Exports	($)	3·1	3·1	2·3
OECD Imports	($)	1·3	1·6	1·5
LDC Exports	($)	1·4	1·7	1·4
LDC Imports	($)	8·4	7·1	4·6
OECD GNP (real)		0·5	0·6	0·4
LDC GNP (real)		1·7	1·8	1·5

[a]The final two lines are calculated from data given in later tables of the report.
Source: US Bureau of Intelligence and Research (1978), p. 3.

These simulations consider a transfer of an additional $20b. a year to non-OPEC developing countries sustained for three years. Three ways of financing the transfers were simulated: (1) a 'costless' transfer, analogous to transferring profits from the sale of IMF reserves of gold or allocating newly created SDRs to the developing countries. In essence, this corresponds to a Keynesian stimulus to demand which calls into use resources that would otherwise be idle. The results shown in Table 17.1 correspond to these simulations. Exports and imports in both developed and developing countries would rise considerably. So also would GNP: by roughly 0·5 per cent p.a. for three years in the industrial countries; by 1·5 per cent p.a. or slightly more for those years in non-OPEC developing countries. The employment impact of such increases was not calculated but, following Okun's rule of thumb, the increase in GNP might be the equivalent to a direct increase in employment of perhaps 0·2 per cent or roughly 500,000 jobs throughout the industrial countries.

The other two simulations are based on alternative ways of raising the finance: (2) assumes that $20b. is obtained by diverting government expenditures from domestic goods and services to the transfer programme in each of the thirteen industrial countries. The sum involved is roughly about 1 per cent of GDP in these countries, so the net effect is also roughly just over twice that of increasing official development assistance (ODA) from the present average level of 0·31 per cent of GNP in the DAC donor countries to the target level of 0·7 per cent of GNP. Simulation (3) assumes that the $20b. is raised from additional direct taxation.

In both these simulations, the net impact on the developed and developing countries is substantially smaller than that of the first simulation, essentially because the positive impact of the transfers on economic activity in both developed and developing countries is offset by the negative impact of the withdrawals of effective purchasing power in the industrial countries. In the case of the transfer financed by a diversion of government expenditures the combined effect on the GNP of the developed countries is negative: total GNP with the programme would be something under 0·1 per cent *less* than without the transfer – though, of course, GNP in developing countries would be 1·5 per cent higher.

In the case of the transfer financed by increasing direct taxation, however, the impact on both developed and developing countries would be positive: on developed countries by some 0·2 per cent of GNP, and on developing countries by about the same amount as in the other simulations.

These simulations only offer a rough guide to the possible effects of transfers of resources but they can help to illuminate some of the issues, particularly the differential impact on the various parties involved.

Structural Change – the Second Objective

Development, however, means much more than a Keynesian expansion of demand. If a programme of additional transfers is to stimulate more balance and sustainable growth in the longer run, the transfers must be directed towards restructuring, to deal with structural problems and global imbalance in key sectors such as energy, agriculture, certain sectors of industry and certain, but not all, raw materials and commodities. Imbalances in all these sectors are considerable, often the result of long-term trends to imbalance exacerbated over the last few years. A start on restructuring could be assisted if these sectors in developing countries were made a focus for increased investment under the transfer programme.

In more general ways, a massive transfer of resources could also assist restructuring. To the extent that a higher level of economic activity was stimulated in the industrialised countries, unemployment would be reduced and thus also one of the main factors which leads to popular and political opposition to imports and restructuring. The link between unemployment and opposition to restructuring and adjustment is worth stressing. More adjustment took place in the 1960s in most industrial countries than has occurred in the last five years. Yet there was relatively little opposition, a comforting contrast with the present, usually attributed in part to the lower unemployment and greater economic dynamism of the late 1960s.

Taken together, under-utilisation of capacity and the need for restructuring provide the possibility of, and suggest the need for, a new international initiative, under which a major increase of transfers from developed to developing countries would be combined with measures to stimulate investment in developing countries in projects or sectors which would ease structural bottlenecks in the medium and longer run. If on a reasonable scale, the transfers and investment could provide an important stimulus towards higher levels of economic activity in the industrial economies of the West – though their probable scale and timing suggest that any initiative should primarily be judged for its medium-term impact than for its short-term counter-cyclical efforts.

Various policy instruments would be available to implement such a programme of transfers: major increases in ODA, especially but not only from Germany and Japan, which currently combine relatively low ODA performance with very large balance-of-payments surpluses; additional flows of private finance, possibly stimulated through new institutional mechanisms or a major increase in co-financing; an increase in SDRs, made possible by more ambitious reforms of the international monetary system; or a combination of such instruments and measures, old and new, but operated on a much larger scale than at present and adding up to a co-ordinated, identifiable international initiative.

In my view the critical points for such an initiative to be politically acceptable and economically effective number four:

(1) That the programme combine additional flows of private finance with at least some reasonable proportion of additional ODA. Without this, the poorer countries of the Third World are likely to receive very little benefit and there will only be capacity to stimulate additional investment in activities which are important for development and structural change but only intrinsically or initially only marginally viable in commercial terms, such as small-scale agriculture, small-scale transportation, or even energy exploration.
(2) That the programme clearly be directed towards stimulating investment of a sort that promotes structural change internationally. The particular sectors to be covered could be reserved for later discussion – though investment (and other related supporting expenditure) to increase Third World production in

agriculture, energy and some sectors of industry and raw material production and processing should certainly qualify. So also would the support of any major regional or global projects and programmes, of the sort which have been proposed for the Third Development Decade, and the support of international stockpiling schemes which might form part of international commodity agreements.

(3) That responsibility for initiating the programme and control of its key operations clearly involve both developed and developing countries on an equitable basis. This is more important than the question of where administrative responsibility for the initiative would rest. As regards administration, it would obviously be desirable to work through existing institutions, possibly relying considerably upon the regional development banks as a way of incorporating greater developing country involvement and of strengthening the regional focus.

(4) In magnitude, the total programme well justifies a sizeable, not a minor, initiative. The Brandt Report itself has recommended a total additional flow of funds from a variety of sources rising to a sum of the order of $50b. or $60b. annually by 1985, of which about half would be from aid and half from sources outside government aid budgets (Brandt, 1980, p. 278).

The number of voices, official and non-official, calling for such a programme has been growing: President Kreisky in 1976, Cheysson in 1977, the Swedish proposal for a massive programme in 1978. Over the last eighteen months there have been proposals from Nakajima for a Global Infrastructure Investment Fund, from Senator Javits for a $25b. Growth Development Fund, for an OPEC/OECD global stimulation plan, for a twenty-year Marshall Plan for the Third World. The 1978 ICFTU *Review of the World Economic Situation* states: 'There has been growing recognition over the past year of the need for a massive, planned international effort to assist the developing countries – for a new, world-wide "Marshall Plan", as advocated by the ICFTU for some years' (ICFTU, 1978, p. 23).

Mr Roy Jenkins said in the first Jean Monnet Lecture (Jenkins, 1977, p. 17):

We also need to view the present economic recession in a longer-term perspective. The extent and persistence of unemployment can no longer be seen as an exceptionally low and long bottom to the business cycle. To restore full employment requires a new impulse on a historic scale. We require a new driving force comparable with the major rejuvenations of the past two hundred years; the industrial revolution itself, the onset of the railway age, the impact of Keynes, the need for postwar reconstruction, the spread of what were previously regarded as middle-class standards to the mass of the population in the industrial countries. I believe that the needs of the Third World have a major part to play here. Two sources of new growth have in the past sometimes come together, the one worldwide and the other regional.

M. de Larosière, managing director of the IMF, stated in 1979 in Manila:

> It is paradoxical that the industrialised countries, most of which are not using their production potential to the full, are hesitating to increase their financial aid to poor countries. This is despite the fact that such aid could result in increased global demand and thus contribute to reactivation of world trade in a recovery of production. There is nothing in the present state of deflationary chain reactions in the industrialised world, stagnation feeding stagnation, which would argue against such an increase in financial aid.

Since then, with no easing of stagflation in spite of heavy doses of monetarist medicine in many countries, the world economy has moved closer to recession. Aid transfers are being restrained – and sometimes cut – and other financial flows are increasingly put in jeopardy by fears of mounting debt.

In fact, a consensus resolution was reached on these matters at UNCTAD V, in the committee on the transfer of real resources. Amongst other points, this stated that 'substantially increased transfers of resources to developing countries are an indispensable factor for accelerating their pace of development and could help stimulate global economic activity, particularly in a medium to long term perspective'. The committee noted that 'Several approaches including co-financing with private resources, could usefully be combined for substantially increasing transfers of resources, largely raised on the financial markets and without prejudice to official development assistance'.

Yet, in spite of these attempts to stimulate serious action on these broad lines, most governments of industrial countries have to date been cautious and hesitant. Among the industrial countries, caution has, I believe, been mainly the result of three concerns: the fear of inflation; the uncertainty of the impact on the balance of payments of different countries; and the reluctance to consider any initiative that might involve increasing public expenditure. These genuine concerns may also, one suspects, be compounded by a general attitude towards developing countries that they are a peripheral part of the world economy, to be considered as part of aid or diplomatic policy but not as serious patterns in a strategy for reviving the industrial economies.

As indicated at Arusha and Manila, Third World governments have been more open to such proposals – but not without conditions. Third World responses have been particularly sensitive to a strong emphasis on transferring resources in ways which would support international structural change – the inclusion of a component of ODA in order that poorer as well as better-off developing countries may benefit from the initiative and a broad base of control which will provide for strong participation by developing countries in the management of any such scheme.

The risk of inflation is in my view the most legitimate of such objections. There is no strong evidence to suggest that a stimulus to greater economic activity within the industrial countries would be less inflationary if effected by means of a transfer to developing countries than by a direct expansion of domestic demand. This had led some critics to argue that a major transfer to developing countries must be rejected for the simple reason that industrial countries have 'obviously been unwilling to undertake major domestic programmes of Keynesian expansion'.

In my view it is the general argument that almost any expansion of demand, output and production would be inflationary that needs to be challenged. The evidence for such a rigid view of a Phillips curve relationship does not exist – and to base policy on the belief that the higher the rate of unemployment the lower will be the rate of inflation is both oversimplified and misleading (Santomen and Seaton, 1978). In contrast one can argue that continuing high unemployment stimulates uncertainty and generates increasing reactions within the organised section of the labour force and among companies with monopolistic power in ways which may result in more wage-push, cost-push and inflationary effects rather than less. Moreover, these reactions often lead to institutional changes which create further imperfections and rigidities within both labour and other markets, thus adding to inflationary tendencies and mechanisms, built into the economic and social structure over the longer run.

In contrast, clear evidence exists of the favourable effects of structural adjustment and trade links with developing countries on inflation. The 1978 *World Development Report* showed that textile prices over the past five years had risen by 26 per cent compared with a general rise in the wholesale price index of 66 per cent. A recent Brookings study shows that imports from less developed countries into the United States sell at 16 per cent lower retail prices than comparable domestically produced goods. The OECD itself has recognised that trade with the NICs has provided a 'curb to inflation' within the industrial countries both in the short run and, by encouraging increases in productivity and efficiency, over the longer run.

Except for inflation, the other effects of the programme are matters of policy not inevitability. The impact on the balance of payments of different industrial countries, for example, will primarily reflect how the size of each country's 'contribution' to the programme compares with the amount of additional exports it gets from the programme, which in turn will primarily reflect the sectors and countries supported and the institutional arrangements governing the use of the transfer funds. All these are matters of policy, which can be adjusted to match the goals and constraints affecting the countries participating in the programme. So also is the form in which the funds are raised and administered.

The need now is for one of the major governments of the industrial powers to give a strong political lead: to recognise the need for a significant international initiative along the lines proposed and to provide the impetus and leadership for it to be converted rapidly into a programme for implementation. The ideas in general terms have already been much debated, but over the years not really engaged because strong political leadership has been lacking. For a proposal now to be seriously developed:

(1) a time limit should be set for preparing a specific programme;
(2) a clear mandate should be given for an international group or groups to work out the elements of a feasible programme within clear and broad basic guidelines, which recognise the different interests of the various parties involved;
(3) both North and South should be involved in whatever formal meetings are required to reach agreement on the proposal.

It is not argued that an initiative on these lines would solve all the major economic problems of the North or the South. In particular, special attention would be needed if the mass of the rural population in the poorer developing countries were to gain much benefit. But a major initiative for restructuring out of recession could provide a more dynamic context in which other long-standing problems could be tackled.

References: Chapter 17

Brandt, W., *et al.* (1980) *North-South: A Programme for Survival* (London: Pan).
Holsen, J. A., and Waelbroeck, H. L. (1976), 'The LDCs and the international monetary mechanism', *AER Papers and Proceedings*, May.
ICFTU (1978), *Review of World Economic Situation* (Brussels: ICFTU).
Jenkins, Rt Hon. R. (1977), 'Europe's present challenge and future opportunity', First Jean Monnet Lecture, Florence, 27 October.
Santomen, A. M., and Seaton, J. J. (1978), 'The inflation, unemployment trade-off – a critique of the alternatives', *Journal of Economic Literature*, June, pp. 499–544.
UNCTAD (1976), *Trade Prospects and Capital Needs of Developing Countries, 1976–80*, TD/B/C.3/134 (Geneva: 15 April).
US Bureau of Intelligence and Research (1978), INR Report No. 1081, Department of State, Washington DC.

18

Government Responsibility for Industrial Restructuring

JAN TUMLIR

Let me begin with the word 'adjustment' which is now employed to denote a special problem. The whole discipline of economics is simply a study of adjustment in the most general sense. The word itself could stand as a generic term for all the particular changes and processes the totality of which constitutes economic growth. Then why has it come to denote a problem? When we define a social problem, the assumption is that there must be something that government can and should do about it. Our question is simply: what can government do to assist industrial adjustment? Nobody has a convincing answer to it – which, I shall try to show, is not surprising.

Why there exists a substantial backlog of industrial adjustment in the rich countries – which, unless allowed to proceed, will disrupt the precarious economic order we have maintained for some thirty years – is easy to understand. There has been unprecedented economic growth in this period, and although all countries participated in it, the initial distribution of productive capacities was such that the bulk of the incremental income accrued to the rich countries and more particularly to their labour. Yet in the meantime an industrial base has been created in the populous so-called Third World which now makes it possible for its labour and enterprise to claim a growing share in future increments. And that seems to be the root of our adjustment difficulties. A number of interesting recent international initiatives can be explained from this perspective: the proposal by the US Secretary of Labor for a $1 international minimum wage, the labour union proposal that an international fair labour standard be established as a criterion of acceptability of imports, and even the drive for industrial democracy, with workers' representatives on corporate boards of directors co-deciding where new investments should be made.

Global Economic Change

We keep discussing how, or whether, 'adjustment' or 'restructuring' can be planned or at least facilitated by government. There is a prior question: adjustment to what? What is the nature of the change behind the need to 'restructure'?

Individuals and societies seek to improve their position by reacting – more or less alertly, more or less creatively – to their perceived opportunities. From this effort, innovation is continuously generated; and the very laws which guarantee individual freedom and national sovereignty ensure that this continuous and ubiquitous effort results in a massive flow of economic innovation which no one – no government and no group of governments – can control.

If we cannot control the global flow of change, we must adapt to it; *there is no other way to maintain order.* What can a refusal to adapt mean? Two different cases should be distinguished. Imagine a world in which only one country – a Himalayan kingdom or a small, quaint Old World country – refuses to adapt to the economic and social change proceeding abroad. First, either its citizens must be unanimous in refusing the change, or the refusal must be enforced on an unwilling minority. Secondly, the refusal implies a growing discrepancy between the country's actual and potential income as more efficient methods of production are foregone and an increasing part of the country's foreign trade is subjected to controls. This growing social cost is bound to increase the proportion of population resenting it, and preferring to adjust to change. Thus persistence in the refusal necessitates an increase in coercion, and one can easily imagine a growing tension which the social fabric can eventually no longer bear.

This was the relatively favourable case. Imagine, instead, that a number of large industrial countries find it difficult for political reasons to adjust to economic change generated elsewhere. Since in each the attained level of prosperity (and to an even larger extent future growth) depends essentially on foreign trade, there will immediately arise two kinds of friction or tension, internal and external, each exacerbating the other. Internally, there will be distributional problems as economic growth at the rate to which their societies have grown accustomed slows down. (It will have to be decided politically, in other words, who can benefit from foreign trade and who cannot.) Externally, the countries might agree that somewhat more organised trade would be a good idea; frictions are bound to arise, however, on the questions of who is to do the organising and which products are to be organised.

These considerations lead to the following conclusion. It is as illusory to think that a relatively affluent society has a choice between somewhat more efficiency and growth, on the one hand, and somewhat greater stability and comfort from dampening change, on the other, as it is to think of choosing between somewhat more inflation and somewhat less unemployment. In both these cases the choice is only between somewhat less discomfort now and much more of it later.

Time Rate of Adjustment

The notion of a given rate of global economic change to which national economies are continuously adjusting is, of course, a simplification, since this change is generated by the very economies which have to adjust to it. It is, none the less, a useful notion for it directs attention to its logical counterpart, the rate of adjustment.

There is a widespread belief among economists, not to speak of politicians, that a slow adjustment is always preferable to a quick one – from which it would seem to logically follow that no adjustment is the best of all. This is in part a professional bias: it comes from studying in detail, step by step, the process of adjustment *to a particular disturbance*. However instructive that may be for the theorist, it would be an impossible luxury for economic policy to be concerned with adjustment to particular disturbances. Economic policy must view adjustment as an unending process, a flow, a constant condition of the economy.

The pairing of these two rates should make it immediately obvious why it could not be a legitimate objective of public policy to slow the adjustment process down – to depress, so to speak, the rate of adjustment below the rate of global change. Such a policy must result in a growing maladjustment. It would amount to pushing into the future a growing cost which at some point must become unsupportable.

It is more difficult, though more interesting, to contemplate the effects of a policy that would attempt to raise the rate of adjustment above the rate of change. (Should we call it anticipatory adjustment policy?) It could be done in two ways. Adjustment within a particular economy could be accelerated relative to the global flow of economic change when that economy would begin to liberalise its imports and/or reduce the duties payable on them. Alternatively (or in addition) such an acceleration could be achieved by offering subsidies or other inducements to stimulate the withdrawal of factors of production from the import-competing industries. There are significant differences between these two methods of raising the rate of adjustment above the rate of change.

The second alternative would represent a policy innovation so radical that its consequences cannot be foreseen in full, principally because different assumptions can be fed into the forecasts. What can be foreseen are the immediate, or impact, effects of such a policy and the general tendency of its consequences. An industry experiencing a pressure from imports, if left to its own devices, can adjust only by innovating. It will abandon certain lines of production and concentrate on improving others, trying to offer some additional quality or service to distinguish its own from the imported product. In this effort it is aided by its own labour force which adapts its wage-bargaining strategy to the perceived danger of the industry's market – and *a fortiori* employment –

shrinking in consequence of comparative advantage shifting against it. As a recent GATT study explains, the rate at which comparative advantage changes can be to a considerable extent *controlled* by the import-competing industry: its position relative to growing foreign competition is largely determined by the relation between the growth of the wages it pays and the labour productivity it generates (GATT, 1977, pp. 46–8). If public subsidies are used to promote the withdrawal of productive factors from the industry under import pressure, some of the innovations which otherwise would have been made will not occur, for the dual reason that subsidies for the scrapping of capital installations will reduce the pressure on enterprise and management, and the availability of additional benefits to workers made redundant by imports will influence the bargaining strategy of unions in the import-competing industries. This will have two consequences.

The foregone innovations, and the 'defensive' investment in which they would have been embodied, would have raised, or postponed the decline of, the rate of return on the capital already invested in the import-competing sector. In their absence, not only the write-downs from the private book-values of that capital, but also the shrinkage in its physical volume, still retaining some social usefulness, will be larger (because subsidised) that they would have been in the case of purely market-dictated adjustment. There is a waste of capital involved here.

At the same time, subsidising the withdrawal of production factors from the import-competing industries will maximise the number of job changes which until now it has been the main – and on the whole equally uneconomical – effort of public policy to minimise. Eventually, the growth of imports will bring about an increase in demand for the country's exports, and factors leaving the import-competing sector can be reabsorbed in the export and home market goods sector. To this extent the same adjustment forces will operate which do not allow trade liberalisation to result in permanent or long-lasting unemployment. In the case of subsidised anticipatory adjustment, however, the process of the reabsorption of these resources may be more difficult for three reasons, which represent a major difference between this situation and the much simpler one of trade liberalisation.

(1) From the description of the policy's effects so far it follows that when full employment is regained, the economy will be more trade-intensive – importing and exporting more – than it would be in an equilibrium attained spontaneously, without subsidies paid for withdrawal of import-competing resources. As economists we have to believe that the spontaneous equilibrium is the more efficient one in the microeconomic sense. The increased trade intensity of the economy then implies that some of its resources now employed in the export sector would be yielding a higher product in the import-

competing sector; and therefore they could be maintained in their existing unemployment only by a *continuing* subsidy. For this reason alone the economy would not be yielding its full potential product.

(2) In a fully employed society, there are only two sources of growth of income per head: innovation, and the rise of average productivity resulting from the reallocation of productive factors from lower-to higher-productivity employments. Conceivably, a continuing shift of demand could ensure growth from the latter source alone, without innovation. Historically, however, a continuous flow of innovation has been needed to maintain the incentive to invest sufficiently strongly to avoid unemployment from shortfalls of aggregate demand. There is no way of knowing whether the innovations foregone in consequence of subsidised withdrawal of factors from the import-competing sector would be made up in the process of the induced expansion of the export sector; that is, whether the policy would not reduce the overall rate of innovation in the economy.

(3) There is, finally, the cost of the subsidy programme as such. To have the significant impact discussed here, it would clearly have to involve substantial amounts of money. Thus what economists generally acknowledge as the 'dead-weight loss of taxation' would also be significant (see particularly Corden, 1974, p. 64).

This analysis suggests that if society at large desires industrial adjustment to proceed at a rate faster than that indicated by market forces, an additional reduction or removal of protection will attain the objective more reliably and efficiently than government programmes to subsidise the withdrawal of resources from import-competing industries and their re-employment elsewhere.

Conditions of Adjustment

Governments of most industrial countries carry on extensive activities ostensibly to help their economies to adjust. On closer inspection, the majority of these policies actually impede adjustment. So it would seem logical in designing the ideal or most efficient adjustment policy to suggest that, first of all, governments discontinue all their adjustment-blocking activities. Then, after some time has elapsed and experience has been analysed, we might be able to see whether anything more was needed in the way of active policy.

At this point I usually encounter the argument that this might perhaps work in normal times, with an economy close to full employment, whereas in present conditions, with inflation combined with high unemployment, the economy cannot adjust under its own steam. There is a point to the argument. Structural industrial change was certainly proceeding much more rapidly in the 1950s and 1960s than in the 1970s.

Could this have something to do with inflation? Let me note here the enormous information requirements of an effective adjustment policy, and the fact that inflation severely impairs the information function of the price system (see Tumlir, 1979). Most prices rise in inflation but not continuously or in proportion; they are periodically adjusted upwards, and *each with a different lag*. Consequently, relative prices at any moment provide little information about the real relative scarcities, information which is essential for investment planning. The loss of vital information increases uncertainty and reduces foresight. Three distinct effects on investment may be distinguished. Its aggregate flow is diminished. Its timing is adversely affected: with each percentage increase in real GNP new bottlenecks appear which, under a stable price level, changes in relative prices would have made it possible to foresee. Finally, inflation skews the composition of industrial investment towards assets with short write-off periods. In consequence of all three, the growth of labour productivity declines.

With this background, the whole issue can be summarised in two questions. What is it that *has to be done* by government to assist adjustment when the economy is growing rapidly? And what is it that government *can do* to assist adjustment in a stagnating, inflationary economy? My answer to both would be, very little. First things first. We have seen the whole world economy growing rapidly while the key countries in it were able to maintain domestic price levels approximately stable. We may not have much agreed theory to go by, but this experience at least strongly suggests that the present stagnationist tendencies are due to inflation, and not the other way around. From this it would follow that we should keep our governments to their traditional functions and responsibilities, which prominently include the maintenance of the purchasing power of national money, rather than trying to invent new makework for their further expansion.

Adjustment is the proper business of the firms on whom the change impinges. When inflation makes it impossible for industrial firms to plan their investments, and the investment shortfall creates unemployment, it is foolhardy to expect that government, which caused the inflation in the first place and despairs of its own ability to arrest it, can help the general economic situation by devising schemes to promote investments in this or that particular line of production suggested by the civil service.

Information Requirements

Governments feeling compelled to conduct industrial adjustment or restructuring policies which do more than merely provide an economic

climate favourable to smooth and rapid change need even more information than firms have to have when they plan their own adjustment to
the pressures of competition. The information requirements of governments can be divided into two kinds.

The first comprises all the information that firms also have to have.
The very process of collecting this kind of information places governments at a considerable disadvantage. It so happens that the bulk of this
information can only be obtained from the firms and industries concerned. This explains why the resulting policies are in effect negotiated
between government and the industry in the process of restructuring.

Here we may have identified the origin of what is, at the moment, the
main threat to a liberal international trade order, namely, the tendency
toward 'sectoral solutions'. There is no need to document here the trend
in contemporary trade diplomacy to withdraw one sector after another
from the regime of general rules and to subject them to new regulations,
negotiated to reflect the 'merits of the special case'. The world solution
was placed in quotation marks because, from the viewpoint of
economics at least, it is clear that no durable solution can be found in
this direction. The reason is that 'solutions' negotiated with producers
are bound to leave out of account the consumer interest, which is the
only general principle by which the needs felt by individual industries
can be made mutually compatible. The negotiated nature of the solution
also makes it almost certain that the adjustment plan, or restructuring
agreement, will contain elements of additional protection, if only to
'provide a breathing space'. The purpose of the new rules, negotiated on
an *ad hoc* basis, is to make such additional protection possible.

A firm planning its own adjustment in the context of competition
needs information as to what 'the others' are doing, and devotes considerable resources to obtaining it. If several governments decide to
promote, by grants of public assistance, the growth of those industries
and lines of production which the firms experiencing the pressure of
competition thought on pure market considerations to be promising, the
convergent public action would be likely to impair the commercial
viability of the lines it was intended to promote. Indeed, convergent
behaviour of this kind contributed significantly to the emergence of
excess capacity in the four or five 'crisis industries' which the governments of industrial countries presently worry about. International co-
ordination of adjustment policies thus appears to be necessary; but that
only adds more difficulties. It would not only enormously complicate the
information problem; its immediate cost would consist of the
investment-inhibiting uncertainty which would prevail while the
necessary negotiations were going on. And, last but not least, because of
their hold on the relevant information, the industries concerned would
have to be drawn into the negotiation. This explains the tendency
towards international cartel-type arrangements in such industries as

steel, shipbuilding, petroleum products and certain types of petrochemicals.

The second kind of information needed by governments contemplating active restructuring policies is of general equilibrium nature; it is information that firms can do without. What are the inter-industry repercussions of protecting particular sub-sectors, the costs of income transfers, and the 'moral hazards' (effects on incentives) involved? How precise is the information we, professionals in economics, can provide to governments in this need?

Political Ethics, or Long-Range Economic Effects

Modelling economic policies is without doubt the most difficult task demanded from an economist. I cannot get rid of the suspicion that it was made even more difficult than it need be by Milton Friedman's methodological distinction between positive and normative economics. Over the last few years, I have been having increasing difficulties with that distinction.

Take the crudest expression of it: positive economics is about facts and normative about values. The 'facts' of positive economics can only be deduced from, are facts only in, the framework of a competitive free-enterprise economy. This is the order of reality we need for specific economic acts or events to be amenable to analysis, to be calculable. Without that order there cannot be economics, whether in the form of positive science or as a branch of moral philosophy. Yet order – inescapably – is a value.

Modelling policies are being tested as to the reliability and durability of the results they aim at. Such an examination must be framed in the analytical mode we call 'positive', yet it ultimately amounts to examining how consistent the particular proposal is with the order in which it is to be implemented. This, as Hayek keeps repeating, is essentially a matter of extending the time horizon of our analysis. The immediate results of a policy will be a, b, c; but they will have further consequences. In the second round, we will observe not only a, b, c but also d, e, f. In the third round, some of the effects d, e, f may have cancelled some of the effects, a, b, c; in any case, there will also be new effects f, g, h. And so on.

Is there a way of controlling this endless chain of repercussions? We never control anything fully but there is a way at least to minimise the undesired repercussions, namely, by making sure that the proposed policy conforms to the basic principles of the order. Another way of putting it is to say that the proposed policy must be generalisable; and once we put it this way, we are back from Friedman to Kant. In short, the values, principles, or basic postulates which supposedly do not enter into positive analysis, substitute – economically and efficiently – for the laborious analysis of a policy's repercussions through first, second, third to *n*th round. The two must always come to the same thing in the end.

This is by the way of introduction to another view of adjustment or restructuring policy, the policy of paying them off (IBRD, 1979, p. 25):

> In designing a better system of adjustment it can be argued that the market mechanism itself is best equipped to bring about the efficient reallocation of resources, if only it is allowed to work. What is needed, therefore, is a policy that reduces the political resistance to change, which ultimately manifests itself as protection. One possible means of so doing is to compensate those directly affected. To diminish the political support for protection, any program of compensation needs to have a number of characteristics. First, those who are to benefit must be able to rely on the benefits, which entails clear and comprehensible guidelines and speedy administration. Second, compensation must be generous, approximating the private costs imposed on those who are denied protection. Third, the program needs to be seen as fair. Finally, the beneficiaries should probably include all, or at least most, of those who bear major losses and have considerable political power, including owners of capital.

This is often also defended by an equity argument: the benefits of letting trade proceed are substantial and widespread but the costs, though much smaller, are concentrated on particular groups; it is therefore only just ... Well, it is not *therefore* just. The feature of 'widespread benefits – concentrated costs' is common to virtually all economic improvements, both domestic and those achieved abroad, to the secondary repercussions to which the domestic society is exposed. We offer a more or less uniform support to some of the groups adversely affected, namely, unemployment insurance and welfare, but no democratic society has ever contemplated, for very good reasons, a full compensation to all interests adversely affected by economic change. Certain individual risks were accepted in the social contract, so to speak.

In the proposal for an additional generous compensation to those adversely affected by imports we face the following political paradox. As a society we recognise that the proposal does not involve any equity principle because it is not generalisable. It is a short-term expedient – short-term because, if granted, it would lead to escalating demands, not only from the import-affected groups but from other groups as well. In addition, powerful backing for these new demands could be expected to come from the compensation-distributing bureaucracies. In this early stage, the proposal seems a good idea simply because the import competing industries have political clout in being able to appeal to the xenophobia latent in every society. At the conscious level, by the moral standards contemporary democratic societies explicitly uphold, they find xenophobia despicable; yet at the same time they are willing to pay off those who appeal to it. For how long could such a policy continue to yield the results for which it was proposed?

Conclusion

What the economist objects to will of course be justified by political exigencies. And the political angle indeed deserves consideration. Governments realise that for adjustment to proceed relatively smoothly, there has to be sufficient dynamism, sufficient innovation in the economy at large. Adjustment to cheaper imports is always presented as a problem of absorbing externally generated change. Yet an economy which generates rapid innovation from its own resources, or imports new technologies (as Europe and Japan have done since the Second World War), is seen to have little problem in absorbing change. On the contrary, such a change is considered desirable, indeed the goal of policy, even though it will also cause many people to change jobs. It is a change which in no economically significant way differs from that implied in importing the cheaper products resulting from innovations made abroad. There is only a political difference. Government (which always wants to do something), in order to keep its staffs employed and expanding, will justify a new programme, whether of protection or adjustment assistance (there need not be much difference between the two), by appealing to nationalism, pointing out that the action was necessitated by foreigners and is directed against them. But it never is, and cannot be; we always pay for it ourselves in the end.

Note: Chapter 18

The views presented here are the author's own, and do not necessarily reflect the position of the GATT secretariat.

References: Chapter 18

Corden, W. M. (1974), *Trade Policy and Economic Welfare* (Oxford: Clarendon Press).
GATT (1977), 'Trade liberalisation, protection and interdependence', *GATT Studies in International Trade*, no. 5.
IBRD (1979), *World Development Report*.
Tumlir, J. (1979), 'Economics, economic policy and inflation', *The Banker*, October.

Part Seven: What Now?

19

Conclusion: the Management of Surplus Capacity and International Political Economy

SUSAN STRANGE and ROGER TOOZE

Out of a welter of diverse perceptions and interpretations, of opinions and prescriptions, it does not seem easy at first to draw any single clear conclusion. Looking back over the chapters in this volume it is hard to think of one which entirely agrees in analysis, prognosis, or policy recommendation with another. Perhaps the nearest approximation is between the two global Keynesians (Jolly and Nakazawa), on the one hand, and the two liberal market economists (Tumlir and Curzon Price), on the other. But between these two pairs and amongst many of the other contributors, deep gulfs of disagreement yawn.

Perhaps it might help readers to clarify their own thinking if we attempt first to identify and recapitulate the major points of disagreement in several key dimensions and then go on from there to see if there are, after all, *any* points on which all or even most of our contributors are in broad agreement. We shall then conclude with a few observations about the implications of discussions such as this for thinking, research and teaching about international political economy.

It seems to us that we can identify at least three major dimensions of the discussion which constitute axes along which we can locate our contributors and which, taken together, form the basis of any conclusions we might draw from this study. One dimension is in answer to the question of whether the demonstrated existence of surplus industrial capacity is a serious or non-serious problem. Another is whether surplus capacity is an old or new phenomenon and, if new, what is new and significant about it, and why. The third is whether there is a 'solution' to the problem of surplus capacity – both in a conceptual and policy sense – and how, or if, this can be achieved: through market mechanisms, national governments, or both.

The major point of disagreement is over whether the appearance of surplus productive capacity (in primary products and services as well as in the manufactures on which this study has concentrated) is to be regarded as a serious – and, if serious, serious for whom – or as a non-serious problem. For example, M.A. Bienefeld thinks there was and is a long-term crisis in the world economy, and that since Keynesian solutions have failed to eliminate excess capacity while monetarist ones are politically unacceptable, the only cure lies in a considerable destruction of capital, suggesting intensified conflict and the need for major political initiatives. In contrast, Bill Diebold fails to find in the United States that pessimism about the economic future that is so pervasive in Europe and that seems to underlie the preoccupation with surplus capacity – a preoccupation which he reports just does not as yet exist in America.

Jan Tumlir, looking at the problem from Geneva, takes it more seriously, as have the governments of most industrialised countries who have embarked extensively on policies to help their economies to adjust to the appearance of surplus capacity. On closer inspection, however, he thinks that many of these policies have actually impeded adjustment. More than that, 'the present stagnationist tendencies are due to inflation'; in short, the cause of the trouble lies more in the monetary structure of the world economy which governments are neglecting than in the production and trade structure in which they are intervening – a conclusion, incidentally, supported by the argument developed by Martin Gilman.

While Tumlir argues that governments have actually made the problem worse by their intervention, Alan Milward, taking a long, cool historical view, retorts that government policies have rarely made much difference to the long trends of growth or shifting production locations. Nor, he points out, have they changed direction half as sharply as conventional liberal ideology would have us believe. So, just as there was no great contrast in fact between the liberalism of the mid-nineteenth century and the protectionism of the last quarter of the century, so it may be that we exaggerate too easily the contrast between the liberalism of the 1960s and the protectionism of the 1970s. In his view, the differences, such as they are, are of more political than economic significance.

Secondly, though most of the contributors, beginning with Alan Milward, were at pains to stress the problem as an old one, recurring after the long expansionist quarter century following the Second World War, some others found it so changed by the greater integration of the world economy of the 1970s as compared with that of the 1930s as to constitute a problem essentially different from market-share disputes of earlier times. The new features they noted were partly political, partly economic, partly technical. One was the high cost of new industrial plant requiring the rapid exploitation of very large markets; national markets were no longer big enough to yield the necessary quick return on large outlays of capital – outlays on R & D as well as on plant and equipment. Significantly, this is a point often overlooked in much conventional theories of international trade, but it has been well developed by Meyer (Meyer, 1977).

Another point stressed by Milward, Gilman and others, including particularly Jeff Harrod who participated in the conference, was the greater political sensitivity to declining demand and/or market invasion. As Milward puts it, the perception of surplus capacity in the 1970s can be seen 'as a set of stages in the widening participation of different groups in that body politic' (p. 63). In other words, the political costs of adjustment to economic change once rejected by French peasants growing wheat in the 1880s are now equally firmly and vociferously rejected by the textile workers, the shipyard workers and the steelmill workers of Europe and North America.

Yet another point was the new impact of accelerating technological change. As Judy Gurney points out, this creates a situation in which market management requires a much greater degree of anticipation on the part of managers or negotiators. The seeds of conflict over market shares may now be sown as much as a decade before the productive capacity comes on-stream. Yet as Chris Cragg's contribution on shipping and shipbuilding makes clear, the awareness of shortening order books does not necessarily produce any greater readiness on the part of either the shipbuilding enterprises or their governments to act or even to open negotiations in good time. The Japanese are judged, by all accounts – European as well as their own – by far the readiest to act decisively and in time – although, as Tadashi Nakamae emphasises, the cost of doing so has not been insignificant for the majority of Japanese workers not covered by the famous life-employment system of the giant enterprises.

The third major disagreement – predictably – was over the ability of markets, and conversely the ability of national governments, to find answers to the pains and burdens of surplus industrial capacity. On balance, writers tended to conclude either that the market mechanisms would, if left to themselves, reach a new balance between overactive supply and underactive demand; or, alternatively, that markets were no longer sufficiently free to work their invisible magic. This, roughly speaking, is the extreme position taken by Jan Tumlir and generally backed up by the observations of our one practitioner from the world of business, Anthony Lowe. Both bewail and condemn the intervention of governments with integrated world markets on the ground that their measures tend to make adjustment by the producers less likely and more difficult, rather than the reverse.

On the opposite side of the fence, those like Jolly and Nakamae who proclaim a faith in the capacity of the political systems to adapt to new demands upon them did not always find it easy to be sanguine about the adaptability of the international system or about the chances of nation-states preferring the long-term advantages of enlightened self-interest over the short-term advantages of *sauve qui peut* – or in the words of de Musset, the principle of 'Chacun pour soi dans ce désert d'egoisme qu'on appelle la vie'.

The main points of agreement take a little more seeking out, but in retrospect are perhaps no less significant. They tend, however, to be the sort of points so simple and commonsensical that they easily get over-looked. Yet they are worth noting not only for our understanding of surplus capacity but for the pointers they give to future directions for international studies, political, social and economic.

The first point of agreement is that the problem of surplus capacity (assuming one does exist) is primarily political rather than economic. That is to say, most writers accept, explicitly or implicitly, that there are no simple neutral mechanical answers with which any ordinarily rational being must inevitably concur. Even the liberal economists seem to concede that allowing market forces to work freely is itself a political decision, expressing a political preference for the value of economic efficiency (i.e. lowest-cost production) over all other values. And, however regretfully, they find that governments have seldom expressed an unequivocal preference of this kind. Indeed, this is where the value of the sectoral studies stands out most clearly, showing the variety of outcomes emerging from the diverse combinations of political objectives, bargainers and bargaining capabilities. If a wider range of sector studies had been feasible – sectoral studies of how surplus capacity got dealt with in, for example, the market for cars and lorries or for that matter toys or sports goods – they would have shown a still greater variety of outcomes. For example, surplus capacity in automobile production has been far more sharply perceived in Detroit or in Coventry than in Brazil or in Spain: exactly the reverse of the situation in the textile sector where the industrialised countries have found it relatively easy through inter-governmental bargaining to shift the burdens of adjustment from their own to the Third World workers and enterprises.

In the steel sector Warnecke notes the estimate that the US government's reference price policy cost US consumers around $1b.; yet there are only 500,000 members of the United Steelworkers' Union. Indeed, a recurrent theme in several chapters is that the number of special-interest groups wanting and able to impose this sort of cost on the uncomplaining majority (or alternatively to veto moves toward freer trade) keeps on growing. That they can do so is primarily a reflection of political developments, not economic ones. They exert power and influence by gaining access to authorities able to determine the rules of the game, whether by coercion or bargaining or by a combination of both. If anyone wants to know or understand this process of burden-shifting, they will find they get little help from most economic theory.

Some understanding of political structures and processes, both national and international, and a necessary familiarity with economic history, both national and international, is more likely to be helpful.

The second point of agreement is directly opposed to this. It is that economic factors matter a great deal: factors such as price, demand, supply, rates of saving and investment, return on capital and relative changes in productivity – above all, perhaps, the monetary structure and the integrated financial system by which capital flows pass more freely than labour across national frontiers and in which the asymmetries of 'interdependence' are so much more sharply marked than in the trade structure. Perhaps not all the contributors would agree with this observation about the monetary structure, but where all do concur is on the simple point that outcomes are produced by the interaction of economic factors with the political.

Thirdly, we think most would agree that however new/old the problem, its dynamic character makes prediction extremely difficult. As M. A. Bienefeld points out, study of governments' experiences in the 1970s directly refutes the conventional wisdom of the 1950s and 1960s. Then it was generally held that 1929 or 1931 could never happen again. Governments know better these days. Now these is no longer any such certainty.

Such awareness of an uncertain future merges with the final point of agreement between our contributors. They do not on the whole feel confident that there *is* a 'solution' to the problem in the sense of an agreed set of decisions reached by free consensus and without coercion and likely to be similarly sustained once reached. Such a 'solution' appeared to have been reached at Bretton Woods; rather more so than at San Francisco two years later. For the original six members of the European Community this was reached at Messina and subsequently expressed in the Rome Treaty. And it was reached by the main trading countries in GATT and subsequently in at least the earlier multilateral trade negotiations; although it seems to us that the more recent Kennedy and Nixon or Tokyo rounds contained too many 'ifs' and 'buts' and conditional agreements to be real 'solutions'. Opinions continue to differ as to which of the three most often cited factors – the declining power of the United States, the deceleration of growth in the world economy or the relaxation of East–West tension before Afghanistan – chiefly accounts for the current state of global economic anarchy. However, that there is such a state of affairs and that there is little prospect of it changing seems widely – if reluctantly – accepted. In the last resort, the contemporary predicament can be ascribed to an international political system in which the ultimate authorities over individual destiny reside with the governments of territorial states claiming the monopoly of violence and the priority of individual loyalties, in return for greater personal security, psychological reassurance and material welfare than any other authority, including international organisations, can offer.

Implications for International Political Economy

Since neither of the editors of this book is a policy-maker or an entrepreneur or a labour organiser our opinions on the substance of these disputed questions are worth no more than those of the next person. Both of us, though, are professionally concerned with teaching international political economy at undergraduate and graduate levels and with research work in the subject. Sticking to our metier, we have some general but perhaps not entirely original conclusions to offer to our fellow academics, which broadly follow from our general approach outlined in the Introduction and are supported by the various contributions included in this volume.

We think the foregoing chapters demonstrate four points (apart from the obvious link of politics and economics). Briefly summarised, they are: (1) that the division between international politics and domestic politics is less and less tenable or justified in the modern world; (2) that the study of international politics or economics is sterile unless values are brought back into the analysis of issues and of outcomes; (3) that there is no inherent incompatibility between a realist approach to international issues and the structural method of analysis developed mainly by Marxists and dependency theorists – although we would add that structural paradigms should not stop with attention to modes of production but should include as equally important the structures in international society for the provision of security, for the management of money, for the production and distribution of knowledge, the provision of welfare, transport services and communications as well as the exchange and employment structures; (4) that the chapters show that the study of international political economy does not reject but incorporates as an essential part the accumulated wisdom, experience and understanding of international history including, most emphatically, economic history and the history of international politics.

We shall use the following few pages to explain and draw out the implications of these points. It is also perhaps worth mentioning here that apart from highlighting various problems with the way we think about international political economy they might also suggest a few deficiencies in the way we currently view and use theory itself.

As we have already noted, the original justification for international relations as a separate social science rested on two fundamental presumptions which, although once explicit, are now often taken for granted. First was the presumption of the separability of domestic politics and foreign politics. Second was the presumption that domestic politics was about many problems, many different questions of 'who gets what', while international politics was about one specific but vital problem, that of war between states. In other words domestic, or national, politics was about one set of outcomes, and international politics about quite another, with little or no overlap between the two. We have also suggested that these two presumptions have led to the development of a unique set of theories to explain international outcomes, derived from the claims of states to ultimate sovereignty, which focus primarily on the overriding problem of war and peace. All other forms of inter-state intercourse were subservient to this essential problem and had to be constantly referred to it. Trade disputes or territorial disputes were therefore important if, or because, they might lead to war.

From this premiss, two implicit conclusions followed. One was that the issue of peace or war was the prime problematic of international relations and that the other issues were only tangential to it. The other was that since the outcome was determined by states, and the worst wars were fought by states, it was therefore states as the protagonists or actors on whom the analysis must necessarily focus. Not only that but outcomes, too, came to be seen and evaluated in terms of what *states* gained or lost, what *states* risked or secured through their relations with other states.

We think the essays in this book have clearly supported the claim that separability is no longer valid and that international politics is no longer just about peace and war. But what of the presumption that war is a unique kind of social problem? After half a century or more of argument and searching for solutions, none has emerged from the study of international relations. Some hopes still remain, as is only to be expected, but among most of the professional scholars in the field of international relations we think it is now fair to say that the problem of war in an international society of territorial states, each claiming a monopoly of violence within its territory, is more and more widely felt to be insoluble.

At first sight, this would seem to restore the justification for a separation of foreign and domestic politics. Within the state political and economic outcomes are either decided by a hierarchy of authorities or for many issues of material life they are left to the forces of the market; between these two extremes there is sometimes a process of bargaining involved before conflicting authorities determine how far, if at all, the issues shall be decided by market forces. This applies to education systems for instance, or to health care, to the management of sport and the use or abuse of nature and the environment. Although decisions can be taken to reverse or redirect policies so as to produce different solutions to problems, the process by which this can be done in any political system usually changes slowly enough to allow time for academic study and analysis of the way the process works. But in international society there is no such element of continuity and the 'solutions' to problems of war and peace, for example, have by contrast an unavoidable, structural element of the temporary, the precarious, the uncertain. The difference is that whereas national political systems are all able to produce solutions – or rather they all used to be able to do so and sometimes still think they are – the states belonging to international society may desire a solution but cannot be sure to find the means to achieve it; nor, if they could, would they have any certainty that it would last.

The 'precariousness', the makeshift nature of this sort of politics, seems now to be spreading from war and peace and security issues in international politics to a rapidly widening range of other issues, including, of course, surplus capacity. The law of the sea is just one very well publicised issue where all the outcomes regarding, for example, fisheries, oil pollution, the extraction of minerals from the sea bed, safety of ships and the provision of public goods, like marine charts, weather and rescue and salvage services, no longer lie within 'national domains', nor are subject to a clearly defined international regime, in the sense used by Keohane and Nye (1977). Rather all these outcomes have become the object of continuing, multidirectional and complex bargaining processes which take place at the inter-governmental, the national and subnational levels. Just to give one example, apart from the issues considered in this book, the treatment of coastal oil pollution may depend for any stretch of coastline partly on the results of government bargaining, but also to unequal extents on bargaining between a government and oil companies or on bargaining between governments and pressure groups and national or local political organisations.

The outcomes and consequences, therefore, are apt to change much more rapidly and unpredictably than when these matters were more directly under national control. We believe that this element of precariousness has important implications for the study of international politics broadly defined. Precariousness in any political economy is the opposite of stability and reduces confidence in a predictable future. A commonsense and intuitive presumption which follows is that perceptions of wealth, of equity or liberty (in the sense of options for choice), in the system are associated with a given level of stability. If, however, this level of stability changes and is replaced by a sensation of precariousness, so that people fear for the future, they become far more acutely aware of injustice in the distribution of wealth, risks, opportunities and options. They also become more critically aware of inefficiencies in the system and its failures to produce wealth in the present, or of the prospect of it in the future. Their freedom to choose may remain the same objectively, but their perceptions of being cramped, cabined and confined by the system are immediately heightened. The ensuing probabilities of conflict may very likely show in domestic politics – as they did in Iran in 1979 – but no one can now doubt that domestic revolutions and conflicts easily rock the international boat and work through to the old problematic of international relations.

Moreover, 'precariousness' must be understood historically, as a product of the development of and change in a number of structures. The complexity of bargaining at different levels – global, international, national and sub-national – is perhaps a result of the 'internationalisation' of national economic destinies coupled with a renewed demand by all kinds of social groups for participation in the processes which control their life-chances. To the extent that the international economy becomes an integrated world economy, and thereby affects more and more people, the interaction among these four levels will increase, and outcomes and consequences will be more unpredictable. And to the extent that the range of issues widens, as seems likely, achieving solutions (in the sense we have used) becomes that much more difficult.

The essays in this book also seem to us to demonstrate the multiplicity of value-judgements made by different authorities and at different levels with regard to basic structures of the international system. In analysing who gets what, therefore, the first step is to trace these various value-judgements and the relative importance attached by those concerned with the creation of wealth, the preservation of liberty or freedom of choice, the provision of justice and security. Each set of choices must then be related to the respective and relative possessions of political and economic resources, including capital, labour, technology and land or other natural resources as the basis of political power. The third step requires the assessment of these contending value-judgements and power to execute them on the structures. It should then be possible to identify the key bargains affecting first structures and then outcomes.

By implication, this process of analysis radically shifts the focus of research in international relations (and consequently by association the teaching of the subject) away from actors, issues and regimes and towards values, structures and bargains and their consequences. Attention to values necessarily widens the range of issues from those perceived by governments and nation-states to include those perceived by classes, generations and other transnational or sub-national social groups. Therefore by implication it renders obsolete a good deal of the conventional 'issue-area' analysis derived from theories borrowed initially from Robert Dahl and his associates. It also differs quite fundamentally – and in our view advances substantially upon – the form of analysis developed by Keohane and Nye, which asks what causes international regimes to change but seems uninterested in the values expressed by those regimes or in the question of who gains or who loses when regimes do change. An even greater weakness is the way that this analysis takes for granted economic structures and the values which they, too, express. We agree with Robert Cox in thinking that a new synthesis is required between the conventional approaches of international relations and international political economy as it has developed thus far and the broader structural approach attempted by Michalet and others (Cox, forthcoming).

The alternative analytical approach we suggest is ideologically neutral, being unbiased and equally open to use by liberal conservatives or by Marxist revolutionaries. For it does not dictate or presume the priority of one value over another, of order over justice or of wealth over liberty. What is does do is to recognise the reality of trade-offs between values – by no means a new political idea, after all. Thus, you can have a greater justice but it may require sacrifice of wealth and economic growth. Or you can have greater liberty for the state, or for groups within it, that it may require a sacrifice of liberty by other groups or other states.

In short, it does not – as do many existing conventions of analysis in international politics or international economics for that matter – presume agreement on the desirability of order or even of peace. Some people, some social classes, or some states may well conclude that the system and its structures produce bargains fundamentally inequitable for them and therefore in need of reform. The last goal of their policy-making would be the maintenance of a given international regime. Some groups or states may seek the objective of maximum efficiency and fast economic growth and to them order of security, even equity, may seem far less important. The questions to be asked therefore concern the factors likely to affect bargaining; these are the concern for the values sought in the global system, within the state, and for the sub-group and for individuals. Also important are the economic resources available for the pursuit of these objectives at each level.

The concern for bargaining processes rather than for regimes is directed to bringing out the dynamic nature of outcomes. Regime seems to us a concept in itself far too static, emphasising order at the expense of other values, and implying far greater predictability than has ever been present in international relations. Moreover, it may be that the key bargains will not be those between states but between states and enterprises or between management and labour or between branches of national and international bureaucracies, or may be business and financial bargains. Finally, we feel that the nature of the outcome, the effect of the multiple bargaining processes on the values expressed in the various structures and on the distribution of values and their opposite qualities (poverty, injustice, insecurity, risk of all kinds, tyranny and the denial of free choice) must be put once again at the centre of the stage. For only when the study of international relations once again allows and even encourages scholars to pass fundamentally moral judgements, however subjective these may be, on the issues of international public policy will the discipline regain some of its lost appeal.

References: Chapter 19

Cox, R. W. (forthcoming), 'In search of international political economy: A review essay', *International Organisation*.

Keohane, R. O., and Nye, J. S. (1977), *Power and Interdependence: World Politics in Transition* (Boston, Mass.: Little, Brown).

Meyer, F. V. (1977), *International Trade Theory* (London: Croom Helm).

Notes on Contributors

JONATHON DAVID ARONSON is Assistant Professor at the School of International Relations, University of Southern California and director of their mid-career master's programme. He has published widely in the field of international political economy.

MANFRED BIENEFELD is currently Senior Fellow at the Institute of Development Studies, University of Sussex, concerned with business economics, economic history and a range of development issues.

CHRIS CRAGG was formerly a research officer for the International Business Unit at the University of Manchester Institute of Science and Technology and then at the Centre for International Studies, LSE. He is now Associate Editor of *Seatrade,* and specialises in energy and commodity affairs.

VICTORIA CURZON PRICE teaches and researches at the Graduate Institute of International Studies and the Centre for Research into Industrial Studies in Geneva. She has written and published extensively on the politics of international trade.

ANTONIO DA SILVA FERREIRA is a research student at St Catherine's College, Oxford.

WILLIAM DIEBOLD is Senior Research Fellow of the Council of Foreign Relations in New York, and has recently written on the industrial policies of western countries and on US foreign economic policy.

CHRISTOPHER FARRANDS is Senior Lecturer in International Relations at Trent Polytechnic, Nottingham and has written on foreign policy, negotiations and West European politics.

MARTIN GILMAN is a staff economist at the OECD in Paris and teaches political economy at the University of Paris.

JUDITH GURNEY, after doing research at the London School of Economics and Political Science, is now a freelance specialist in international petroleum and energy matters.

RICHARD JOLLY is Director of the Institute of Development Studies, University of Sussex and has written and published extensively on subjects in that field.

ANTHONY LOWE is Head of Planning and Economics, Shell International Chemical Company Limited.

ALAN MILWARD is Professor of European Studies at UMIST and has written several works on twentieth-century economic history and two books on European economic development in the nineteenth century (with S.B. Saul).

TADASHI NAKAMAE is chief economist at Daiwa Europe NV, in London, and has written widely on economic affairs.

KAZUO NAKAZAWA was formerly Visiting Research Fellow at the Rockefeller Foundation, New York and is now Deputy Director of the Economic Co-operation Department of Keidanren (Federation of Economic Organisations) in Tokyo.

SUSAN STRANGE is Montague Burton Professor of International Relations at the London School of Economics and Political Science. She was formerly Senior Research Fellow at the Royal Institute of International Affairs, and began her career as a journalist for *The Economist* and the *Observer*. She has written extensively on the politics of international monetary and trade issues.

ROGER TOOZE is Senior Lecturer in International Relations at North Staffordshire Polytechnic. He has been extensively involved in teaching and research on international political economy, primarily through IPEG, of which he is the convener, and he also set up a research group on Teaching International Relations which is funded by the British International Studies Association.

LOUKAS TSOUKALIS is a Research Fellow at the Royal Institute of International Affairs and at St Catherine's College, Oxford. He is editor of the *Journal of Common Market Studies* and author of two books on the political economy of the EEC.

JAN TUMLIR is Director of Research at the GATT Secretariat and Visiting Professor at the Graduate Institute of International Studies, Geneva.

STEVEN J. WARNECKE is a Visiting Scholar at the Middle East Institute, Columbia University, working on energy and resource issues. He was a Research Fellow at the Royal Institute of International Affairs.

STEPHEN WOOLCOCK is a Research Associate at the Royal Institute of International Affairs and has recently completed a study on the implications of the NICs for trade and adjustment policies.

Index

DATE DUE

APR 11 1988			

HIGHSMITH 45-102